MW00782046

THADDEUS KOSCIUSZKO

Military Engineer
of the American Revolution

He is as pure a son of liberty
as I have ever known.

~ THOMAS JEFFERSON

BOOKS BY
FRANCIS CASIMIR KAJENCKI

Star on Many a Battlefield:
Brevet Brigadier General Joseph Karge
in the American Civil War
1980

"Uncle Billy's War:"
General William T. Sherman's Changing Concept
of Military-Civilian Relations during the
Civil War—from Staunch Civilian Protector
to "Cruel Plunderer"
1989

Poles in the 19th Century Southwest
1990

Across the generations:
Kajencki Family History
1994

Thaddeus Kosciuszko:
Military Engineer of the American Revolution
1998

COLONEL THADDEUS KOSCIUSZKO
*Chief Engineer of General Nathanael Greene's Southern Army, 1781-1783.
Painting by Robert Wilson of Woodruff, South Carolina.
(Courtesy of the artist)*

THADDEUS KOSCIUSZKO

Military Engineer
of the American Revolution

FRANCIS CASIMIR KAJENCKI

Francis Casimir Kajencki

SOUTHWEST POLONIA PRESS
EL PASO • TEXAS

Published by Southwest Polonia Press, 3308 Nairn Street, El Paso, Texas 79925.

Printed in the United States of America

Cataloging-in-Publication Data

Kajencki, Francis Casimir
Thaddeus Kosciuszko: Military Engineer of the American Revolution

Bibliography:
Includes Index

1. United States—History—The Revolutionary War, 1775-1783, Diplomatic Tension with France, 1798.

2. Poland—History—Kosciuszko's Insurrection against Russia, 1794.

3. Biography—Thaddeus Kosciuszko—Correspondence with Thomas Jefferson, 1798-1817.

Library of Congress Catalog Card Number: 97-61982
ISBN: 0-9627190-4-8

In Honor of

THOMAS JEFFERSON

Author of the American Declaration of Independence, 1776
President of the United States, 1801–1809
Staunch Friend of General Thaddeus Kosciuszko

PREFACE

THIS BOOK is a military biography of Thaddeus Kosciuszko. It concentrates on his engineering achievements in the American Revolution over a period of seven years, 1776–1783. For the sake of continuity, the author includes a short account of Kosciuszko's formative years as well as his valiant battle for Poland's independence against rapacious neighbor countries. Kosciuszko's unsuccessful Insurrection of 1794 against the superior forces of Russia and Prussia was added to the present account in order to maintain historical transition for his return to America in 1797.

No American historian ever wrote a biography of Thaddeus Kosciuszko in nearly 200 years. Yet, Kosciuszko's service in the Revolutionary War added significantly to the American effort to gain independence and assuredly deserved to be recorded for generations. Granted that numerous tributes were made and short essays written about Kosciuszko. Notwithstanding, some pages of American history remained blank until the appearance of Polish American historians. The first intensive and scholarly research of Kosciuszko occurred in the 1930 decade when Miecislaus Haiman of Chicago undertook the pioneering effort. His research extended into the archives and libraries of America and Poland where he located and identified letters and fragments of data.

Assembling the results into a meaningful narrative of 176 pages, he had his work published in 1943 under the title *Kosciuszko in the American Revolution* by the Polish Institute of Arts and Sciences in America. Although the book is somewhat brief, Haiman simply put down the facts he found. Not having a military background, Haiman did not try to analyze and evaluate the battle plans and campaigns of American and British commanders. The great value of Haiman's book, though, springs from his determined pursuit and gathering of data and the location of these sources. Haiman's work assisted this author materially, and he found Haiman to be an objective historian. Haiman produced a sequel, *Kosciuszko: Leader and Exile*, published in 1946 by the Polish Institute of Arts and Sciences in America and reprinted by The Kosciuszko Foundation of New York in 1977. Since Haiman's time, only a few books on Kosciuszko have appeared. They are mostly fictionalized accounts published for young readers.

After completing the history of the Kajencki family in 1994, the author of the current military biography set out to research and write a book about Kosciuszko's contribution to American independence. Over the years he had read numerous newspaper articles and short essays about Kosciuszko, and he believed he knew much about the gallant Pole. However, the research uncovered previously unknown facts that enhance Kosciuszko's stature. He determined to write not only what Kosciuszko did but also how his actions contributed to American success during the fight for independence, 1775-1783. Whenever Kosciuszko met with controversy, the author attempted to get beneath the surface and analyze the reasons. This effort caused him to criticize severely Lieutenant Colonel "Light-Horse-Harry" Lee and to take issue with eminent British historians.

Perhaps the first major action of Kosciuszko that stamped him as a tactician and strategist, as well as a military engineer, occurred at Fort Ticonderoga, New York, in 1777. General Horatio Gates directed his engineer, Kosciuszko, to reconnoiter the adjacent Mount Defiance and determine the practicability of dragging cannon up its steep slope to the summit and from there dominating Fort Ticonderoga. Kosciuszko evaluated that possibility positively and recommended that the Americans occupy and fortify Mount Defiance. The recommendation, unfortunately, could not be carried out by Gates and was disregarded by his successor. Consequently, British General John Burgoyne placed his cannon on that summit and forced the Americans to abandon the fort without firing a single shot in defense. Less than three months later at Saratoga, Kosciuszko's strongly fortified position on Bemis Heights, occupied by General Gates's army, blocked Burgoyne's advance on Albany and forced him to make wide sweeps to the west into thick woods and disaster. Kosciuszko's share of victory was much more significant than most historians credit him, for Kosciuszko did more than simply choose and fortify a position. In effect, Kosciuszko destroyed the British Grand Strategy for the conquest of the colonies.

Kosciuszko's second major accomplishment took place at West Point where, as chief engineer for twenty-eight months, he designed and built Fortress West Point. The British never dared to attack the fortress. Thus, he carried out General George Washington's strategy that insured the American control of the vital Hudson River. After Kosciuszko's departure for the Southern Army, French General Le Chevalier de Chastellux visited West Point. He marveled at the brilliantly planned fortifications. However, he took away the achievement from Kosciuszko and credited the work to French engineers.

In the Southern Army commanded by General Nathanael Greene, Kosciuszko gave Greene the mobility he needed with an amphibious army. At Ninety-Six, South Carolina, Kosciuszko carried out a masterful, Vauban-style siegecraft, the only one in the Revolutionary War. As hostilities subsided, Kosciuszko gained the distinction of fighting the British in the last engagement of the war on James Island, South Carolina, 14 November 1782.

Following the cessation of hostilities, Congress promoted Kosciuszko to brigadier general. He joined the Society of the Cincinnati, received gifts from General Washington, and sailed for Europe on 15 July 1784.

In Poland, Kosciuszko led the Polish Army in 1794 against powerful neighbors that sought to destroy his country. Kosciuszko failed against overwhelming numbers of the enemy. He returned to America in 1797, intending to make his home here. However, Vice President Thomas Jefferson asked him to undertake a secret mission to France for the purpose of lessening tension and avoiding war with the French. Kosciuszko left at once and succeeded in his mission. Ironically, historians have ignored yet another of Kosciuszko's significant contributions to America. Most historians also seem to have glossed over or ignored the close and long friendship between Kosciuszko and Jefferson.

The author's military biography presents the results of Thaddeus Kosciuszko's remarkable service to America.

> —*Francis Casimir Kajencki*
> *El Paso, Texas*
> *September 1998*

ACKNOWLEDGEMENTS

THE AUTHOR expresses his deepest appreciation to individuals and staffs of libraries, historical societies, and archival agencies in Poland and the United States for invaluable help in gathering data and documents during the author's three-year period of intensive research. Indeed, the cooperative and ready responses of these individuals were encouraging to the author and eased his labors. He is very grateful for their assistance. In particular, the author would like to thank his cousin Marzena Piasecka of Sopot, Poland, who sought out the names of directors of scholarly institutions and contacted them for the author's specific needs. As a result, he received photo copies and microfilm of required documents.

I would also like to thank my daughter Dr. AnnMarie Kajencki, Professor of English at Bismarck State College, North Dakota. She reviewed my manuscript critically, offering many valuable suggestions.

The list of assisting individuals and agencies is shown in the Appendix.

—*Francis Casimir Kajencki*

CONTENTS

ILLUSTRATIONS

Maps:

CHAPTER ONE

Prelude to Saratoga

N EARLY SEPTEMBER 1777, Major General Horatio Gates, commander of the American Army of the Northern Department, directed his chief engineer, Colonel Thaddeus Kosciuszko, to examine an area of high ground on the west bank of the Hudson River and to select a defensive position. Called Bemis Heights after the owner of a tavern near the river, the site lay about four miles north of Stillwater, where Gates had encamped his army. A few local inhabitants had mentioned Bemis Heights to Gates. Lieutenant Colonel James Wilkinson, Gates's adjutant general, also had suggested this location. Wilkinson had noticed the high ground when the Americans, then under General Philip Schuyler, had retreated past Bemis Heights to the Mohawk River, nine miles north of Albany. Gates asked his ablest lieutenant, Major General Benedict Arnold, to accompany Kosciuszko.[1]

At the site, Kosciuszko observed an east-west ridge running perpendicular to the Hudson and overlooking the river and the road through a meadow below. The commanding heights extended westward for about three-quarters of a mile to a knoll, where farmer Neilson's house and barn stood. About one-half mile farther west, Kosciuszko saw a plateau shaped like a long

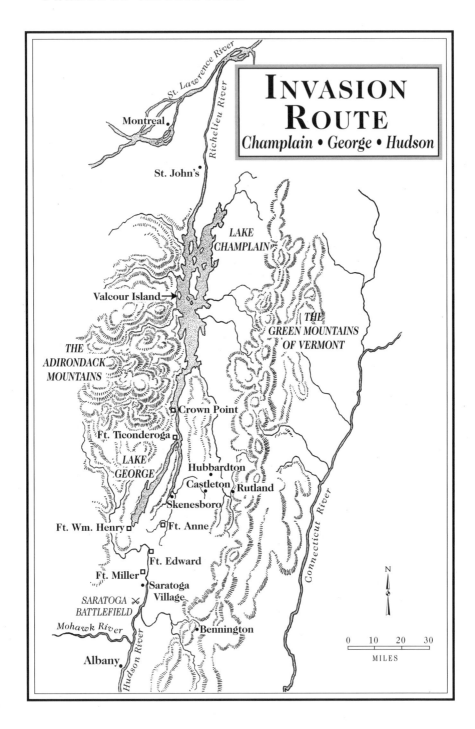

INVASION ROUTE

Champlain • George • Hudson

St. Lawrence River

Montreal

Richelieu River

St. John's

LAKE CHAMPLAIN

Valcour Island

THE GREEN MOUNTAINS OF VERMONT

THE ADIRONDACK MOUNTAINS

Crown Point

Ft. Ticonderoga

LAKE GEORGE

Hubbardton

Castleton Rutland

Skenesboro

Ft. Wm. Henry Ft. Anne

Connecticut River

Ft. Edward

Ft. Miller

Saratoga Village

SARATOGA BATTLEFIELD

Mohawk River

Bennington

Albany

Hudson River

N

0   10   20   30
MILES

oval that could serve as a second line of defense on the western flank. To the north the main position rose above several ravines formed by Mill Creek and its south and middle forks. Still farther north lay the Great Ravine that extended northwestwardly. The entire area was heavily wooded with pine, maple, and oak trees, except for small clearings at several farms in the area. If an observer stood at Freeman's farm and looked south to Bemis Heights, he would see a solid line of trees, screening everything below the tops. To the west of Bemis Heights a heavy forest covered the land. Kosciuszko pronounced the site an excellent position and highly recommended it to General Gates. Historian Lynn Montross called Kosciuszko's position "a strategic bottleneck which could neither be forced nor avoided without difficulty."[2]

The American Army occupied Bemis Heights on September 12. Under the direction of Kosciuszko, the soldiers worked vigorously to dig trenches and built breastworks of logs and earth in the shape of a half-circle. The line of fortifications extended from the eastern escarpment westward along the ridge to Neilson's farm and bent south for a distance. The soldiers converted Neilson's barn of logs into a fort. To the west of Neilson's house the ground descended into a draw and rose again to form a plateau where General Arnold's soldiers occupied the ground after the first battle on September 19. Kosciuszko placed cannon to cover the enemy's avenues of approach, especially on the eastern bluff that overlooked the road and river. To strengthen the defenses down on the plain, Kosciuszko built redoubts on both sides of the road to Albany. A short distance from the redoubts, the Americans constructed a bridge of boats across the Hudson. Kosciuszko's engineering skill converted the high ground into a nearly impregnable position. Consequently, it infused General Gates with a high degree of confidence that allowed him to await the British attack. Bemis Heights became the center of two hard-fought battles whose victories not only decided the fate of a strategic British campaign but also became the turning point of the War of Independence.[3]

Anticipating victory, Lieutenant General John Burgoyne

marched some 7800 British and German professional soldiers
from Canada into New York and south along the invasion route
of Lake Champlain – Lake George – Hudson River. By September 13,
Burgoyne began crossing the Hudson to the west bank at the
village of Saratoga, some eight miles above Bemis Heights.
Burgoyne's objective was Albany, the American base in the State.
However, he was carrying out a much broader mission—the
Grand Strategy for the conquest of the rebellious colonies. The
strategy called for the separation of New England, the hot bed of
rebellion, from the other colonies along the Hudson River line.
Once the Hudson was firmly in their possession, the British
planned to overwhelm the American military units in New
England. Next, the British would turn to the conquest of the
middle and southern colonies. They believed the second phase
would be easier because of the expected support from large numbers of loyalists and the discouragement of the patriots.[4]

Burgoyne promoted the Grand Strategy with vigor, for he
expected to play a key role. He had been in Boston under General Thomas Gage when the patriots fired on the redcoats at
Lexington and Concord in April 1775. Later, he had served in
Canada under General Sir Guy Carleton. Observing the status of
the rebellion, he evolved the Grand Strategy and returned to
England in the fall of 1776 to advocate the plan. Both King George
III and Lord Germain, Secretary of State for the Colonies, were
favorably disposed toward Burgoyne, and they approved the
Grand Strategy. It consisted of three parts: Burgoyne to march
his army from Canada into Albany; General William Howe in New
York to move north up the Hudson and attack the Americans in
their rear; and Lieutenant Colonel Barry St. Leger with a small
force to march from Oswego east along the Mohawk River. St.
Leger's march constituted a diversion. The three armies were to
converge on Albany, where General Howe would assume overall
command.[5] Burgoyne's plan, indeed, was brilliant.

Germain drew up the necessary orders, and Burgoyne departed
on 31 March 1777, carrying a copy of the orders for General
Carleton. Burgoyne believed that Germain had also issued

GENERAL JOHN BURGOYNE
Commanding the British Army at Saratoga
(Photo courtesy of the Library of Congress)

instructions to General Howe for him to join Burgoyne at Albany. Unfortunately, due to a regrettable oversight in Germain's office, no orders were sent to Howe. The omission fatally flawed the Grand Strategy.[6]

In June 1777, General Burgoyne assembled his army at St. John's (St.-Jean) on the Richelieu River in Canada. His first major target was Fort Ticonderoga, built on a peninsula in the narrow waterway that joins Lakes Champlain and George. The French had erected the Vauban-style fort, named Fort Carillon, to protect Canada from British incursions in 1755 – 58. In 1759, during the French and Indian War, the British captured the fort and renamed it Fort Ticonderoga from the Indian name "where the lake shuts itself." Soon, however, the fort was allowed to fall into disrepair. A small unit of about fifty soldiers under Captain William Delaplace garrisoned the fort. In May 1775, immediately after Lexington and Concord, Ethan Allen and Benedict Arnold organized a small force of "Green Mountain Boys" and marched rapidly to the fort. Because of its isolation, the garrison did not know of the outbreak of fighting in Massachusetts. The Americans surprised the British soldiers in a night attack and quickly subdued them. In fact, Allen pounded the door of a lieutenant's quarters and met the bewildered officer in his nightgown. The British officer asked by what authority Allen demanded the surrender. According to tradition that American school children learn, Allen thundered, "In the name of the Great Jehovah and the Continental Congress."[7]

The patriots were delighted with the capture of the massive fort. Its strategic location blocked the likely invaders from Canada. At first, however, the Continental Congress considered abandoning the fort as a gesture of reconciliation with the mother country. Notwithstanding, rapidly developing events pointed to a permanent break. On the military side, General George Washington valued the fort as a great prize. Still, the fort required much renovation, additional fortifications to protect the approaches to the fort, and a large garrison. Major Generals Philip Schuyler and Horatio Gates each requested 10,000 soldiers.

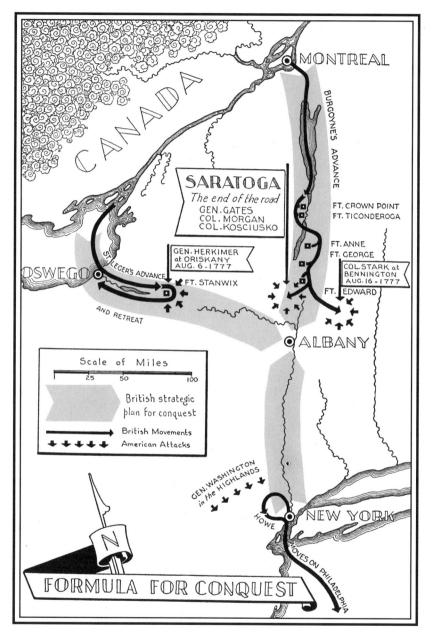

THE BRITISH GRAND STRATEGY
From Lynn Montross, The Story of the Continental Army, 1775-1783.
(Reprinted by permission of Harper/Collins Publishers, Inc)

Unfortunately, Washington could not provide that large number. He himself struggled to contain the British around New York with a grossly inadequate army. Nevertheless, work was now carried on under the supervision of Colonel Jeduthan Baldwin, referred to as the chief engineer of the Northern Department, although he was not professionally schooled.[8]

At the time the British formulated their Grand Strategy in London in the fall of 1776, Major General Philip Schuyler commanded the American Northern Department from his headquarters in Albany. Schuyler, a descendant of an aristocratic Dutch family, was a successful farmer and merchant. He built a mansion in Albany and another imposing house in Saratoga. Because of his gentry manners, some patriots considered him unbending, especially the informal New Englanders who disliked him. Nevertheless, he was a man of character and a patriot.[9]

During 1776 and the first half of 1777, Generals Schuyler and Gates waged a tug of war for the command of the Northern Department. Although Major General Arnold failed to capture Quebec in late 1775, Congress still toyed with the hope of wresting Canada from the British. Congress appointed Gates to command the American Army which had remained on Canadian soil. However, when General Carleton forced Gates to retreat to Crown Point in New York, Schuyler asserted his authority over Gates and his troops, since Crown Point lay in the Northern Department. But Gates disagreed, believing he still commanded an independent army. On 1 July 1776, Schuyler referred the dispute to Congress, which ruled in favor of Schuyler, and Gates accepted the decision. Within his Department, Schuyler gave Gates the command of the important post of Fort Ticonderoga. Four months later General Washington, desperately needing reinforcements, ordered Gates to march 1200 troops to join him near Philadelphia. Having easy access to members of Congress now, Gates agitated for an independent command, and Congress granted him his wish. Congress assigned Gates to Fort Ticonderoga but made his command independent of Schuyler. Gates also received the permission of Congress to take along with him Brigadier General Roche de Fermoy and "such other French officers as he may think proper." One of the "French" officers was Colonel Thaddeus Kosciuszko, whom Gates selected to be his engineer. Gates also chose Major James Wilkinson as his aide-de-camp and adjutant general.[10]

General and Mrs. Gates traveled to Albany, followed by Kosciuszko and Wilkinson. On arriving at army headquarters, Gates found that Schuyler had left to join Congress. Gates, therefore, decided to remain in Albany, a decision that irritated Schuyler's supporters who believed Gates attempted to usurp Schuyler's command. Gates dispatched Wilkinson to Fort Ticonderoga in order to improve the chain of communications between Albany and the fort, as well as to report on conditions there. Kosciuszko accompanied Wilkinson to the fort and reported to Brigadier General John Paterson of Massachusetts.[11]

Gates directed Kosciuszko to make an independent survey of the work in progress at the fort, without upsetting the chief engineer, Colonel Baldwin. Relying on Kosciuszko's modesty and cooperative attitude, Gates still wrote a letter of explanation to Paterson on 8 May 1777:

> Lieut. Col. Kusiusco [sic] accompanies Wilkinson, he is an able Engineer and one of the best & neatest draughtsmen I ever saw. I desire he may have a Quarter assigned him, and when he has thoroughly made himself acquainted with the works, have ordered him to point out to you, where & in what manner the best improvements & additions can be made thereto; I expect Col. Baldwin will [give] his countenance & protection to this Gentleman for he is meant to serve not supersede him.[12]

Gates went out of his way to avoid offending Baldwin. It seems the general deliberately misstated Kosciuszko's rank, addressing him as lieutenant colonel. On May 12, Baldwin greeted Kosciuszko, Wilkinson, and Dr. Jonathan Potts, chief medical officer of the Northern Department. The Pole found General Paterson and all the officers very friendly. Baldwin and he got along well. Three days after Kosciuszko's arrival, Baldwin escorted the new engineer on an inspection of the fortifications. The next

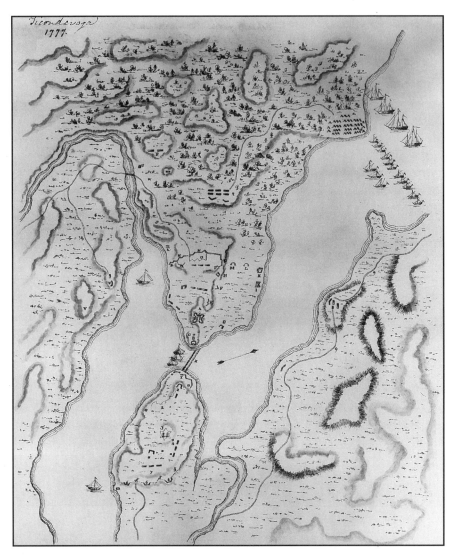

Area around Fort Ticonderoga and Mount Independence on two peninsulas jutting into Lake Champlain. Colonel Thaddeus Kosciuszko introduced this map on behalf of Major General Arthur St. Clair at his court martial in 1778. (Map courtesy of Cornell University Library, Ithaca, New York.)

day Paterson hosted a dinner for Kosciuszko, Wilkinson, Baldwin, and Major William Hull, who later became governor of Michigan Territory. Undoubtedly, the group discussed the strengths and weaknesses of the fort.[13]

Kosciuszko sent Gates a lengthy report in French on the state of the fortifications at Fort Ticonderoga, recommending changes, additions, as well as a plan of his own. "In consequence of your Orders I have visited every part or place," Kosciuszko said, "& from My remarks I send you the plan. What appears in black is what actually remains, what you see in red is my Scheme." Kosciuszko also was not satisfied with the French Lines:

> As I perceived, my Gen'l, that the french lines are not properly defended, & that they are in a situation to be repaired. I think necessary to make some alterations at the same time in some places.

Kosciuszko continued with proposals for defenses manned by a large garrison and those with a small garrison, and the smaller number he believed to be the more likely case. He kept referring to his plan on which he had drawn defense lines and labeled them with letters of the alphabet. Although Kosciuszko's letter has survived, the plan apparently has not. Without Gates's approval and orders for implementation, Kosciuszko hesitated to disclose the plan to General Paterson and Colonel Baldwin. He explained, "Being a stranger, I am convinced how much I ought to be on my Guard, as also have regard to nationality."[14]

Colonel Baldwin seemed unwilling to adopt Kosciuszko's changes, and the Pole was reluctant to force them on the resident engineer. The standoff provoked Wilkinson to complain to Gates, " I wish to Heaven, either yourself or General St. Clair were here for a few days. Colonel Kosciuszko is timidly modest; Baldwin is inclosing the lines on a plan of his own."[15]

Kosciuszko expressed optimism about converting Mount Independence into a stronghold. He wrote General Gates on 18 May 1777:

> My Opinion may be dangerous. I say if we have time to make an Entrenchment like what I had the honor to send you a Model

of; with the addition of a trifling thing towards the Lake to prevent the passage of shipping. I say the enemy cannot hurt us; we have an excellent place not only to resist the Enemy, but beat them, but Courage and more artillery men will be necessary, for we have only one Company & that is not enough; we ought to have three.

Kosciuszko added that "the Bridge is not yet finished, nevertheless it must be." Criticizing Baldwin's lack of competence, he told Gates, "I say nothing of what unnecessary works have been carried on, you will be a Judge yourself my Genl. We are very fond of making Block houses, and they are all erected in the most improper places." Historian William Sterne Randall calls Baldwin "the incompetent American engineer at Ticonderoga" for failing to fortify Mount Defiance. Randall further states that Baldwin "ridiculed Kosciuszko's observation that a few siege guns atop Mount Defiance could pulverize all the forts in short order."[16]

General Gates showed great concern over the unfinished work at Fort Ticonderoga, although he personally was absent and was represented there by his adjutant general, Wilkinson. On 23 May 1777, Gates wrote Paterson to continue to strengthen the fort. "Perhaps the Enemy may give us Two Months, before they come again to look at Ticonderoga," he cautioned. And he urged Paterson "to order Lieut. Colonel Kosciusko's plan to be immediately put into Execution, doing the most defensible parts first." Gates attempted to win Baldwin's cooperation by including some soothing words: "Colonel Baldwin will gain my Affection and Esteem, by cultivating the friendship of that Capable Young Man; and he may be assured he can in nothing serve his Country more, than in going hand and hand with him, in improving the Fortifications of Ticonderoga."[17]

On 23 May 1777, Kosciuszko traveled with General Paterson to Skenesborough (Whitehall) and continued to army headquarters in Albany where he made a personal report to Gates. Wilkinson had planned the visit. "Thinking that Col. Kusiusco would be of more Service by personally representing to you the Situation of this Place," he wrote, "I have obtained leave for His Return."[18]

Gates's instructions to Kosciuszko on examining the fortifications at Fort Ticonderoga included a very key provision: to determine whether it was practicable to place guns of large caliber atop Sugar Loaf Hill. Renamed Mount Defiance, it faced Fort Ticonderoga from across a narrow body of water, and it towered over the fort. In the past, however, French, British, and American commanders dismissed the idea of placing cannon on Mount Defiance, believing the mountain was simply too steep and rugged for artillery occupation. Nonetheless, some lower-ranking officers thought otherwise, including Colonel John Trumbull, Gates's aide. Trumbull had stated his belief earlier in 1776: "I had for some time regarded this eminence as completely overruling our entire position." He presented a recommendation to Gates at a meeting of his principal officers. "I ventured to advance the new and heretical opinion," Trumbull said, "that our position was bad and untenable, as being overlooked in all its parts by this hill." After Gates and the officers reacted scornfully, Trumbull remarked, "I was ridiculed for advancing such an extravagant idea." Nevertheless, the threat of Mount Defiance in the hands of the enemy worried Gates. On his return to the command of Fort Ticonderoga in April 1777, Gates had with him the engineer Kosciuszko, in whom he placed his trust and confidence. Gates charged Kosciuszko to conduct a military evaluation of Mount Defiance.[19]

After making his engineering assessment of the key mountain, Kosciuszko concluded:

1. The steep slopes of the mountain could be shaped by fatigue parties, so as to allow movement of the heaviest cannon.
2. The sharp and pointed summit could by similar means be leveled for emplacing a battery properly.
3. A battery so sited would cover completely both Fort Ticonderoga and Mount Independence, the bridge of boats between them, and the adjoining boat harbor.[20]

General Gates approved Kosciuszko's conclusions. However, before he could carry out his engineer's recommendation, Gates lost his command to General Schuyler. On 22 May 1777,

Congress abolished Gates's independent command of Fort Ticonderoga and placed it again in the Northern Department under the authority of Schuyler. Even after being replaced, Gates urged Major General Arthur St. Clair to occupy Mount Defiance. St. Clair took command of the fort on 12 June 1777. Unfortunately, the politicking activities in Congress of both Schuyler and Gates resulted in frequent changes in command that prevented a continuity of effort in the Northern Department. The need to occupy and fortify Mount Defiance fell by the wayside. General John Armstrong, former major and Gates's aide at Fort Ticonderoga, explained that General Schuyler,

> ...reasoning from the fact that no Engineer hitherto, French, British, or American, had believed in the practicability of placing a battery on Sugar Loaf hill, was not disposed to embarrass himself or his means of defense, by making the experiment; and the less so, as he was fully convinced that, between two and three thousand men, could effectually maintain Fort Independence and secure the pass."[21]

During Kosciuszko's absence from Fort Ticonderoga, Colonel Baldwin himself supervised the construction of fortifications, and Wilkinson did not like what he saw. He wrote an urgent letter to Gates on 31 May 1777, not knowing that Gates had been superseded by Schuyler. "The works are now being pushed on Baldwin's unmeaning plan. For God's sake," he cried, "let Kosciuszko come back as soon as possible, with proper authority." Kosciuszko returned to Fort Ticonderoga on 6 June 1777, keenly disappointed that he lost his commander. Nevertheless, his first priority lay with the cause of American independence, and he applied himself vigorously to the work at the fort.[22]

On June 8, Kosciuszko accompanied General Paterson to Crown Point, eight miles north of the fort, to take measurements of the surrounding waters. Colonel Baldwin, Major Armstrong, Dr. James Craik, and thirty soldiers were also in the party. Shortly, General St. Clair assumed command of Fort Ticonderoga, and, in response to his orders, Kosciuszko concentrated his effort on Mount Independence. Baldwin and he reconnoitered the mount

MAJOR GENERAL ARTHUR ST. CLAIR
St. Clair took command of Fort Ticonderoga, 12 June 1777
(Photo courtesy of the Library of Congress)

to determine the most advantageous areas to be fortified.[23]

Colonel Trumbull had earlier reconnoitered the hill on the Vermont side of Lake Champlain. He described Mount Independence, named in honor of the American Declaration of Independence:

> At the northern point, it ran low into the lake, offering a good landing place; from thence the land rose to an almost level plateau, elevated from fifty to seventy-five feet above the lake, and surrounded on three sides, by a natural wall of rock, everywhere steep, and sometimes an absolute precipice sinking into the lake. On the fourth and eastern side of the position ran a morass and deep creek at the foot of the rock, which strengthened that front, leaving room only, by an easy descent, for a road to the east, and to the landing from the southern end of the lake. We found plentiful springs of good water, at the foot of the rock. The whole was covered with primeval forest.[24]

Baldwin had begun the fortifications on Mount Independence in the summer of 1776. A year later, however, General Schuyler found his work unsatisfactory and far from complete. In the company of Generals St. Clair, Roche de Fermoy, Enoch Poor, and John Paterson, Schuyler inspected the defenses of the fort and the companion mount on 19 June 1777. The generals concluded, among other measures, "That the fortifications and lines on Mount Independence are very deficient; and that repairing the old and adding new works, ought to claim immediate attention; and that the engineers be directed to repair and make the necessary fortifications."[25]

A short time before the inspection, General Schuyler decided to make Mount Independence the primary American defensive position. In a letter to Congress, 8 June 1777, Schuyler wrote, "I have directed that Mount Independence should be the primary object of attention." Because of the gross shortage of soldiers, Schuyler and St. Clair believed that they could not defend both Fort Ticonderoga and Mount Independence against a determined enemy. Of the two positions, the Mount would be the final one. St. Clair admitted to Schuyler that both sites were interdependent, and he, St. Clair, would continue to occupy Fort Ticonderoga. "I design, however, to make the appearance of doing it," he wrote Schuyler, "and after defending Ticonderoga as long as possible retreat to Mount Independence."[26]

Although Baldwin was the ranking engineer, General St. Clair turned to Kosciuszko to carry out the necessary engineering work. From the numerous references to Kosciuszko's activities at this time, St. Clair clearly relied on the Pole. For example, Major Isaac B. Dunn, aide to St. Clair, made the rounds of the lines and "on Mount Independence he found a party of about one hundred men, under the direction of Colonel Kosciuszko, erecting three redoubts in the rear of the Mount, and forming an abbatis."[27] Additionally, to accelerate the work on the batteries of Mount Independence, St. Clair placed a force of 500 to 600 soldiers under Kosciuszko's supervision. The indefatigable engineer carried out the assignment rapidly and confidently, having already developed his plan that he had submitted to Gates in May 1777. Although the assigned priority was Mount Independence, Kosciuszko erected "some additions to the works on the Ticonderoga side...between the west end of the French Lines and the Lake."[28]

The work on Mount Independence continued. Lieutenant Colonel Henry B. Livingston, aide to General Schuyler, observed: "No measures were neglected to strengthen the works on both sides of the Lake. Fatigue parties were daily employed in this duty, and the direction of them generally committed to Colonel Kosciuszko, an active officer, who acted as an assistant engineer in the northern department."[29] Historian Hoffman Nickerson writes that the stone breastwork on the land side of Mount Independence "follows the military crest very cleverly so as to avoid leaving dead ground in its front, showing that its trace was laid out by a competent military engineer, probably Kosciuszko."[30]

Kosciuszko succeeded in the race to create a formidable defense on Mount Independence. When the British appeared, the summit was crowned with a star-shaped fort. Trenches lined the foot of the hill on the lakeside and were fortified with heavy

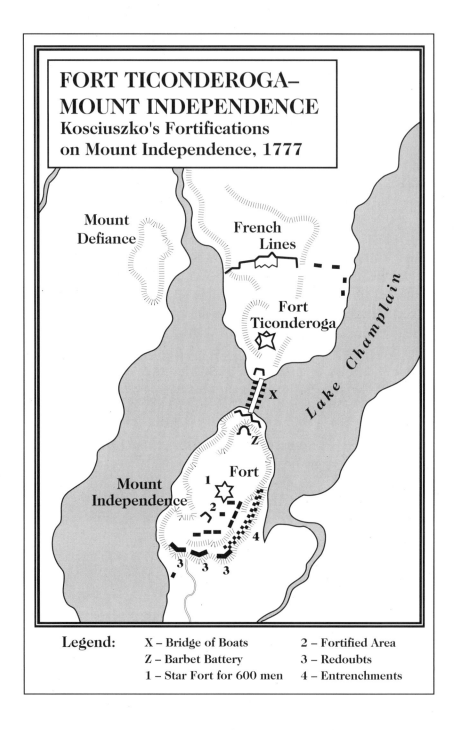

**FORT TICONDEROGA–
MOUNT INDEPENDENCE**
Kosciuszko's Fortifications
on Mount Independence, 1777

Mount Defiance

French Lines

Fort Ticonderoga

Lake Champlain

X

Z

Fort

1

Mount Independence

2

3 3 3

4

Legend: X – Bridge of Boats   2 – Fortified Area
Z – Barbet Battery   3 – Redoubts
1 – Star Fort for 600 men   4 – Entrenchments

cannon, pointed in the direction of the expected attack. Another battery of guns about halfway up from the water line reinforced the lower-level guns. A heavy barrier of logs, chained together, protected the bridge of boats to Fort Ticonderoga.[31] Unfortunately, Kosciuszko's defenses were never tested in battle, but they later prompted a favorable response from the enemy. Lieutenant August Wilhelm Du Roi (the Elder) of General Riedesel's Prince Frederick Regiment described the fortifications at Fort Ticonderoga:

> Not only the old fortifications of Fort Ticonderoga and the so-called French lines, had been renewed and increased during this time, but the hill just opposite the fort had been cleared of the wood, and a wooden fort been erected there, strengthening the whole with trenches and batteries.

Du Roi, whose regiment occupied Mount Independence after its capture, praised the excellence of the engineering work. "The whole was well done," he wrote, "and showed no lack of clever engineers among the rebels." He was especially impressed with the bridge between Ticonderoga and the Mount that Kosciuszko had improved upon. Du Roi said the bridge did "honor to human mind and power" and "It may be compared to the work of Colossus in the fables of the heathen."[32]

Generals Schuyler and St. Clair vigorously directed the construction of defenses on Mount Independence and on the Fort Ticonderoga side, but they neglected Mount Defiance. Historian John C. Miller writes, "Although Kosciuszko, the Polish engineer, General Gates, and other officers had pointed out the importance of fortifying Sugar-Loaf Hill, nothing had been done toward rendering it inaccessible to the enemy; the supposed impossibility of dragging cannon up its steep slopes quieted the patriots' apprehension from that quarter." Still the 2000 Continental troops, augmented by about 900 militia, were not sufficient to man Fort Ticonderoga, Mount Independence, as well as Mount Defiance. Historian Henry Carrington comments on the decision of Schuyler and his generals to ignore Mount Defiance: "The troops could not be spared, it is true; but the possibility of its occupation by

View of Mount Defiance from Fort Ticonderoga (restored), showing its commanding height over the fort. Colonel Thaddeus Kosciuszko reconnoitered Mount Defiance, recommending that it be occupied and fortified. American commanders, however, neglected the site. But British General John Burgoyne placed cannon on the summit and forced the American garrison to abandon Fort Ticonderoga without firing a single shot in defense, 6 July 1777. (Photo by the author, 18 September 1995).

a hostile force was not considered a serious question of fact."[33]

As the Americans awaited the enemy invasion, General John Burgoyne prepared to launch his combined British/German Army from St. John's. On 1 July 1777, his soldiers numbered nearly 8000. Of these, some 3700 were British, 3000 Germans, 400 artillerymen, 250 Canadians and Tories, and 400 Indians. The British and Germans were experienced professional soldiers. The officers were very capable. Burgoyne's second-in-command, Major General William Phillips, was an accomplished artillery-man. Burgoyne's brigadiers were Simon Fraser, Henry Powell, and James Hamilton. All would perform prominent roles in the approaching battles.[34]

Major General Baron von Riedesel commanded the German force, which, with the exception of one regiment from Hesse-Hanau, had been hired from the Duke of Brunswick. The 39-year-old Riedesel was considered a more experienced and versatile officer than Burgoyne. Von Riedesel's two brigadier generals were Johann Friederick von Specht and Wilhelm von Gall. Two other German officers would play key roles in the battles— Lieutenant Colonels Friederick Baum at Bennington and Heinrich von Breymann at Bemis Heights.[35]

From St. John's on 21 June 1777, Burgoyne's army sailed on a flotilla of vessels down Lake Champlain. Nine days later the army reached Crown Point, which General Schuyler had abandoned. Here, only eight miles north of Fort Ticonderoga, the soldiers disembarked and marched on both shores of Lake Champlain, the British on the western shore and the Germans on the eastern. On July 2, Captain Alexander Frazer's lead unit of marksmen, with several hundred Indians, attacked Mount Hope, high ground to the west of Fort Ticonderoga. The American garrison withdrew to the main fort. Shortly, the whole British force stood before the French Lines.[36]

On the morning of July 5, General St. Clair unsuspectingly looked up at Mount Defiance and to his consternation saw British cannon pointing down at Fort Ticonderoga. The British fired a round at a vessel in the lake, as if to announce their presence. At once St. Clair realized that he had been defeated. He called a council of his brigadier generals and Colonel Pierse Long. All unanimously agreed on an immediate evacuation so that the garrison of some 2000 Continentals and the militia would be saved. That night the Americans quietly abandoned Fort Ticonderoga and crossed the bridge of boats to Mount Independence. Fortunately, the route of escape remained open; Von Riedesel's Germans had not reached the bridge of boats on the Vermont side. General St. Clair hurried his soldiers twenty-four miles through wilderness along a trail of a road to Hubbardton and continued another six miles to Castleton, which he reached at dusk on July 6. Although they were pursued by the British, the Americans escaped.[37]

Congress, General Washington, and, indeed, all patriots were shocked. The commander-in-chief had considered Fort Ticonderoga impregnable. Before the British invasion took place, Washington had questioned Brigadier General Anthony Wayne, who had commanded the fort for several months, about conditions there. Wayne assured Washington that the fort possessed strength. Wayne's overly optimistic report conveyed a false sense of security. Governor George Clinton likewise was stunned by the great loss in his backyard. Notwithstanding his friendship for Schuyler, Clinton wrote critically of the general's judgment in a letter to James Duane, member of Congress, on 27 August 1777: "How he could be so mistaken about the strength and defensibleness of the posts, is a matter of no small wonder to me." On the international front, the loss of Fort Ticonderoga dampened the French desire to turn their secret aid into open support. General St. Clair, too, felt the devastating result of his abandoning Fort Ticonderoga and Mount Independence. In his letter to Washington of 17 July 1777, St. Clair pointed to his inadequate army of some 2000 Continentals, with which to defend lines and redoubts of more than three miles in extent. He said he could not bring in the militia because he lacked provisions for them. When a scanty supply arrived, he called in 900 militia, which joined him a day before evacuating the two posts. The most telling reason sprang from the powerful threat of British artillery. St. Clair explained: "The batteries of the enemy were ready to open in three different quarters, and our whole camp, on the Ticonderoga side, was exposed to the fire of each." The debacle of Fort Ticonderoga also damaged General Schuyler's reputation. Congress removed him from command of the Northern Department and ordered that St. Clair and he face court martials. Despite the gloom, the misfortune aroused the patriots to renewed effort. They raised militia units and marched them to Albany to reinforce the Northern Army.[38]

Kosciuszko felt sad over General St. Clair's misfortune. From his close association with the general, he had observed St. Clair's strenuous efforts to improve the defenses of Fort Ticonderoga, despite the meager number of soldiers he commanded. Kosciuszko came to admire his zeal and leadership. Notwithstanding the chaos of the retreat, Kosciuszko found time to write him words of encouragement at Fort Edward: "My General—Be well persuaded that I am wholly attached to you for your exceptional merit and knowledge of the military art that you most assuredly possess." He told St. Clair that some have severely criticized him for abandoning the fort, but these individuals, speaking from ignorance of the facts, had to be informed. Kosciuszko offered to help: "I am well persuaded my general that you are in a position yourself to give reasons for the retreat, but as it is a matter which touches my condition, I shall wish to be useful to you here in some way, therefore, make use of me." With other witnesses, Kosciuszko testified in behalf of General St. Clair at his court martial presided over by Major General Benjamin Lincoln at White Plains, New York, in August and September 1778. The board of officers cleared St. Clair of all charges and acquitted him "with the highest honour."[39]

On the British side, General Burgoyne was jubilant over his quick capture of Fort Ticonderoga. He had expected a relatively long siege and had equipped his army with a large number of cannon. In his report to Lord Germain on 11 July 1777, Burgoyne explained the key role of Mount Defiance. He wrote: "Lieutenant Twiss, the commanding engineer, was ordered to reconnoiter Sugar Hill, on the south side of the communications from Lake George into Lake Champlain, which had been possessed in the night by a party of infantry." He continued: "Lieutenant Twiss reported this hill to have the entire command of the works and buildings of Ticonderoga and Mount Independence...that the ground might be leveled so as to receive cannon, and that the road to convey them, although difficult, might be made practicable in twenty-four hours." The report of Twiss reads very much like the findings Kosciuszko had made to General Gates two months earlier. But, instead of a long siege, Burgoyne acted at

Letter of Colonel Thaddeus Kosciuszko (in French) to Major General Arthur St. Clair [Fort Edward, New York, July 1777]. Kosciuszko offers his help over the general's loss of Fort Ticonderoga to the British. (Collections of the Manuscript Division, Library of Congress)

once to occupy Mount Defiance and forced the Americans to abandon the fort. Burgoyne acknowledged the American awareness of Mount Defiance, telling Lord Germain: "It is now known that the enemy had a council some time ago about the expediency of holding it; but the idea was rejected upon the supposition that it was impossible for a corps to be established there." Unaware that Kosciuszko had urged Gates to occupy and fortify Mount Defiance, Burgoyne blamed the Americans for having among them "no men of military science."[40]

The easy capture of Fort Ticonderoga had a downside for General Burgoyne. It reinforced his contempt for the Americans. He considered their army a rabble, bound to stampede upon the first contact with British regulars. Burgoyne grew overconfident. A short time later, when he learned that General Howe set sail for Philadelphia instead of marching his army for Albany, Burgoyne still felt confident that he and his own force alone could defeat the American Army.[41]

Saratoga:
The Turning Point

ENERAL ARTHUR ST. CLAIR retreated through Hubbardton, Castleton, and Rutland to Fort Edward. His rear guard under Colonel Ebenezer Francis fought a skirmish at Hubbardton with a pursuing enemy force that suffered more casualties than the Americans. Reaching Fort Edward on 12 July 1777, St. Clair joined his weary soldiers with those of General Philip Schuyler, who himself could muster only 2100 troops. Meanwhile, General Burgoyne's confident army marched into Skenesborough (Whitehall) and tarried there for two weeks.[1]

Although he was devastated by the unexpected loss of Fort Ticonderoga and Mount Independence, Schuyler nevertheless sought to stem Burgoyne's march to Albany. He planned to impede and delay the British along Wood Creek, from Skenesborough to Fort Edward, for a distance of twenty-three miles. Schuyler assigned the difficult task of creating obstacles to Kosciuszko. Both Colonel Baldwin and he retreated with St. Clair's garrison to Fort Edward. Although Baldwin was nominally the chief engineer of the Northern Department, Schuyler called on the more talented Kosciuszko. Colonel James Wilkinson, Gates's adjutant general, always looked to the Pole, calling him "our chief engineer."[2]

While Kosciuszko directed the construction of obstacles and the destruction of bridges along the road, Schuyler busily rounded up axes for the crews. On 16 July 1777, Schuyler wrote Kosciuszko: "I have sent one of the Quartermasters to Saratoga and the post below to bring up all the Axes which can be collected and to deliver them to you." Evidently Kosciuszko had lost his horse during the hectic retreat from Fort Ticonderoga and asked Schuyler for a replacement, for in the same letter Schuyler added: "Col. Lewis has my orders to send you a horse immediately." To carry out Kosciuszko's plan of delaying the British, Schuyler gave him temporary command over two brigades of soldiers. He informed his engineer: "I will give the orders for moving General Fermoy's and General Paterson's Brigade[s] tomorrow, and dispose of them in the manner you wish."[3]

The road from Skenesborough to Fort Edward was only a trace through a primeval forest of tall pines and hemlock. Historian Don Higginbotham writes: "The ring of American axes and the crash of giant trees felled across the enemy's path echoed through the wooded country." The historian properly credits the initiative to Schuyler, but he fails to mention that Kosciuszko planned and carried out the work.* Historian John S. Pancake also attributed the work solely to "a thousand axmen." Kosciuszko destroyed some forty bridges over ravines, and he directed his soldiers to roll rocks and boulders into Wood Creek, thereby making it unusable for any navigation. The soldiers also dug ditches to run the creek water to low areas, already soggy from the heavy July rains, and created additional marshes, such that British engineers were forced to build laboriously two miles of corduroy roads. Writing from Skenesborough, Lieutenant Thomas Anburey recorded the delay:

---

*The six-hour documentary "The Revolutionary War," produced by Real TV of Los Angeles, California, and telecast on the Arts & Entertainment Network (A&E) in November 1995, included an account of Schuyler's obstruction of the British route of advance. Historian Robert Wright spoke of the thousand axmen but did not mention the Pole, who planned and carried out the destruction.

We are obliged to wait some time in our present position, till the roads are cleared of the trees which the Americans felled after their retreat. [One] would think it almost impossible, but every ten or twelve yards great trees are laid across the road, exclusive of smaller ones, especially when it is considered what a hasty retreat they made of it. Repairing the bridges is a work of some labour, added to which a stock of provisions must be brought up previous to our marching to Fort Edward.

When Burgoyne's army marched out of Skenesborough, the soldiers soon wilted from the sultry summer heat, and they were further tormented by swarms of gnats and mosquitoes. Burgoyne finally reached Fort Edward on July 29.[4]

"In the retreat of the American army Kosciusko was distinguished for activity and courage," wrote Major John Armstrong, aide-de-camp to General Gates, "and upon him devolved the choices of camps and posts and everything connected with fortifications."[5] On 17 July 1777, Schuyler's army retreated to Moses Creek, about five miles south on the Hudson River. Kosciuszko selected the camp because of the proximity of hills to the river that together formed a natural defense against a superior enemy. Here Schuyler again supported Kosciuszko fully, giving him the manpower, oxen, and carts for the engineering work. On July 19, Schuyler directed his quartermaster "to send eight carts & forty-eight oxen, with yokes, chains, drivers, and an overseer to Moses Creek, to be employed as Colonel Kosciuszko Engineer shall direct." On July 29, Schuyler assigned his engineer a force of 343 officers and soldiers levied upon the brigades of Generals Nixon, Fermoy, Poor, Patterson, and Ten Broeck. Through his aide, Lieutenant Colonel Henry B. Livingston, Schuyler ordered: "The fatigue party is, till further orders, to be furnished in the following proportions" [which he lists] "and is to proceed at seven o'clock, and receive orders from Colo. Kosciusko Engineer."[6] Schuyler, though, believing he still was too weak to oppose Burgoyne, retreated successively down the river to Saratoga, Stillwater, and finally to the Mohawk River, nine miles north of Albany. Here on Van Schaick's Islands, Kosciuszko erected fortifications.[7]

At this camp Schuyler received reports of the march of Lieutenant Colonel Barry St. Leger along the Mohawk River toward
the British objective of Albany. St. Leger reached Fort Stanwix
(Schuyler), near the present city of Rome, and placed the American garrison under siege. Meanwhile, Brigadier General Nicholas
Herkimer raised a force of 800 New York militia and marched to
relieve the besieged Americans. At Oriskany Creek, Herkimer
ran into a British ambush, and a hard-fought battle followed,
6 August 1777. St. Leger stopped Herkimer from reaching Fort
Stanwix. However, General Schuyler ordered Benedict Arnold
with 2000 soldiers to rush to the aid of the beleaguered fort.
Abetted by rumors of a disaster to Burgoyne, St. Leger suddenly
became unduly alarmed. He abruptly abandoned the siege of Fort
Stanwix and retreated to Oswego. Thus, the diversionary tactic
of the Grand Strategy ended in failure.[8]

Before Burgoyne got involved seriously in battle with his main
army, he suffered another heavy loss at Bennington, Vermont.
Von Riedesel had been urging the commander to order a foraging
expedition into the Connecticut River Valley for the purpose of
rounding up horses for his dismounted dragoons. These heavily-
equipped Germans had stumbled along the route of march, and
as infantry they were almost ineffective. Burgoyne agreed to the
German's request; however, in addition to mounting the dragoons,
Burgoyne sought to enlist Tories and to seize cattle, more horses,
and wagons. He ordered Lieutenant Colonel Baum to head the
foray of some 900 soldiers and dragoons. Burgoyne's choice of
the Germans was a mistake. They carried too much gear and
marched too slowly. And Baum proved to be an unlikely commander for the mission. He had to operate in an English-speaking
environment, and he did not speak that language. In addition,
Burgoyne's intelligence of rebel strength in the expected area of
operations was faulty. He did not know of the presence of John
Stark, a fighting general, and his New Hampshire militia brigade.
At Bennington, Stark destroyed Baum's total force, 16 August
1777. Earlier, Burgoyne ordered Lieutenant Colonel Breymann
to reinforce Baum, but Breymann arrived too late to save Baum.

MAJOR GENERAL HORATIO GATES

Commanding the American Army at Saratoga, he destroyed the British Grand Strategy upon Colonel Thaddeus Kosciuszko's stronghold on Bemis Heights, 19 September and 7 October, 1777. (Photo courtesy of the Library of Congress).

The loss was serious. Some 200 Germans were killed and 700 taken prisoner. Despite this defeat, Burgoyne vowed to carry out the mission of marching to Albany.[9]

Although Schuyler with Kosciuszko's help did his utmost to stem Burgoyne's advance down the Hudson River, he was severely criticized by members of Congress for the loss of Fort Ticonderoga. Congress resolved to try Schuyler by court martial. Replacing him, Congress again gave the command of the Northern Department to General Gates, 4 August 1777. Gates arrived in Albany on August 19 and found the army dispirited. The continual retreats, although tactically sound for an under strength army, contributed to low morale.[10] Gates decided to advance the army up river toward the enemy. The aggressive movement immediately lifted the spirit of the soldiers. At Stillwater, Gates called on his engineer to fortify the camp, and Kosciuszko laid out a trace of trenches. However, the river meadows were so extensive that Gates's small army could not occupy the position in sufficient strength to keep Burgoyne from outflanking the Americans. Kosciuszko condemned the position, and Gates looked for another. He dispatched Kosciuszko up river another four miles to Bemis Heights. After a thorough reconnaissance, Kosciuszko found the position an admirable one. "Patriots would fight and die on the ground he [Kosciuszko] selected," Colonel Red Reeder wrote, "and the fate of the campaign, indeed the war, would rest in large part on the way he laid out the defenses."[11] The foreign volunteer would justify the confidence of the Americans.

Gates received reinforcements of state militias as well as from General Washington. Although the commander-in-chief did not choose Gates to replace Schuyler, he was not indifferent to the plight of the Northern Army, for it was a key unit of the Continental Army. He now ordered Colonel Daniel Morgan's corps of riflemen to join Gates. Frontiersmen from Pennsylvania, Maryland, and Virginia, Morgan's soldiers were crack shots with the Kentucky rifle and experienced Indian fighters. These rugged woodsmen were the elite of the Continental Army.

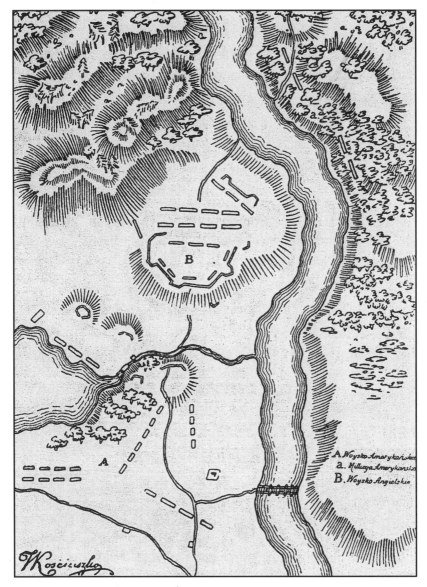

KOSCIUSZKO'S DISPOSITION OF FORCES AT SARATOGA
Translation of Legend:
A. *American Army*   a. *American militia*   B. *English Army*

(*Courtesy of National Library, Warsaw. The original drawing was in the Zamoyski Library but is now lost, following the German wanton destruction of Warsaw in World War II.*)

Washington told Gates: "This corps I have great dependance on, and have no doubt but they will be exceedingly useful to you." To Morgan's 330 soldiers, Gates added the 250 sharpshooters of Major Henry Dearborn. Gates employed this capable force well in the upcoming battles.[12]

Gates gained additional reinforcements. To Schuyler's original army of about 4500 soldiers, over which he assumed command, Gates obtained Brigadier General John Glover's brigade of Massachusetts Continentals (750 men), and the 2nd and 4th New York Regiments (400 men) plus Morgan's frontiersmen and Dearborn's sharpshooters. Thus, Gates's army grew to about 6300 soldiers; of these, seventy percent were Continentals. In number, Gates fielded about the same as Burgoyne. Nevertheless, with the continual arrival of militia units in September and October of 1777, the American Army soon surpassed that of the enemy.[13]

From Fort Edward, Burgoyne marched his army of some 6000 soldiers on the east bank of the Hudson River to Batten Kill. At this point his engineers built a bridge of boats, and on 13 September 1777, the army crossed to the west bank at the village of Saratoga. Burgoyne continued the march to Sword's House, within four miles of the American position on Bemis Heights. Here he paused to develop his plan of attack. The American east flank could be seen from the river. Mostly clear of trees, the bluff bristled with Kosciuszko's cannon and entrenchments. The center of the American defense was screened by tall trees and brush; the west flank disappeared into thick woods. Burgoyne's shortest and direct axis of advance lay along the river road for an attack on the American fortifications. He had forty-two pieces of cannon, including large 24-pounders that could bombard that flank. In contrast, the Americans had only twenty-two cannon, of which Kosciuszko positioned fourteen on the river flank. A supply of ammunition and provisions was readily available to the British in bateaux on the river. By concentrating his troops along the river road, Burgoyne's span of control would be excellent. Nevertheless, the British commander rejected that option of attacking the forbidding American right flank.

Historian Benson Lossing describes Kosciuszko's river fortification:

> Along the brow of the hill toward the river a line of breast-works was thrown up, about three-fourths of a mile in extent, with a strong battery at each extremity, and one near the center, in such position as to completely sweep the valley and command even the hills upon the eastern side of the river.[14]

Burgoyne was not alone in his assessment of the strength of the American east flank. Captain John Money, deputy quarter-master who had reconnoitered that flank, testified later that the top of the hill was fortified with a strong breastwork, and at the foot, an abatis. He stated categorically, "I do think that we could not have attacked the right flank of the rebel entrenchment without risking the loss of the whole army, and with little probability of success." Lieutenant Colonel Robert Kingston, Burgoyne's adjutant general, also testified at the same hearing. In answer to Burgoyne's question, "Was not the right of the enemy deemed impracticable?", Kingston answered, "I had no opportunity myself of seeing the right flank of the enemy; but I understood from others that the position was too strong to be attacked with any prospect of success." The eminent British historian Sir Edward Creasy *(The Fifteen Decisive Battles of the World)* confirmed Burgoyne's assessment of the American right flank. "The right of the American position, that is to say the part of it nearest the river," Creasy writes, "was too strong to be assailed with any prospect of success, and Burgoyne therefore determined to endeavor to force their left."[15]

On the critical river flank, Kosciuszko set up a clever trap for Burgoyne. Taking advantage of Mill Creek as an obstacle, the engineer built a redoubt along the creek and across the Albany road (Position 1 on the map, First Battle of Saratoga, page 36). Should Burgoyne choose to attack along the road, he could undoubtedly break through the redoubt with a sufficient force. His troops could then march down the road for nearly a mile until blocked by the second redoubt (Position 2). Burgoyne now would have entered the trap. Unable to move forward, even for a short time, and hemmed in by the Hudson River, the British units in the pocket

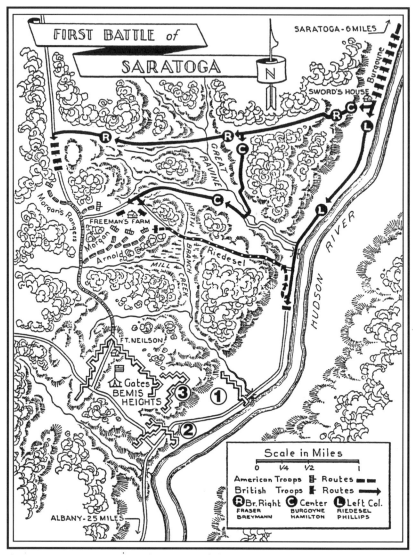

(From Lynn Montross, The Story of the Continental Army, 1775-1783, and reprinted by permission of Harper/Collins Publishers, Inc.)

could be raked with fire of fourteen cannon that Kosciuszko had positioned on the bluff (Position 3). Wisely, Burgoyne did not take the bait, and Kosciuszko, therefore, canalized the British attacks to the inhospitable terrain of the west.

Burgoyne was not sure of the location and extent of the American position on the west, having lost his scouting capability when practically all of his Indian allies deserted him. But surely there was an end to its western extension. None the less, the decision that Kosciuszko forced him to make became a disaster. The heavy woods disorganized the ranks of the redcoats, and they stumbled into the sights of Morgan's screened sharpshooters.

Burgoyne launched his first attack on 19 September 1777. It became known as the Battle of Freeman's Farm. He organized three wings. The right wing of light infantry, some 2000 strong, was commanded by Brigadier General Fraser. Brigadier General Hamilton commanded the center wing of about 1100 soldiers. Burgoyne marched with this wing. The left wing, led by Major Generals Phillips and Von Riedesel, consisted of some 1100 German troops. They were making a feint on the American right flank.[16]

On a sunny day the three columns marched out—Fraser moved westward for nearly three miles before turning south. Von Riedesel followed the river road, and Burgoyne with Hamilton in the center marched south and then swung west in support of Fraser. By about one o'clock Burgoyne concluded that Fraser and he had reached the temporary positions from which to begin the attack. Meanwhile, American scouts spotted the British and immediately notified Gates, who hesitated to act just yet. But relenting to Arnold's strong pleas, Gates ordered out Morgan's riflemen, who sped through the woods to near Freeman's farm, where they engaged the redcoats. The battle was joined. (Wilkinson said that Gates did not hesitate but "immediately ordered Colonel Morgan to advance with his corps"). Morgan's sharpshooters picked off soldiers but concentrated mostly on officers. Gates now ordered out Arnold's division, which fiercely attacked the British. Late in the afternoon, Gates threw General Ebenezer Learned's brigade into battle. Unfortunately, Learned struck at Fraser's right flank instead of joining the fighting at Freeman's farm. Fraser beat off Learned's attack. Meanwhile, Von Riedesel got a report of the heavy fighting and marched his force in support of Burgoyne. Von Riedesel's unexpected attack drove the

Americans into the woods. Because of the approaching darkness, the fighting ended. The Americans returned to Bemis Heights while the British kept possession of the field. British losses were unusually heavy, some 600 killed, wounded and captured. The center wing of 1100 soldiers lost more than half its force. On the American side, some 320 were killed, wounded, and missing.[17]

Burgoyne planned to resume the battle on the following morning, but his generals dissuaded him. Their soldiers lay dead or dying on the battlefield. Duty and compassion called for the burial of the dead and alleviating the suffering of the wounded. Much work lay ahead. The British soldiers also needed a pause. They were stunned by the ferocity of the American attack. The redcoats had been led to believe that the Americans were a ragtag army that would flee rather than fight. Burgoyne himself witnessed the fighting ability of the Americans, and he later testified in 1779 before a committee of the House of Commons: "Eleven hundred British soldiers, foiled in these trials, bore incessant fire from a succession of fresh troops in superior numbers, for above four hours." Junior officers, too, changed their opinion of American soldiers. Lieutenant Anburey of the 24th Regiment said in his published account:

> The courage and obstinacy with which the Americans fought were the astonishment of everyone, and we now become fully convinced that they are not that contemptible enemy we had hitherto imagined them, incapable of standing a regular engagement, and that they would only fight behind strong and powerful works.

With the end of the fighting on September 19, Burgoyne set up camp on the high ground near the Hudson River and south of the Great Ravine. The soldiers of Lord Balcarres built a redoubt on Freeman's farm, and Colonel Breymann's Germans erected a wall of defense north of Balcarres. The two positions protected Burgoyne's army from the vulnerable west.[18]

More aggressively-minded than his generals, the spirited Burgoyne had planned another attack for the following day. But he had experienced the disorganization of his units and the danger of hidden fire from the forest. Perhaps he again considered

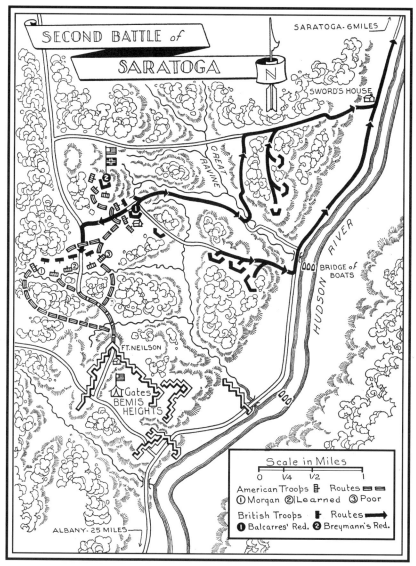

On 7 October 1777, Burgoyne conducted a reconnaissance in force in a continuing effort to determine the western limit of the American position. Unexpectedly he found himself in full battle when Gates attacked him near Freeman's Farm. Gates defeated Burgoyne and forced the British to retreat. (From Lynn Montross, The Story of the Continental Army, 1775-1783, *and reprinted by permission of Harper/Collins Publishers, Inc).*

the route along the river for a direct attack on the American right flank. Kosciuszko's formidable defenses, however, were still too intimidating. Lieutenant Anburey held the same view. Writing of the results of the Battle of Freeman's Farm, he said, "We have gained little more by our victory than honour, the Americans working with incessant labour to strengthen their left; their right is already unattackable." Burgoyne again decided to turn the American western flank. He planned a reconnaissance in force and, with the information gained, to launch a major attack the following day. However, the reconnaissance mission unexpectedly developed into full scale battle.[19]

On the morning of October 7, Burgoyne led 1500 soldiers with ten guns to the west. His units marched in an extended line of about three-quarters of a mile. Reaching the Barber farm wheat field, Burgoyne rested the troops. Meanwhile, out on reconnaissance, Wilkinson observed the British formation and galloped to army headquarters to report to Gates. The commander immediately ordered Morgan to attack the British advance and Brigadier General Enoch Poor's brigade to strike the rear of the column. Poor mauled and drove back a grenadier unit while Morgan delivered a hard blow against Fraser's light infantry. Astride a horse and wearing a bright uniform, Fraser became the target for an American sharpshooter. The general fell mortally wounded from his horse. Burgoyne now withdrew his force to Freeman's farm and gave up any attempt at continuing the reconnaissance.[20]

To the surprise of the Americans on the battlefield, General Arnold galloped into their midst and assumed command. He had no authority, having been relieved of his division after quarreling with Gates. Arnold felt resentful that the commander failed to recognize his part in the first battle. Notwithstanding, Arnold's fearless presence inspired the Americans to greater effort. Gates ordered out more troops: General Learned's brigade of three Massachusetts regiments and Brigadier General Ten Broeck's 3000 New York militia. Seizing command of nearby troops, Arnold attacked the Balcarres redoubt but was repulsed. Not giving up the fight, Arnold led his soldiers in a furious assault on Breymann's redoubt and captured it. In this final action, Arnold received a serious leg wound, and Breymann was killed. The American casualties were about fifty killed and 150 wounded. British losses were heavier, 175 killed, 250 wounded, and 200 taken prisoner. Perhaps as serious were the deaths of senior officers General Fraser and Colonel Breymann as well as many junior officers whose loss created a gap in leadership. Burgoyne's second failure to turn the American west flank doomed his ambitious campaign. He now sought to save his devastated army.[21]

During the night of 7 and 8 October, Burgoyne abandoned the Balcarres redoubt and withdrew his army to the high ground north of the Great Ravine. He paused long enough to bury General Fraser and then began to retreat north in a downpour of rain. American units followed the British. By the evening of October 9, Burgoyne's exhausted soldiers reached the village of Saratoga, crossed the Fish-Kill, and established a fortified camp on the high ground north of the creek. The next day, October 10, Gates's army arrived at the Fish-Kill. Although a continuing retreat seemed to be his only course of action, Burgoyne anxiously awaited word from General Henry Clinton who might have ordered a relief force to Albany. However, by this time Burgoyne's situation was hopeless. Gates had encircled the British camp, posting Colonel Morgan's corps on the high ground to the west of the British camp. Brigadier General John Fellows' Massachusetts militia brigade kept watch of enemy activities from the east bank of the Hudson. To the north, Stark's militia and Colonel John Bayley's New Hampshire militia held Forts Edward and George.[22]

General Clinton did conduct a diversionary attack up the Hudson River during the period of the Battle of Bemis Heights and the British retreat to the Fish-Kill. Clinton believed that his superior, General Sir William Howe, should have launched a major campaign to join Burgoyne at Albany. Instead, Howe sailed with 12,000 troops for Philadelphia, which he captured easily. The city possessed little strategic value. (It appears that Howe desired a pleasant social environment for the winter months of

1777–78). Clinton understood better than Howe the significance of Burgoyne's campaign. As soon as reinforcements from England reached New York, Clinton began his march. With 4000 soldiers, he sailed up the Hudson and captured Forts Clinton and Montgomery near Bear Mountain on 6 October 1777. The next day he seized the weakly-held fort on Constitution Island, opposite West Point. He then dispatched troops under Major General Sir John Vaughn to burn Esopus (Kingston). Clinton's diversion ended here. In the meantime, Gates, although worried over Clinton's movements, refused to divide his army. He correctly evaluated Clinton's march as a diversion. Nevertheless, Clinton influenced the terms of Burgoyne's surrender.[23]

Indeed, Burgoyne contemplated surrender. He was frustrated "by the total defection of the Indians, and the desertion or timidity of the Canadians and Provincials, some individuals excepted." His regulars had been reduced to 3500 fighting men, 2000 of whom were British. Only three days of provisions remained, and Burgoyne's routes of escape had been blocked. Meanwhile, Gates's army had grown to 16,000 soldiers.[24]

Burgoyne asked Gates for terms. Gates answered immediately: "Unconditional Surrender." Burgoyne rejected this harsh condition. During several negotiations between James Wilkinson and Major Robert Kingston, Gates moderated his terms to Burgoyne's satisfaction. The final agreement was called a "Convention" rather than a surrender, allowing Burgoyne's soldiers to return to England on the promise that they would never serve in North America again. Later Gates was severely criticized by Congress for his lenient terms. However, the specter of General Clinton's marching to Albany troubled Gates deeply during the negotiations. Gates was anxious to have Burgoyne's army lay down its arms. No doubt, the surrender of an entire army on 17 October 1777 and the demise of the Grand Strategy constituted an enormous victory.[25]

In his summation of the British Strategy, historian John Sweetman labels the strategy "completely unrealistic." He explains that although it was "attractively simple on a small-scale map, it was utterly impracticable on the ground." Sweetman's assessment is false. In fact, the strategy almost succeeded in spite of St. Leger's failed diversion and Burgoyne's disastrous foray for horses into Vermont. Burgoyne had marched to Bemis Heights, only thirty miles from Albany. From the south, General Vaughn reached Esopus and further to Tivoli, only about forty miles from Albany, and his march, too, was a diversion. But suppose that General Howe had led an army of 12,000 soldiers supported by a powerful naval force up the Hudson River in accordance with the strategy. The outcome could have been vastly different. Kingston stated the case forcefully to the committee of the House of Commons in 1779. He answered the supposition of simultaneous marches of Howe and Burgoyne on Albany: "I should think most certainly that a great army upon the Hudson's River near Albany would have contributed very much to our making our way to Albany." Therefore, the failure of the Grand Strategy resulted primarily from a violation of a cardinal, military principle —Unity of Command. The intended commander was General Howe, but the British government never told him his role. The Grand Strategy became essentially an individual effort by Burgoyne, and Gates destroyed that strategy.[26]

Gates achieved his resounding victory through Colonel Thaddeus Kosciuszko's exceptional choice of Bemis Heights and the well-planned fortifications. The brilliant military engineer created a bastion that Burgoyne dared not attack directly. Kosciuszko forced the British commander twice to try wide sweeping movements to the west and into heavy woods that disrupted his ranks and offered excellent cover for Morgan's riflemen. Historians have criticized Gates for relying too heavily on his strong defensive position and thus making himself too cautious. Admittedly, Gates showed caution at times; for example, not launching his own attack on the morning of September 20, the day after the first battle. However, Gates shouldered tremendous responsibility and could not risk an unexpected defeat. The fate of an infant nation depended on victory. Furneaux says much the same:

Gates's position was very strong. To gain a decisive victory, he needed only to stand fast and allow Burgoyne to batter his head against his defences. Prudently, Gates awaited attack; he was the only commander on either side who could lose the war in one afternoon.[27]

Despite his caution, Gates acted decisively at critical times. He did not wait in his strongly-fortified position for Burgoyne to complete the turning movements and attack him in the flank and rear. On the contrary, at the right time Gates ordered Morgan to stop the British sweep, followed by strong units that inflicted heavy casualties and defeated the movements. On October 7, Burgoyne was forced to try the same unsuccessful tactic and suffered a disastrous defeat. His campaign was over.

Gates was generous in his praise of Kosciuszko. At a meeting with Dr. Benjamin Rush, eminent physician and signer of the Declaration of Independence, Gates reacted to the doctor's profuse compliments, exclaiming, "Stop, Doctor, stop, let us be honest. In war, as in medicine, natural causes not under our control, do much. In the present case, the great tacticians of the campaign were the hills and forests, which a young Polish Engineer was skillful enough to select for my encampment.[28]

United States Marine Corps historian Lynn Montross credits the victory at Saratoga to Generals Gates and Schuyler and Colonels Morgan and Kosciuszko.* Similarly historian Edward Channing states unequivocally, "The credit of Saratoga belongs to Horatio Gates, and with him to Daniel Morgan, Benjamin Lincoln, and Thaddeus Kosciuszko." On the other hand, Furneaux, attributing the result to a makeshift army of amateur soldiers who fought for a principle and freedom, is correct but incomplete. Major John Armstrong, an eye-witness and participant in the campaign, wrote in retrospect that Kosciuszko's strong position on Bemis Heights "had no doubt much influence on the subsequent events of the campaign."[29]

---

* In the television documentary "The Revolutionary War," produced by Real TV and shown on the A&E Channel in 1995, narrator Charles Kuralt said nothing of Kosciuszko at Saratoga.

Colonel Rufus Putnam, American commander and engineer who assisted Kosciuszko at Saratoga, modestly gave full credit to the Pole. Putnam states in his *Memoirs:*

> the worthy Kusesko the famous Polander was at the head of the Engineer department in Gates army; we advised together with respect to the works necessary to be thrown up for the defence of the Camp but he had the over Sight in executing them. I therefore have no claim to extra Service this year, nor did I receive any particular notice from Gen. Gates.[30]

The capture of an entire British army was a magnificent victory for the Americans. Conversely, the failure of the Grand Strategy was an enormous defeat for the British. Most important, however, Saratoga lifted the American cause onto the international stage. France, previously aiding the Americans secretly, declared its open support, recognized the infant nation as an independent country, and joined the war with soldiers and warships. On 6 February 1778, France and the United States signed a treaty of commerce and alliance. Spain and the Netherlands cooperated with France, and Great Britain felt threatened. Although several more years of fighting remained, the American victory at Saratoga became the turning point of the War of Independence.[31]

BURGOYNE'S PLAN OF ATTACK

Battles of 19 September and 7 October 1777

Why Did Burgoyne Twice Attack To the West?

1. Premise.

The author concludes that Colonel Thaddeus Kosciuszko's exceptionally strong fortifications of the American position on Bemis Heights, especially on the river flank, forced General John Burgoyne to abandon a direct attack along the river road and, instead, to attempt twice, turning movements of the western flank. The near-impregnable eastern flank was the sole reason for Burgoyne's decision.

Several British historians and American Christopher Ward, too, introduced an "unoccupied hill," located immediately west of the fortified heights at Neilson's farm. These historians state that Burgoyne knew of the unoccupied hill and set it as an intermediate objective for his flanking attacks. If true, Burgoyne had some reason for directing the two attacks to the west, and Kosciuszko's river fortifications, although a powerful incentive for Burgoyne's decision, were not the sole reason.

2. Views of British Historians.

a. Sir George Otto Trevelyan in *The American Revolution* (1907) explains Burgoyne's three-pronged attack of 19 September 1777: "Phillips undertook to keep Gates in play. In the meantime Burgoyne and Fraser would occupy the high ground immediately to the west of that intrenched enclosure in which the Americans were penned." Trevelyan goes on to theorize that the British Army, having captured the hill, would "enfilade their lines with cannon, assail them with the bayonet in flank and

The "unoccupied hill"—the low, elongated rise of ground on the horizon. Located about one-half mile to the west of Neilson's farm on Bemis Heights. Preoccupied with this hill, British historians maintain that the "unoccupied hill" was Burgoyne's intermediate objective. (Photo by the author, 21 September 1996).

rear, and push their ill-commanded and disheartened army into and across the Hudson River."[32] Trevelyan's enthusiastic conclusion, however, is mere conjecture.

b. Sir John Fortescue in *History of the British Army*, Volume 3, praises Kosciuszko's strong fortifications but attempts to show how they could have been circumvented. Fortescue writes, "Burgoyne, however, was a better soldier than the Pole. He remarked very quickly that there was a hill on the American left which commanded the whole of their position, but which was still unoccupied."[33]

c. James Lunt* in *John Burgoyne of Saratoga* (1975) repeats the presence of an unoccupied hill. Lunt writes that Burgoyne's "scouts had reported an unoccupied hill lying to the west of

---

* Major General James Lunt, British Army, served two successive American Supreme Allied Commanders, Europe—Generals Lyman L. Lemnitzer and Andrew J. Goodpaster —as their Chief of Staff for Contingencies Planning.

Gates's line, and doubtless with the occupation of Sugar Hill at Ticonderoga in mind, this hill became Burgoyne's objective."[34] Lunt's conclusion, nevertheless, raises a pertinent question: On the evening of September 17, did Burgoyne have the time to order out his scouts when he reached Sword's House, about four miles north of the American position? Only one day remained for him to develop and coordinate with his commanders the plan of attack set for the morning of September 19. Major General Baron von Riedesel, for example, recalls in his *Memoirs*, "That night [September 17], however, passed quietly—still no particulars of the enemy's position among the hills were yet known."[35]

d. Gerald Howson in *Burgoyne of Saratoga: A Biography* (1979) is less certain of an "unoccupied hill." He states that if Burgoyne "did not know of an actual hill…he did suspect that there probably was one." Howson mentions in a footnote that General Simon Fraser bought information on Gates's position from unidentified persons on September 17. Nevertheless, Howson seems convinced that "Burgoyne did not know the exact position or extent of the American lines, for his Indians and auxiliaries were never able to get within sight of them.[36]

e. John Sweetman in *Saratoga 1777* (1973) introduces yet another unoccupied hill located farther west of the ground feature mentioned by the other authors, as shown in his map sketch below:[37]

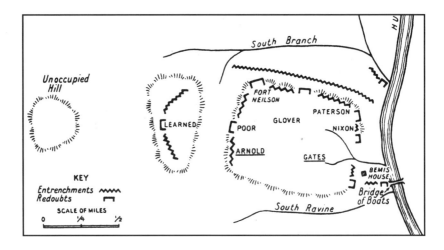

3. *View of American Historian Christopher Ward.*

He interprets the British plan of attack of September 19 in these words:

"Burgoyne planned an attack. Phillips and Riedesel were to advance along the river road to engage the American right. Burgoyne and Hamilton, with their four regiments, were to attack in the center, while Fraser's light infantry and grenadiers, the 24th British regiment, and his mixed auxiliary force of Tories, Canadians, and Indians swept around the American left and occupied that undefended higher ground to the west of the fort [Neilson's barn]."

In support of his stated British plan, Ward cites three sources:

(1) Benson J. Lossing, *The Pictorial Field Book of the American Revolution*, 2 Vols. (New York, 1850-51), I: 51.

(2) Isaac N. Arnold, *The Life of Benedict Arnold* (Chicago, 1880), pp. 170-71.

(3) George O. Trevelyan, *The American Revolution,* 6 Vols. (London, 1909-14), III: 162.

Neither Lossing nor Arnold mention an "unoccupied hill" as an intermediate objective of Burgoyne; however, Trevelyan does. Therefore, Ward bases his account on Trevelyan. Moreover, just like Trevelyan who indulges in possibilities, Ward also expands on the likely results flowing from the capture of the unoccupied hill: "From it Fraser could bring his guns to bear on the entrenchments, enfilade their front lines, and finally assault them in flank and rear, in the hope of pushing the Americans down the slope and into the river."[38]

4. *General Burgoyne's Own View.*

If Burgoyne received information of the American position on Bemis Heights by unknown civilians, he never admitted it, and he marched as if he were unaware of any high ground on the American western flank. Information from civilians is usually sketchy and unreliable since they may not know what a commander needs. As an experienced professional soldier, Burgoyne relied on his own trained engineers. At the hearing before a committee of the House of Commons in 1779, Burgoyne disclosed a great deal of his thinking and planning. He posed a key question to Lieutenant Colonel Robert Kingston, adjutant general:

Question: "From your conversation with the chief engineer and from other circumstances, have you reason to know, that every possible means were used after the 19th, to obtain a knowledge of the ground on the enemy's left?"

Kingston: "I had frequent conversation with the chief engineer on that subject. I believe his attention was given to that point almost every day, and a knowledge of that ground I understood to be very difficult to obtain."[39]

Therefore, Burgoyne conducted a reconnaissance in force on October 7, still trying to define the American position and determine the most effective manner of attacking it.

5. *Views of American Historians.*

a. James Wilkinson (*Memoirs*) discloses Burgoyne's weakness in the number of scouts. He writes: "The greater number of General Burgoyne's Indians had long before deserted him and the few who remained had lost their spirit of enterprise."[40]

b. Rupert Furneaux (*Battle of Saratoga*):

(1) "Deprived of his Indian scouts, Burgoyne had no knowledge of the American position, and he knew only that they were in strength a few miles ahead."

(2) "Nor could Burgoyne had intended, as is frequently suggested, to occupy the small height to the extreme left of Bemis Heights, the existence of which he could hardly have known, as Gates's fortified position was completely screened by woods from Freeman's Farm."[41]

c. Don Higginbotham (*The War of American Independence*): "With only the vaguest notion of Gates' whereabouts, Burgoyne groped forward for a showdown on the morning of September 19."[42]

d. Willard Sterne Randall (*Benedict Arnold: Patriot and Traitor*): "But Burgoyne wanted to see if there was some way around the Americans, even if his plan was vague and open-ended. He ordered a reconnaissance in force for the 7th; he himself would lead it. He simply had to get close enough to the Americans to see how powerful their defenses were...."[43] (Randall does not mention an "unoccupied hill.")

    e. Hoffman Nickerson (*The Turning Point of the Revolution*):

    (1) "In order to reach Albany, Burgoyne must beat Gates... his difficulty in doing so was his ignorance of his enemy's position."[44]

    (2) *Author's Comment.* Only the American right (east) flank was visible from the river. Nickerson believes that Burgoyne's best course of action was a direct attack along the river road because of certain advantages that it gave him (employment of a large number of cannon, proximity to supplies and ammunition on the bateaux in the river, and the exercise of effective command and control). Nevertheless, Howson flatly asserts that Burgoyne's direct attack along the river road would have led to disaster: "One has only to stand on the heights overlooking the Albany road to see the fatuity of the idea."[45] This author concurs with Howson.

6. Conclusions.

    a. Kosciuszko's admirable choice of Bemis Heights and his strong fortifications, especially on the east flank, dissuaded Burgoyne from attacking along the Albany road and forced him to turn to the west and into disaster.

    b. It appears that British historians Trevelyan, Fortescue, Lunt, and Sweetman discovered the "unoccupied hill" *after* the two battles.

    c. If not a better soldier than Burgoyne, Kosciuszko was a match for the Briton.

CHAPTER THREE

From Poland to America

Freedom Motivates Kosciuszko

THE NOBLE VALUES of liberty, individual dignity, and patriotic service for one's country shaped idealistic Thaddeus Kosciuszko's character during his formative years. As a student at the private school of the Piarist Fathers in Poland, young Tad read about the ancient Greek hero Timoleon the Corinthian and admired his valiant defense of the Greeks in Sicily against the forces of oppression. Plutarch wrote that Timoleon was noted for his love of country and gentleness of temper, except in his extreme hatred of tyrants and wicked men. In 344 B. C., Timoleon, an accomplished and courageous warrior, answered the pleas of the Greek colonists of Syracuse to defend them against the tyrant Dionysius II. Timoleon defeated Dionysius as well as the Carthaginians and organized the Greeks into a military league against Carthage. He also set up a semi-democratic government in Syracuse, after which he retired from public life. Timoleon became a model for Kosciuszko.[1]

The future engineer was born 4 February 1746 in the village of Mereczowszczyzna (Me-re-chov-chez-na) in the Polesie region of eastern Poland. The village lies midway between the towns of Brzesc Litewski and Nowogrodek. (The Russians seized the

entire region in the infamous Partitions of the late eighteenth
century and again in 1939). His parents, Ludwik and Tekla nee
Ratomska Kosciuszko, were Polish gentry of limited financial
means, living on their modest estate of Siechnowicze. Thaddeus
was the youngest of four children. His sisters were Anna and
Katarzyna. Brother Jozef was three years his senior. Thaddeus
was baptized Andrzej Tadeusz Bonawentura, but he preferred
the name of Tadeusz. During the Revolutionary War in America,
he habitually signed his name "Thad Kosciuszko."

The parents enrolled Tadeusz and Jozef at the school in
Lubieszow, near Pinsk, run by Father Stanislaw Konarski, headmaster, of the Piarist Order. The dynamic Konarski was adopting
many reforms of the Enlightenment. The students were taught
Latin, Polish, mathematics, and the natural sciences. Above all,
the headmaster sought to teach the young people how to be good
citizens. After five years the two brothers left the school in 1758
when their father died and returned to Siechnowicze to help
their mother run the estate.

In 1765, at age nineteen, Kosciuszko expanded his opportunities by enrolling in the newly-created Knights School, or Cadet
Corps, in Warsaw. At the time, King Stanislaw August Poniatowski,
patron of the arts, was changing the capital into a progressive
and intellectual center. He invited many artists from abroad, one
of whom was the renowned Bernardo Belloto-Canaletto, whose
beautiful paintings of the city became indelibly etched into the
history of Poland.[2]

King Stanislaw August established the school of cadets and chose
the very capable Prince Adam Czartoryski as commandant of the
Cadet Corps. Kosciuszko found himself in an exceptional environment where he received a thorough grounding in military
engineering from the best instructors of Western Europe. One year
later Kosciuszko was commissioned ensign and, as a gifted student,
took special engineering courses. He became an instructor of the
school and was promoted to captain. King Stanislaw August noted
Kosciuszko's performance by awarding the brilliant officer a royal
scholarship of studies in engineering and art in France.

Arriving in Paris in the fall of 1769, Kosciuszko enrolled in the *Academie Royale de Peinture et de Sculpture.* His foreign status made him ineligible for the *Ecole de Genie* at Mezieres, the famous school of military engineering. However, he was able to continue military science with private lessons from the instructors of that school. During his five years in France, Kosciuszko immersed himself in the pre-revolutionary environment that began to envelop the nation. The philosophy and political thinking of the French Enlightenment impressed and molded his thinking. He espoused the belief of the equality and participation of all society in the governing of a nation.

Kosciuszko returned to Poland in 1774, two years after the First Partition of his country. National and family affairs were both in shambles. He could not join the army. In fact, there was no army to speak of. Jozef's mismanagement left the family estate saddled with heavy debt. Kosciuszko depended on the hospitality of relatives and friends. Fortunately, the lord of the region, Jozef Sosnowski, engaged Thaddeus to give French lessons to daughter Ludwika. As a powerful magnate, Sosnowski possessed wealth and land. King Stanislaw August made him *hetman* (military commander) of Lithuania, and he enjoyed prestige in the Polish Commonwealth.* Thaddeus enjoyed coming to Ludwika's home in Sosnowice. Polish writer Antoni Gronowicz describes the pastoral setting:

> The Sosnowice estate was situated in the midst of lovely country beside the banks of a quiet rivulet bordered and invaded by flag. Young willows swung in stately measure as the wind led. The garden beds held millions of marsh marigolds. All around, as far as the eye could see, stretched the great rich fields. When the season was right, colored shadows raced away perpetually over the ripening rye, barley, and oats. In the center of the estate lay the well-kept park lined with many ancient trees whose leafy arches provided much needed shade during the summer months.

---

* As the Commonwealth of Poland, the country consisted of three nations: Grand Duchy of Lithuania, Ruthenia, and the Kingdom of Poland.

Here stood the imposing mansion with high, white columns. In this place lived the lovely Ludwika of the jet-black hair.

Tadeusz and Ludwika fell in love and planned to marry. But *Pan* Sosnowski, believing the marriage would not bring him any material gain, opposed the union. According to a popular saying, Sosnowski told the young man, "Ring-doves are not meant for sparrows, and the daughters of magnates are not meant for minor gentry." Unable to marry the beautiful Ludwika and with no opportunity to apply his engineering ability in Poland, Kosciuszko left for France in the fall of 1775. At age twenty-nine, he looked for another future.[3]

According to historian Miecislaus Haiman, Kosciuszko traveled south to Krakow, former medieval capital of Poland, and then west into Saxony. In Dresden he met Nicholas Dietrich, Baron de Ottendorf, and traveled with him to Paris. A French artillery captain, Charles Noel Romand, Sieur de Lisle, accompanied them. Neither of the American commissioners, Silas Deane nor Benjamin Franklin, had arrived in Paris, as yet; Kosciuszko therefore did not obtain a letter of recommendation to Congress, as foreign volunteers did later. With his two companions, Kosciuszko sailed for America by the end of June 1776. One account has the vessel encounter a violent storm that diverted the passengers to the island of Santo Domingo in the Caribbean Sea. Even so, the three travelers reached America, and Kosciuszko arrived in Philadelphia before 30 August 1776.[4]

Although Kosciuszko had no letter of recommendation from Deane or Franklin, the Pole is believed to have carried a letter of introduction from Prince Adam Czartoryski to Major General Charles Lee, second in command to General George Washington. Lee was well-known in Poland, having served King Stanislaw August as aide-de-camp and major general in the Polish Army, 1765–69. In Philadelphia, Kosciuszko planned to offer his services directly to the commander-in-chief, but neither Washington nor Lee were available. At the time, Washington's army was being chastised by superior British forces on Long Island and New York. Instead, Kosciuszko presented a memorial, stating his qualifications and experience, directly to the Continental Congress. The letter was read in Congress on 30 August 1776, and referred to the Board of War.[5]

While Kosciuszko waited for an answer from Congress, the Pennsylvania Council of Safety engaged him to plan and develop fortifications at Billingsport Island on the Delaware River. Congress had authorized the construction and agreed to fund it. Kosciuszko first reviewed the engineering plans of a Frenchman, Chevalier de Kermovan, that he submitted to Congress in July. Congress had appointed Kermovan an engineer in the Continental Army with the rank of lieutenant colonel and pay of sixty dollars a month. A Committee of the Pennsylvania Assembly and Kermovan jointly examined the existing defenses in the Delaware River and:

> judged it necessary, for further security, that a redoubt should be erected at Billingsport, on the New Jersey side, and that a boom should be thrown across, or some other obstructions fixed in the channel...and that Congress would direct these works to be done at the continental expense.

Congress so resolved on 14 June 1776. Next, Kermovan's plan of implementation was read in Congress and referred to the Board of War on 29 July 1776. Whether the Board acted on Kermovan's plan is not known, but the French engineer was now at Perth Amboy, New Jersey, facing Staten Island. From there, on 26 July and 12 August 1776, Kermovan wrote two letters to Benjamin Franklin concerning his work on the fortifications at Perth Amboy. Thus, Kosciuszko filled the vacancy of engineer in Philadelphia.[6]

Before proceeding with his work, Kosciuszko analyzed the American strategy for the defense of Philadelphia. If the British sailed up the Delaware River to Philadelphia without opposition, the Americans would be seriously threatened. He, therefore, drew a plan for the construction of parapets, batteries, and redoubts at Billingsport that could delay, if not stop, an attack along the Delaware. Kosciuszko's companion, Captain Romand de Lisle, assisted him in the work. Meanwhile, the Board of War reported favorably on Kosciuszko's memorial, and Congress passed the

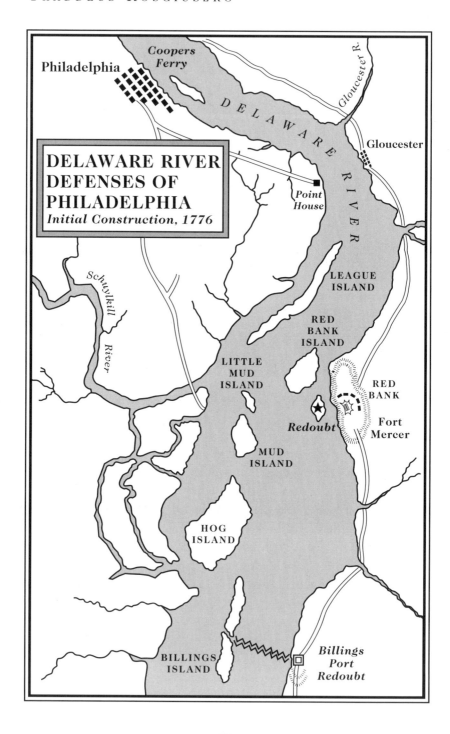

Philadelphia

Coopers Ferry

Gloucester R.

DELAWARE RIVER

Gloucester

DELAWARE RIVER DEFENSES OF PHILADELPHIA
Initial Construction, 1776

Point House

Schuylkill River

LEAGUE ISLAND

RED BANK ISLAND

LITTLE MUD ISLAND

RED BANK

★
Redoubt

Fort Mercer

MUD ISLAND

HOG ISLAND

BILLINGS ISLAND

Billings Port Redoubt

following resolution 18 October 1776: "*Resolved*, That Thaddeus Kosciuszko, Esq., be appointed an engineer in the service of the United States, with the pay of sixty dollars a month, and the rank of Colonel."[7]

Congress became alarmed when Washington retreated with his army into New Jersey and the British pursued him. As the danger to Philadelphia grew, Congress removed itself to Annapolis, Maryland, and Washington ordered Major General Israel Putnam to Philadelphia to "superintend the Works and give the necessary directions."[8]

General John Armstrong also worried over the safety of the city. He was the father of Major John Armstrong with whom Kosciuszko would serve in the Revolution. General Armstrong called on Kosciuszko to apply his engineering skill to the defenses of Philadelphia. Washington, too, took further action in the matter. On 9 December 1776, he wrote John Hancock, President of Congress, "If the Measure of fortifying the City should be adopted, some skillful person should immediately view the Grounds and begin to trace out the Lines and Works. I am informed there is a French Engineer of eminence in Philadelphia at this time. If so, he will be the most proper." Washington looked for another engineer when Colonel Rufus Putnam quit to take command of a Massachusetts regiment. Washington wrote Hancock again on December 20: "None of the French Gentlemen whom I have seen with appointments...appear to me to know anything of the Matter. There is one in Philadelphia who I am told is clever, but him I have never seen."[9]

In addition to Billingsport, Kosciuszko began the construction of fortifications at Red Bank on the New Jersey side of the Delaware River. He planned and directed the laying of the foundation of the site, named Fort Mercer, during the winter of 1776–77. Fortunately, Washington's victories over the British at Trenton on 26 December 1776 and Princeton at the start of 1777

Map, opposite page: *Thaddeus Kosciuszko first applied his engineering skill in designing defenses at Billingsport and Red Bank.*

forced the British away from Philadelphia for the time being. Although fear of the British subsided, Kosciuszko continued the work already begun.[10]

In early February of 1777, General Horatio Gates succeeded Putnam in command of Philadelphia. Kosciuszko met the new commander, and a close friendship developed that lasted throughout the war. When Congress ordered Gates to assume the command of Fort Ticonderoga, Gates took Kosciuszko along as his engineer.[11]

CHAPTER FOUR

Kosciuszko and the French Engineers

THADDEUS KOSCIUSZKO had been in America for one year when four French engineers joined the Continental Army. They arrived in Philadelphia in July 1777 at the request of the American Commissioner in Paris, Benjamin Franklin, who let the French government know that trained engineers were desperately needed in the American Army. Selected and approved by the French government, the four were Major Louis Lebeque Duportail, Captains Louis de la Radiere and Jean Baptiste Joseph de Laumoy, and Lieutenant Jean Baptiste de Gouvion. Duportail, spokesman for the group, had insisted before leaving France that they be promoted one grade by Congress (on top of the brevet promotion the French Army gave them before their leaving France).[1] Congress confirmed Franklin's agreement with France, and the four officers were commissioned in the Continental Army at two grades higher than their regular ranks in the French Army. Later, Congress appointed Duportail chief engineer.[2] Even before these engineers had the chance to demonstrate their talent, Duportail again asked for promotion. He had become alarmed when the Marquis de Lafayette and other companions arrived from France to join the American Army. These volunteers were promised the rank of major general by Silas Deane, American

DU PORTAIL.

MAJOR GENERAL LOUIS LEBEQUE DUPORTAIL

As commandant of engineers, he schemed and pressured the Continental Congress repeatedly for promotions for himself and his French engineers. (Photo courtesy of the Library of Congress).

Commissioner with Franklin in Paris. Provoked by Deane's promise, Duportail petitioned Congress at once for another round of promotions for himself and his three companions.[3]

When Congress delayed action on the promotions, the French engineers became unhappy and threatened to return to France. Meanwhile they performed odd jobs but kept up their demand. In November 1777, Congress asked General Washington for his opinion as to the worth of Duportail and his colleagues. Knowing that they had no chance to demonstrate their capability, Washington was reluctant to rule for or against them. Nevertheless, he believed that these foreign officers would prove their value to the Continental Army in time, and he pointed to Kosciuszko's contribution to victory at Saratoga the previous month. Washington remarked, "I would take the liberty to mention, that I have been well informed, that the Engineer in the Northern Army (Cosieski, I think his name is) is a Gentleman of science and merit." The outstanding performance of Kosciuszko in shaping the decisive victory over the British may have influenced Congress to keep the Frenchmen, who, undoubtedly, never learned of the crucial, indirect role Kosciuszko had played in their lives.[4]

While Congress temporized with the second round of promotions for the French engineers, Duportail kept up the pressure. He wrote a long letter that was read in Congress on 13 November 1777. Much of the contents was nonsense. He claimed, for example, that the chief engineer must have "a respectable rank in the army," and such standing is more necessary in America than elsewhere. "Have I not seen the colonels of the army," he asked rhetorically, "and even the militia colonels refusing to follow my directions about the works?"[5] Duportail's reasoning reflected that of a rank-conscious monarchist suitable for currying favor in the courts of Europe and alien to independent-minded Americans. Rather than let the merit of his engineering performance convince the Americans, Duportail believed he had to assert superior rank. (In contrast, Kosciuszko did not experience any of Duportail's problems. Americans took to the modest and accomplished Pole.[6]) Swayed by Duportail's arguments, the members of Congress promoted the Frenchman to brigadier general and his companions one grade again.[7] As a brigadier general, Duportail ranked Kosciuszko. General Washington, however, concurred in the need to have one senior officer in charge of the corps of engineers.

The unwarranted promotion of the French engineers provoked Colonel John Laurens to complain to his father, Henry Laurens, President of Congress. Colonel Laurens wrote:

> It is a pity that Congress should grant any promotion but upon the recommendation of those superior officers, who have known or seen the feats upon which these pretensions are founded. The present way of proceeding is productive of great confusion and much uneasiness. It is complained that whoever will go to York and speak loudly to members of Congress, of his own abilities and eminent services, will obtain what he intrigues for...The august representative body of thirteen free states is said to be bullied by every man who is impudent enough to make his own panegyric, and represent his own importance.[8]

Nevertheless, the presence of the French engineers and their good fortune of generous promotions had no immediate affect on Kosciuszko. His association with Duportail and La Radiere did become a source of trouble. They did not accept Kosciuszko as a fellow engineer. In fact, they sniped at his reputation and derogated his capability, even though Kosciuszko had studied military engineering in France for five years. His problems with his fellow engineers began at West Point in March 1778, and Kosciuszko found the arrogance of the Frenchmen insufferable.[9]

General Washington considered West Point the key to the continent. The British strategy to seize control of the Hudson River and thereby divide New England from the middle and southern colonies failed at the Battle of Saratoga in 1777. Notwithstanding, the inspiring victory underscored the absolute necessity of defending and maintaining control of the waterway. The Americans chose West Point, some fifty miles above New York, for the site of the bastion. In response to instructions from Congress, Washington dispatched La Radiere to Fort Montgomery in the Hudson Highlands.[10]

Thus far, the four French engineers had been marking time, but they expended much effort in pressuring Congress about promotions. In fact, La Radiere was lobbying for a colonelcy on his way to the Highlands. Historian Dave Richard Palmer writes, "The officer who had been a captain in France only months before, who was now a Continental lieutenant colonel for doing nothing more than crossing the Atlantic, threatened to embark for France in January if he were not elevated to full colonel." As events unfolded, La Radiere had been unduly impatient. A short time later Congress promoted all four engineers one grade higher on 17 November 1777.[11]

La Radiere's first major assignment called for him to assist the Americans in selecting a site on the Hudson River. He joined a high-level group composed of Major General Israel Putnam, New York Governor George Clinton, the Governor's brother General James Clinton, and several other prominent individuals. The group reconnoitered the Highlands and narrowed their choices to two locations: West Point and Fort Clinton, located a few miles down river from West Point at Bear Mountain. Earlier, Fort Clinton and the companion Fort Montgomery were seized by General Sir Henry Clinton during the attempt to rescue General Burgoyne at Saratoga. However, when Burgoyne surrendered his army, the British destroyed the forts and retreated to New York.[12]

The Americans unanimously chose West Point over the loud objections of Colonel La Radiere, who insisted on Fort Clinton. But West Point was an excellent choice. Not only was the terrain very suitable for erecting fortifications but also for stopping warships and firing on them. At this location the river makes two abrupt turns that cause ships to lose sail and slow down to a crawl. However, La Radiere was not convinced of the value of the site. He took time to prepare a memorial—a written statement—in which he strongly advocated the choice of Fort Clinton. In addition, he requested that the reasons for the selection of West Point be put in writing even though the group had discussed these reasons among themselves for many days. As expected, General Putnam ignored La Radiere's arrogant demand.

In deference to the French engineer, however, Putnam asked the Council and Assembly of New York to make a final determination. The appointed five commissioners conducted a three-day reconnaissance of the river and unanimously confirmed the choice of West Point.

Rebuffed and humiliated through his own stubbornness, La Radiere began to plan the fortifications at West Point. But his heart was not in his work, and the gruff, sixty-year-old general lost patience. Putnam complained to Washington, "I have directed the Engineer to lay out the fort immediately—but he seems disgusted that everything does not go as he thinks proper, even if contrary to the judgment of every other person." Putnam derided La Radiere as "an excellent paper Engineer."[13]

The Frenchman labored under the false assumption that as the schooled engineer he had the authority to make decisions for the army. A staff officer, however, no matter how sound his judgment, makes only recommendations to the commander, who is the final authority. Clearly La Radiere did not understand the difference when he tried to explain his right of command to the President of Congress.[14]

La Radiere also wrote to General Washington, asking for time to speak with him personally about the situation at West Point. In response, Washington sided with Putnam. The commander-in-chief explained that the time for decision-making had passed, and the construction of a fortified site demanded immediate action. La Radiere set to work during February 1778, but he had no enthusiasm for his role. General Samuel H. Parsons, in command at West Point and noting La Radiere's distaste for his assignment, let him go. Parsons explained to Washington that La Radiere did not wish to risk his reputation on a fortification that differed from the accepted European model.

Everyone except La Radiere seemed aware that the Frenchman's plan of a massive, Vauban-type fort would not meet Washington's urgent time schedule for a blocking position on the Hudson and that La Radiere's grandiose scheme called for resources and costs beyond the means of Americans. Colonel

David Humphreys, Washington's aide-de-camp, concluded that La Radiere's plan was totally impractical, and he expressed disgust for La Radiere's arrogance: "His petulant behaviour and unaccommodating disposition added further embarrassments."[15]

The problems with La Radiere became more complicated by an independent action of Congress. When General Gates became President of the Board of War, he ordered Colonel Thaddeus Kosciuszko to West Point, believing that the important post on the Hudson would benefit from Kosciuszko's engineering skill. Gates probably was influenced by Governor George Clinton's utter disgust with La Radiere. Clinton wrote Gates,

> I fear the Engineer who has the direction of the works is deficient in point of practical Knowledge; without which altho [sic] possessed of ever so much scientific I need not mention to you, Sir, how unfit he must be for the present Task, the Chief Direction & Management of which too requires a Man of Business & Authority.[16]

Kosciuszko traveled to the Highlands, calling first on Governor Clinton in Poughkeepsie on 26 March 1778. Impressed with the Pole, Clinton handed him a letter of introduction to Parsons. The Governor wrote, "I believe you will find him an Ingenious Young Man & disposed to do Everything he can in the most agreeable Manner."[17] In turn, Parsons greeted West Point's new engineer cordially. At dinner that evening the two talked about the task that lay ahead. They formed a good rapport, and Kosciuszko seemed pleased to be at West Point.

The Pole's pleasure turned to dismay when La Radiere showed up the next day. Believing that La Radiere's problem with General Putnam sprang from a personality clash, Washington ordered La Radiere back to West Point. Washington, meanwhile, had assigned a new commander for the Highlands, Major General Alexander McDougall. Unfortunately, La Radiere again caused trouble. As a trio of West Point historians remarked, "From La Radiere's viewpoint, the very idea that a French engineer could be replaced by a non-Frenchman was enough to make Vauban turn over in his grave." Although he was junior in rank to Kosciuszko, La Radiere fancied himself superior to Kosciuszko not only in rank but also in engineering ability. McDougall had to keep the two apart.[18]

Learning of Kosciuszko's assignment to West Point, Washington became irritated by the lack of coordination that resulted in two chief engineers there. He at once ordered McDougall to send Kosciuszko to army headquarters. The commander-in-chief wrote McDougall on 6 April 1778, "The presence of Colonel de la Radiere rendering the Services of Mr. Kosciousko as Engineer at Fishkill unnecessary—you are to give him immediate orders to join this army without loss of time." Always the diplomat, Washington caught himself and added a postscript: "However desirous I am of having Mr. Kosciousko here, if he is employed in any special device by order of Congress or the board of War, the above order you will set aside."[19] Meanwhile, General Parsons sent La Radiere, the day after his arrival, to McDougall at Fishkill. Parsons opposed La Radiere and penned a strong letter of support for Kosciuszko. He told McDougall:

> Colonel Kosciuszko, sent to this place, is particularly agreeable to the Gentlemen of this State and all others concerned at this post; you will, Sir, readily find by a little enquiry that altho' Col. La Radiere appears to be a man of Some Learning and Ingenuity, an attachment to his opinion in his Profession & Some other Matters have rendered him not so suitable as some other Persons to have the Principal Direction at this Post…As we are desirous of having Col. Kosciuszko continue here & both cannot live upon the Point, I wish your Honor to adopt such Measures as will answer the wishes of the People & garrison; & best Serve the public good. Col. La Radiere will be with you tomorrow.[20]

Likewise stating his preference for Kosciuszko, General McDougall perhaps was influenced by the enclosures of Parson's letter—the resolutions of Congress and the Board of War that appointed Kosciuszko the chief engineer at West Point. Though McDougall was partial to La Radiere, he knew better than to oppose Congress. In his reply to Washington on 13 April 1778, he wrote:

> Mr. Kosciousko is esteemed by those who have attended the works at West-point, to have more practice than Col. Delaradiere.

And his manner of treating the people more acceptable than that of the latter; which induced Genl. Parsons and Governor Clinton to desire the former may be continued at West-point. The first has a Commission as Engineer with the rank of Colonel in October 1776—Colonel Delaradiere's Commission I think is dated in November last, and disputes rank with the former, which obliges me to keep them apart; and avail the services of their assistance in the best manner I can devise.[21]

General McDougall's letter convinced the commander-in-chief to reverse himself. On 22 April 1778, Washington replied: "As Colo. La Radiere and Colo. Kosiusko will never agree, I think it will be best to order La Radiere to return, especially as you say Kosiusko is better adapted to the genius and temper of the people."[22]

According to historian Elizabeth Kite, Kosciuszko lost a golden opportunity for advancement when he remained at West Point rather than return to army headquarters at Valley Forge where he could have been close to General Washington. As a consequence, she writes that Kosciuszko "was never the recipient of any mark of recognition from General Washington, and he remained only a Colonel to the end."[23] Clearly Kite misjudges Kosciuszko's character. The Pole never schemed to advance himself, unlike Duportail and La Radiere.

La Radiere failed to maintain his status at West Point, first against General Putnam and then against Kosciuszko. The Frenchman had created his own problems. Perhaps if he had possessed some of Kosciuszko's modesty, he would have gotten along with Americans and contributed his talent to the building of the river fortification. Following his second rejection from West Point, La Radiere was bitter, and his feelings against the Pole surfaced again in the summer of 1778. Kite asserts that "pressure was brought to bear upon Congress to have Col. Kosciuszko made brigadier general." However, she does not disclose the names of those who applied the alleged pressure nor does she offer any proof. However, the rumor was enough for La Radiere to become alarmed. He dashed off a letter directly to Congress, bypassing his superior, Duportail, and even General Washington.

Writing from White Plains, New York, 10 August 1778, La Radiere said, "It is reported here that Congress will appoint several Brigadier generals five or six days hence...I see that I am in the right to beg the Congress to be appointed Brigadier general in this promotion." La Radiere's intervention in the alleged promotions evidently stopped them. "Needless to say," Kite concludes, "there was no more talk of raising Kosciuszko to a rank that would have necessitated at once a train of elevations not only among the French Engineers but among the American officers as well, causing endless dissatisfaction and jealousies on every hand."[24]

Precisely for the reasons Kite presents, Kosciuszko never tried to advance himself. He had come to America to help the patriots gain independence. He wanted Americans to accept him so that he could work harmoniously with them. He was well aware of the resentment of American officers toward foreigners receiving quick promotions and thereby, as Washington was wont to say, "upsetting the tranquility of the army." Like other Continental Army officers, Kosciuszko undoubtedly knew the shock that three prominent generals caused Congress with their protest of the political appointment of foreign officers to high rank. The three, Major Generals Nathanael Greene and John Sullivan, and Brigadier General Henry Knox, voiced their displeasure when Congress was about to confirm the promise made by Silas Deane to Monsieur Philippe Charles Du Coudray. The Frenchman expected to be made chief of artillery in place of Knox and given the rank of major general, to date from 1 August 1776. Thus, Du Coudray would rank both Greene and Sullivan. Moreover, Du Coudray would supplant Knox, who was well-liked by Greene. Biographer Francis Vinton Greene explains that General Greene was not xenophobic, but he "did not relish the idea of being overslaughed, and though he afterward conceived great admiration and friendship for Lafayette, Steuben, and Kosciuszko, at this time he looked with distrust upon the advent of foreign adventurers." On 1 July 1777, Greene penned his letter of indignation to John Hancock, President of Congress, threatening to leave the army: "If the report be true, it will lay me under the necessity of resigning my Commission, as his appointment supersedes me in command. I beg you'll acquaint me with respect to the truth of the report, and, if true, inclose me a permit to retire." Generals Sullivan and Knox added weight to Greene's letter by submitting similar letters.[25]

The letters of the generals provoked Congress into anger. On 7 July 1777, it unanimously passed a strong resolution, telling the three protesters to submit to the authority of Congress or resign. The resolution read:

> That the president transmit to General Washington copies of the letters from Generals Sullivan, Greene, and Knox, to Congress, with directions to him to let those officers know that Congress consider the said letters as an attempt to influence their decisions, and an invasion of the liberties of the people, and indicating a want of confidence in the justice of Congress; that it is expected by Congress the said officers will make proper acknowledgments for an interference of so dangerous a tendency; but, if any of those officers are unwilling to serve their country under the authority of Congress, they shall be at liberty to resign their commissions and retire.[26]

General Greene responded in a polite and dignified manner, acknowledging his willingness to serve under the authority of Congress. At the same time, he emphasized the case for the soldier: "In my military capacity I have and will serve my Country to the utmost of my ability while I hold it, but I am determined to hold it not a moment longer than I can do it unsullied and unviolated." The protest of the three generals helped the cause of the army. Congress made key changes to the original expectations of Du Coudray, insuring that Greene and Sullivan continued to outrank Du Coudray as major generals. Congress also preserved Knox's position as chief of artillery by coming up with a novel office for Du Coudray, that of "Inspector General of Ordnance and Military Manufactories." Major General Du Coudray served barely a month. On 15 September 1777, he accidentally drowned in the Schuylkill River near Philadelphia.[27]

American opposition to foreign officers and their promotions did not cease with the case of the three generals. In fact, Greene himself experienced opposition from a subordinate. Upon assuming command of the Southern Army in early December 1780, he faced the hostility of Major General William Smallwood to serving under the foreigner, Major General Baron von Steuben. At the time, the German was in Virginia recruiting soldiers for the Southern Army. He expected to march with the recruited force to join Greene and serve as his principal assistant. Greene expressed his dilemma to Washington:

> I find when the Baron Steuben comes forward there will be a difficulty between him and General Smallwood. The latter declares he never will submit to the command of the former, and insists upon his commission dated back to as early a period as he had a right to promotion. When that was I know not; as I know of no principles of promotion from brigadiers, majors, generals, except their seniority or special merit. What is best to be done in the affair? Before I order the Baron to come forward, I wish your Excellency's advice in the matter.

The Baron never left Virginia. Nevertheless, Greene grew pessimistic about the future: "I fear our army is always to be convulsed by extraordinary claims and special appointments."[28]

Unlike the French engineers and others, Kosciuszko dissuaded friends from agitating for his promotion. When his backers, including General Gates, recommended Kosciuszko for promotion to members of Congress, following Duportail's advancement to brigadier general, the Pole begged Gates to cease his efforts. Kosciuszko wrote to Colonel Robert Troup, aide to Gates, "My dear Colonel, if you see that my promotion will make a great many jealous, tell the General that I will not accept of one, because I prefer peace more than the greatest rank in the World."[29] On this occasion Kosciuszko made a mistake. Certainly, clamoring for promotion like Duportail was unbecoming. However, he should have allowed his demonstrated capability and his appreciative supporters to work in his behalf. As a consequence, Kosciuszko was not promoted for seven years.

Although Kosciuszko had nothing to do with La Radiere's

relief from West Point, the Frenchman nevertheless blamed the Pole for his misfortune. He bore a grudge that surfaced a few months later when General Washington marched the Continental Army to the Hudson Highlands. General Duportail and La Radiere came with the army headquarters. La Radiere now vented his malice in a letter to General Gates, temporarily in command of units around West Point. Deriding Kosciuszko's engineering ability, La Radiere warned Gates "not to risque his reputation for a gentleman who does not know his duty." Gates paid no attention to La Radiere's insinuation, having come to respect and admire the brilliant engineering that Kosciuszko had demonstrated at Saratoga.[30]

Asserting his own engineering superiority and that of his companions, Duportail bothered Congress again shortly after La Radiere's false alarm over promotions. From Camp White Plains on 27 August 1778, Duportail wrote that some officers (probably having Kosciuszko in mind) were designated engineers by Congress, but they really did not possess the schooling and experience necessary for the practice of the art of engineering. Consequently, the placing of French engineers under them, due to seniority, "would abase our abilities on a level with theirs, and therefore hinder our being more useful than they." Continuing in a highly-opinionated mode, Duportail made a hair-line distinction. Those outside the French circle, he maintained, should be called officer-engineer, like colonel-engineer. But the French were really officers of the Engineers. In his prattling, Duportail never conceded the possibility that a non-French engineer could be just as competent as, or more than, a Frenchman.

In addition to the assumed French superiority in capability, Duportail demanded that their status extend into the matter of seniority, as well. Without naming Kosciuszko but referring to the recent difficulty at West Point between Kosciuszko and La Radiere, Duportail stated, "A Col. Engineer would not acknowledge Mr. de la Radiere, Col of the Engineers, for his Superior." The Continental Congress chose to overlook the petty and troublesome behavior of Duportail and La Radiere. No doubt, international politics influenced Congress. The new nation desperately needed the substantial support of France, a European power and sworn enemy of Great Britain.[31]

General Washington sought to establish a relationship between Kosciuszko and the French engineers. The opportunity arose when Duportail informed Congress (and Washington) of the special seniority that the French engineers should be accorded. Washington, in turn, advised the President of Congress that any promise made to Duportail was a matter for Congress. However, on the subject of seniority, Washington stated that "the Commissions of Officers were the only rule of precedency and command I had to judge by; and while others hold superior appointments I must consider them accordingly in the course of service." He also expressed his policy specifically for Kosciuszko: "At the same time I think it right to observe, that it cannot be expected that the Colo. Cosciusko, who has been a good while in this line and conducted himself with reputation and satisfaction will consent to act in a subordinate capacity to any of the French Gentlemen except General Portail."[32]

Washington's statement of policy followed the principles of seniority, since Duportail was a brigadier general and ranked Kosciuszko. Nevertheless, Washington sought to protect Kosciuszko's standing in the Continental Army. A striking example occurred in September of 1778 when Kosciuszko served as chief engineer at Fortress West Point. Always concerned with the security of the Hudson River, Washington ordered the chief of the Corps of Engineers, Duportail, "to the Highlands and examine the several fortifications carrying on there for the defense of the river."[33] Duportail made the inspection of West Point on 9 and 10 September 1778. He timed the visit to Kosciuszko's absence, occasioned by the Pole's presence in White Plains, where he testified at the court martial of General Arthur St. Clair. Undoubtedly Duportail wished to avoid Kosciuszko, even though, by doing so, he failed to carry out one of Washington's requirements—to determine the cost of construction at West Point. Duportail explained his failure as follows: "It is not in my power to present anything on this subject [costs], not having seen Col. Kosciusko, who alone is possessed of these facts—I am going to write to him for this purpose."

Duportail should have alerted the West Point commander or Kosciuszko of the upcoming inspection. Duportail needed the presence of Kosciuszko who could escort the inspecting officer around the fortifications, answer questions and clarify the status of construction, and receive personally the inspector's comments and recommendations. In military circles, inspections are not a time for destructive criticism but, rather, an opportunity for improvement. Evidently Duportail did not allow proper military procedure to influence his biased conduct.

Following the inspection visit, Duportail submitted a lengthy report to Washington. He found mostly minor "deficiencies" that pertained in large measure to unfinished work of on-going construction, although Duportail did not identify them as such. One project Kosciuszko considered vital to the defense, and that Duportail dismissed as unnecessary, was the plan to fortify Rocky Hill, high ground that rose above Fort Putnam. Duportail concluded that Rocky Hill, despite its commanding height and nearness to Fort Putnam, would not give the enemy any advantage. "It would be very difficult for an enemy," Duportail stated, "even when master of it, to bring heavy cannon there." Duportail made the same mistake that American commanders committed at Fort Ticonderoga when they ignored Mount Defiance in 1777. A trio of West Point historians termed Duportail's report "a good account of the state of the fortifications." Nevertheless, Duportail destroyed Kosciuszko's defense design when he ruled out the need to occupy and fortify Rocky Hill. Duportail's comments in his report, for example, whether the walls of forts should be one thickness or another, or one height or another, pale into minutia when they are added up and compared to the gross military error he committed. Whereas Duportail turned out to be a technician, Kosciuszko proved himself a military planner. Fortunately, Washington later restored the soundness of Kosciuszko's design.

Duportail's engineering thinking was heavily influenced by the schooling he received at *Ecole de Genie* at Mezieres where the staff stressed Vauban's design of massive fortifications built like regular polygons. However, the Marquis de Vauban began to experiment with variations in his latter years. Professor Henry Guerlac writes that Vauban "had freed himself from reliance on the main *enceinte*" [walled fort] "and taken the first steps toward a defense in depth. He had gained a new flexibility in adapting his design to the terrain without imperiling the main line of defense." Guerlac adds that Vauban's new flexibility in depth, unfortunately, was rejected by the staff at Mezieres "whose ideas dominated the eighteenth century, and whose schemes of fortifications were based squarely upon Vauban's first system." It appears that Kosciuszko, while studying engineering in France, received more than the dogmatic teachings of Mezieres.[34]

Although Washington approved Duportail's report of West Point, he ruled out any significant changes to Kosciuszko's engineering plan. He told Duportail that the great progress already made "would render any alteration in the general plan of work of too much time." Historian Palmer explains how Washington diplomatically changed Duportail's criticism into praise for Kosciuszko:

> Next, the General blandly told Duportail: "The favorable testimony which you have given of Colonel Kosciousko's abilities prevents uneasiness on this head." Duportail, of course, had paid no such compliment, not intentionally at least. But he could hardly refute it.[35]

Thus, Washington managed to satisfy both engineers. With some exceptions, the commander-in-chief approved the inspection report (thus satisfying Duportail), and he upheld Kosciuszko's reputation (pleasing his West Point engineer).

Shortly after the inspection, Kosciuszko unburdened himself to his friend, General Gates: "His Excellency was here with General Portail to see the works, after all Conclusion was made that I am not the worst of Inginier." In the same letter Kosciuszko criticizes Duportail's rigid insistence on transferring a planned fortification from the drawing board to its construction on the ground. Kosciuszko maintained that a proposed plan, of necessity, must be adjusted to fit the geography of the land. He cautions

Gates, "That is between us."[36] [Colonel La Radiere, too, behaved rigidly like his superior, Duportail.]

Another instance of Washington's concern for Kosciuszko's standing in the Continental Army occurred in 1781 when Kosciuszko served under Major General Nathanael Greene in the Southern Army. The Marquis de Lafayette asked for Colonel Gouvion to join his division that Washington had ordered to Virginia to stop the deprivations of the traitor, General Benedict Arnold. Virginia was part of the geographical area of the Southern Department, although Greene's army operated primarily in North and South Carolina, some 200 miles from Richmond. Nevertheless, Washington refused Lafayette. Washington informed Lafayette that Duportail wanted Gouvion at army headquarters and added, "Independent of that occasion which there may be for him here, there is another reason which operates against his going with you, it is, that he would interfere with Colo. Kosciusko who had been considered as the commanding Engineer with the southern Army." Thus, the commander-in-chief allowed Kosciuszko to act essentially independent of Duportail.[37]

Although Duportail often showed his dislike for Kosciuszko, and sometimes envy, the Frenchman was not unwilling to use Kosciuszko's reputation to advantage. On 16 January 1780, Duportail asked General Washington's help for the transfer of Captain Daniel Nevin to the Corps of Engineers. Nevin, an American of Huguenot descent, was appointed a captain in Colonel William Malcolm's regiment, which served at West Point. Lieutenant Colonel Gouvion and Nevin worked as engineers for Kosciuszko, who treated them well. They did their work capably, and Kosciuszko supported Nevin's request for transfer. In his letter to the commander-in-chief, Duportail wrote, "Col. Koskiuszko has told me much in his favor and Col. Gouvion with whom he was employed all last winter at King's Ferry has spoke to me of him in a manner still more favorable." Captain Nevin got his transfer and a promotion to major.[38]

Following the series of rapid promotions, Duportail made no further demands for advancement until the surrender of Lord

Cornwallis at Yorktown, 19 October 1781. Barely a week later he asked Washington for a promotion to major general for himself and to colonel for Gouvion. Duportail also requested a furlough of six months so that Gouvion and he could visit France. At this time Colonel La Radiere was deceased. Two other engineers, Colonels Laumoy and Cambray, were prisoners of the British and had not been exchanged, as yet. Washington had no objection to the furlough. However, he balked at recommending promotions to Congress for the two Frenchmen, offering the following reason:

> In the present instance the infringement of the rights of seniority in so many individuals, and the pretensions of some who have particular claims upon their country, convince me that your desires could not be accomplished but at the expense of the tranquility of the army.[39]

Clearly Duportail was again scheming for a promotion, but he was not dissuaded by Washington's reason. The very next day he answered him, introducing a motive that had no relevance to his service in the American Army. It had to do with the prestige he wished to enjoy in the French Army. "When i am going to france," he wrote, "it is so important for me to have here the rank of major general that i cannot easily give up the idea of getting it." He expressed fear that his fellow engineers and he would be reduced in grade once they rejoined the French Army. He would become a lieutenant colonel, although he was a major at the time he agreed to come to America.

Duportail attempted to get Washington to act as a channel for his correspondence to Congress. He did not ask Washington for a recommendation but only for his neutrality. He simply wanted Washington's great prestige, resulting from the decisive victory at Yorktown, to be associated with his bid for promotion. Desperate for two-star rank, Duportail even stooped to putting words in Washington's mouth. "so all what I beg of your Excellency," he pleaded, "is not to interfere in this affair...if Congress requires your opinion about my demand, may not your Excellency be so good as to say something like this: that this promotion being not in the ordinary course, you have nothing to do with it, but you do not pretend to set limits to the favours of Congress, and it should be easy for you not to compromise yourself...." Duportail also sought the help of the French Minister, Monsieur le Chevalier de la Luzerne, suggesting that he influence some member of Congress.[40]

Washington, caught in a euphoric mood after the great victory at Yorktown, unfortunately succumbed to Duportail's pressure. The substantial help of the French Army under Rochambeau and the powerful French Fleet of Admiral De Grasse insured the surrender of General Lord Cornwallis. Washington felt grateful to the French, and Duportail took advantage of Washington. Congress promoted Duportail to major general and Gouvion to colonel by brevet without delay.[41]

Duportail's latest promotion aroused the latent feelings of General Gates about Kosciuszko's overdue promotion. He and other friends were ready to take up the matter with Congress. However, because of Kosciuszko's adamant opposition to advancing ahead of American officers, Gates first wrote Kosciuszko to learn his current thoughts. The letter reached Kosciuszko at the camp of the Southern Army at Bacon's Bridge, South Carolina. He answered Gates on 8 April 1782, telling his friend, "The promotion of General Du Portail I don't think would be the consequence of mine, as the Congress lately resolved to make no more Brygadier Generals." He adds that "I am extremely obliged to you for your kind offer." Nevertheless, he reaffirms his unchanging view when he states, "the recommendation in my favor am entirely against, what I beg of you, will always be denied to the others."[42]

Kosciuszko's insistence that he not be promoted was a mistake, for he was carrying his modesty too far. He need not have stooped to Duportail's level. Rather, he should have allowed his friends to intercede on his behalf. He deserved to be promoted. Not until the end of the war did Kosciuszko seek a promotion, but then he would find the climate in Congress had changed.

Despite Duportail's success in amassing promotions, the memory of his service faded in America. Kite laments the lack of recognition from American historians. "This seems curious," she writes, "when one considers that the names of de Kalb, of Pulaski, of von Steuben, of Kosciuszko, not to mention Lafayette, are known to every one."[43] Perhaps Duportail's arrogance, self-importance, and obsession with promotions tarnished the record of his service in the American Revolution.

CHAPTER FIVE

West Point:
Key to the Continent

Kosciuszko Builds a Fortress

THE BRITISH GRAND STRATEGY failed at Saratoga but highlighted the great military value of the Hudson River, both to the British plans for conquest and to the American hopes for independence. Perhaps no other person was more acutely aware of this fact than General Washington. To deny the enemy the waterway (also called North River), the Americans must insure its control. New York Governor George Clinton and army commanders agreed that the Highlands of the Hudson offered the best defensive location, but not everyone moved with alacrity. Washington urged the new commander in the Highlands, General Gates, to begin the work. However, Congress appointed Gates the President of the Board of War, which met in Philadelphia. Hence, Gates never superseded Major General Israel Putnam. But Washington had exhorted Putnam, too. Stressing the importance of the Hudson River, Washington made a clear and strong case:

> These facts at once appear, when it is considered that it runs thro' a whole State; That it is the only passage by which the Enemy from New York or any part of our Coast can ever hope to Cooperate with an Army that may come from Canada; That the possession of it is indispensibly essential to preserve the Communication

between the Eastern, Middle and Southern States; And further, that upon its security, in a great measure, depend our chief supplies of Flour for the subsistence of such Forces as we may have occasion for, in the course of the War, either in the Eastern or Northern Departments....

For the next three years, Washington encouraged and closely followed the progress of construction at West Point and with his army safeguarded the site against the enemy during that time.[1]

When Kosciuszko arrived at West Point on 26 March 1778, he saw a rugged area alongside a wide and beautiful river, and surrounded by almost inaccessible mountains. Undoubtedly he was struck by the tumultuous scene of hills, mountains, and rock interspersed with deep valleys, meadows, and swamps; and the jumbled terrain impeded the movement of travelers. Dependent on one's point of view, a person could find solace or despair here. General Samuel Holden Parsons, upon taking command of West Point, described his impressions: "To a contemplative Mind which delights in a lonely Retreat from the World to view and admire the stupendous and magnificent Works of Nature, 'tis as beautiful as Sharon, but affords to a Man who loves the Society of the World a prospect nearly allied to the Shades of Death." Replacing Parsons, Colonel William Malcolm lamented his misfortune. From West Point on 3 August 1778, he wrote to Parsons: "Send me news and newspapers, anything to keep me alive; this is actually t'other end of the world."[2]

At West Point, Kosciuszko learned that the great chain was being forged at the Sterling Ironworks at Chester, New York, and preparations were underway to place the chain across the Hudson by the end of April. The army entrusted the task to Captain Thomas Machin, who earlier had laid a chain at Fort Montgomery.

OPPOSITE PHOTO: *GENERAL GEORGE WASHINGTON, Commander-in-Chief, American Continental Army. Convinced of the absolute necessity of controlling the Hudson River Valley, Washington strongly supported Colonel Thaddeus Kosciuszko, chief engineer, during the construction of Fortress West Point. (Collections of the Library of Congress).*

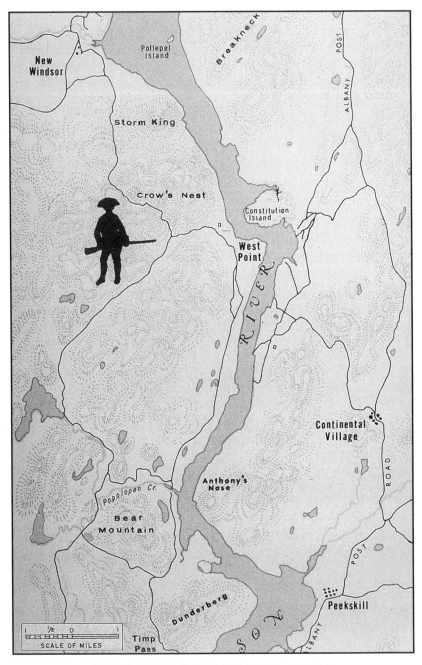

THE HUDSON HIGHLANDS

As part of their attempt to aid Burgoyne at Saratoga, the British from New York destroyed the chain and temporarily seized Forts Clinton and Montgomery. Machin used the experience at Fort Montgomery to double the strength of the chain for West Point. Machin had the trust of Governor Clinton and the army officers associated with the project. While La Radiere remained at West Point as chief engineer, the Board of War confirmed Machin's responsibility in an obvious move to prevent the Frenchman from meddling in Machin's work.[3]

Once placed across the river, the Great Chain required an annual procedure of picking it up in early winter and laying it down again in the spring. During the time the river was frozen solid, the ice could damage the chain and especially the wood sections supporting it. The twice-a-year ritual consumed time and challenged one's ability to prognosticate a severe change in temperature. Picking up the chain too soon in the winter or laying it down too late in the spring would give the British navy an opportunity for a surprise visit. The chain measured more than 500 yards in length. The links were two feet long and made of Sterling iron, and in thickness two and one-quarter inches square. A swivel was added every 100 feet and a clevis to every thousand weight. The chain was floated on huge logs cut to sixteen-foot sections that were anchored at selected distances so as to provide the chain with stability. Invariably, damaged logs had to be replaced every spring. The same procedure was followed—trees were felled, shaped and sharpened, dried and treated with tar and oakum. In front of the chain, the Americans placed a boom

----

MAP, OPPOSITE PAGE: *Americans chose the site of West Point, over the loud objections of French engineers, for the construction of fortifications that insured the control of the Hudson River. Here, Chief Engineer Colonel Thaddeus Kosciuszko proved the French wrong. He designed and built a fortress the British dared not attack.(Map by Edward J. Krasnoborski, courtesy of Dave Richard Palmer and the Association of Graduates, USMA. From Palmer's masterful book,* The River and the Rock: The History of Fortress West Point, 1775-1783*).*

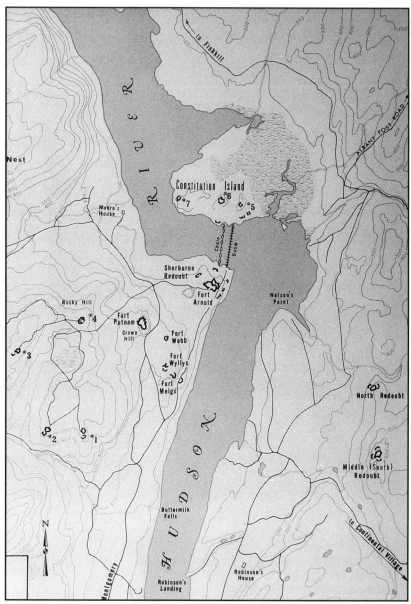

Fortress West Point with three defensive rings of forts and redoubts —to delay, disrupt and defeat British attacks mainly from the southern (and most likely) avenue of attack. (Map courtesy of Dave Richard Palmer and the Association of Graduates, USMA. Cartography by Edward J. Krasnoborski)

that gave the chain some protection. The Great Chain was an important element of the defense of West Point, and it clearly lay in the area of responsibility of the chief engineer. Nevertheless, Kosciuszko respected the decision of Congress, Governor Clinton, and the army to give Machin an independent project. Even after the chain was stretched across the river in April, Machin continued to labor on a boom. With the help of garrison soldiers, he laid the boom down in July 1778. At the end of the year, however, General McDougall suddenly thrust the responsibility for the chain onto Kosciuszko.[4]

Meanwhile, the chain had to be secured from enemy land attacks, too, for it was only one part of the defensive bastion. When General Putnam let the uncooperative La Radiere leave West Point, and before Kosciuszko's arrival, General Parsons looked for engineering help, and he summoned Machin. Parsons also asked for Colonel Rufus Putnam's 5th Massachusetts Regiment to perform the labor of construction. Machin's priority centered on water batteries at West Point and Constitution Island, as well as a more substantial fort near the chain. He had barely begun when the newly-designated chief engineer arrived, Colonel Thaddeus Kosciuszko, who assumed supervision of the planning, design, and construction of an integrated defense of West Point. Kosciuszko concurred with Governor Clinton and the American generals that West Point, at the double bend in the river and surrounded by rugged terrain, was an admirable defensive site. Although he was a product of French military schools, like Duportail and La Radiere, he was flexible and open-minded to the advantages of each situation. Massive, Vauban-style forts were not always the best solution. He proved the value of adaptation at Fort Ticonderoga, but the French engineers apparently never learned the lesson. Palmer calls Duportail "a good engineer," and the Frenchman possessed a measure of expertise that was useful to the American Army. Nevertheless, Duportail displayed rigid thinking and a distinct partiality for Vauban-style fortifications.[5]

General Washington replaced the old soldier General Putnam with Major General Alexander McDougall as commander in the Highlands. His area included West Point, but here Brigadier General Parsons remained in command. From his headquarters in Fishkill, New York, McDougall crossed the Hudson to West Point for his first visit on 8 April 1778. He was accompanied by La Radiere, whom Washington had not relieved, as yet. The next day Governor Clinton and brother Brigadier General James Clinton joined McDougall. They found the initial construction work on the point to be satisfactory. Next, McDougall, James Clinton, Parsons, and La Radiere climbed to the tops of Crown and Rocky Hills, located to the southwest of the plain. The four officers sought to determine whether the two hills ought to be fortified. La Radiere already recorded his opposition to any work on these hills. They need not be fortified, he maintained, because their steepness would preclude the enemy from emplacing artillery on the summits. The Americans seemed to be convinced, and they accepted La Radiere's assessment. As McDougall noted in his diary: "They all agreed it was inexpedient to make any works on those hills, and the direction of cannon from there would be very uncertain."

That April morning Kosciuszko was not among the four officers who conducted the reconnaissance. As chief engineer, Kosciuszko should have been in the party, but McDougall kept him away because of the hostility of La Radiere. When Kosciuszko learned the results of McDougall's survey, he became alarmed that his planned defense would be seriously compromised. Tactfully and persuasively he convinced Parsons to retain the two hills in the ring of defenses. James Clinton became persuaded, too, and before McDougall returned to Fishkill, he had changed his mind.[6]

Kosciuszko drew a design for Crown Hill. He planned a strong fort on the very top, an area of about 200 feet in diameter. The walls of the fort became an extension of the vertical cliffs of the hill, except for one approachable side from the direction of the plain. When the work on Crown Hill was completed, the fortification became a formidable site at West Point. General Parsons assigned the construction work to Colonel Rufus Putnam and

Section of the Great Chain near Trophy Point, U. S. Military Academy, West Point, New York. (Photo by the author, 25 September 1996)

his regiment of some 300 soldiers and named the site Fort Putnam in the colonel's honor. The fort, as Putnam described it, stood "on a high hill, or rather rock, which commands the plane & point. The rock on the Side next the point is not difficult to assend but on the other Side where the fort Stands the rock is 50 feet perpendiculer." Kosciuszko knew Colonel Putnam from Saratoga, where he assisted Kosciuszko in fortifying Bemis Heights. Putnam was both a line officer and an engineer. Of the two duties, he preferred command. He was immensely proud of his 5th Massachusetts Regiment. In June 1778, after only three months at West Point and before Fort Putnam was built, Putnam received orders to march his regiment to Peekskill and report to General Gates, who then joined Washington at White Plains in July.[7]

Before Kosciuszko began work on the other hill (Rocky Hill), General Duportail, as directed by Washington, came to West Point to inspect the defenses. He timed his visit to Kosciuszko's absence, September 9–10, when the engineer testified at the court martial of General Arthur St. Clair at White Plains. One of Duportail's recommendations to Washington countermanded Kosciuszko's selection of Rocky Hill as an integral part of the defense. Duportail concluded that Rocky Hill was not necessary because the British could not possibly scale that steep hill with cannon to neutralize Fort Putnam. Washington undoubtedly did not realize the implications of Duportail's destructive conclusion at the time, and the commander-in-chief gave a blanket approval to the report. Kosciuszko put the design for a redoubt on Rocky Hill aside. However, the following year Washington made West Point the army headquarters, from 19 July to 30 November 1779. His presence stressed the importance of West Point and spurred his commanders to furnish levies of soldiers for the construction. He frequently noted Kosciuszko's progress. While visiting Fort Putnam, Washington evaluated the defensive capability of the fort. Perhaps for the first time he was struck by the nearness of Rocky Hill and its towering elevation. If the British should capture that hill, they could render Fort Putnam ineffective, in the manner in which they had captured Fort Ticonderoga without a fight after first occupying Mount Defiance. Reversing Duportail's recommendation, Washington ordered Kosciuszko to fortify Rocky Hill, too (Redoubt No. 4). Washington stated his conclusion: "The possession of this Hill appears to me essential to the preservation of the whole post and our main effort ought to be directed to keeping the enemy off of it." (As Palmer writes: "General Duportail might have seen a smirk flash across Colonel Kosciuszko's face when Washington made that decision.") Stressing the importance of Redoubt No. 4, Washington tasked General St. Clair and his division to build the redoubt. And Kosciuszko was ready. He had anticipated eventual approval of his plan for Redoubt No. 4, having submitted it to General McDougall on 6 February 1779.[8]

Although Fort Putnam and Redoubt No. 4 were formidable elements of Kosciuszko's defense, still they were part of a total design. On the plain near the Great Chain, Fort Clinton was under construction by General James Clinton and his New York militia. (General McDougall named it Fort Arnold.) Near this fort,

Sherburne's redoubt was added to the river defense. To further strengthen the capability along the Hudson, Kosciuszko placed three small forts below Fort Arnold. These three, named Webb, Wyllys, and Meigs after the regiments that built them, were within supporting fire from Fort Putnam. Kosciuszko designed an ambitious defense that would require a great amount of work.

Within two weeks of his arrival at West Point, Kosciuszko developed his initial plan of defense and undoubtedly presented it to General McDougall. On 11 April 1778, the general expressed his own plan and execution in written instructions to General Parsons:

> The hill which Colonel Putnam is fortifying is the most commanding and important of any that we can now attend to.... The easternmost face of this work must be so constructed so as to command the plain on which Colonel Putnam's regiment is now encamped, and annoy the enemy if he should force the works now erecting by Colonel Meigs's and Colonel Wyllys's regiments....
>
> The next principal ground to be occupied for the safety of the post is the rising ground to the northward of the fort near the northwest corner of the Long Barracks.
>
> This redoubt [Sherburne's] is so important that it must be finished without delay.... The water batteries now erected on the point to be completed as soon as possible and two cannon placed in each...Should the enemy force the regiments of Colonels Wyllys, Meigs and Webb from their works, it will be most advancive to the defense...that those corps retire to defend to the last extremity the avenues leading to Colonel Putnam's redoubt....

Designing a superb defense, Kosciuszko developed it without any future changes. Later, he planned Redoubts 1, 2, and 3 to the south for more depth, as well as Redoubts 5, 6, and 7 on Constitution Island.[9] (See map, page 86.)

Due to a scarcity of housing at West Point, Kosciuszko roomed with General Parsons, Dr. Timothy Dwight, and Major Samuel Richards, senior officer of Parsons' brigade. Richards left an account of his impressions of Kosciuszko:

> I quartered a considerable time with him in the same log hut, and soon discovered in him an elevation of mind which gave fair

Colonel Kosciuszko's design
for Redoubt No. 4 atop Rocky Hill.

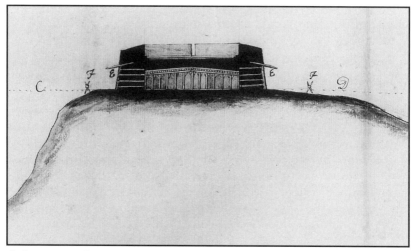

Sideview with protective walls up

Sideview with walls down to illustrate the firing of a cannon.

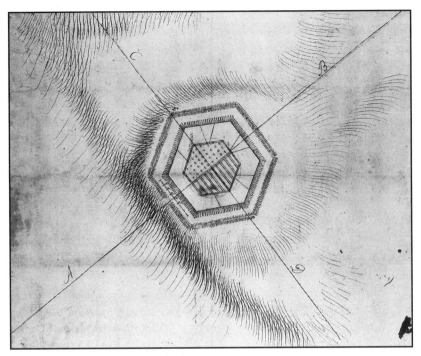

View above shows vertical plan.

A VITAL LINK *in the defense of West Point, Kosciuszko's Redoubt No. 4 was disapproved by General Duportail, commandant of engineers, as unnecessary in September 1778. Fortunately, General Washington overruled Duportail and directed Kosciuszko to build the redoubt.*

Schooled in the design of massive Vauban-type fortifications, Duportail looked with disfavor on Kosciuszko's (and American) design of an extended defense with mutually supporting forts and redoubts at West Point, but they gave the site depth and defensibility.

(Collection of the New-York Historical Society.)

promise of those high achievements to which he attained. His manners were soft and conciliating, and, at the same time, elevated. I used to take much pleasure in accompanying him with his theodolite, measuring the heights of the surrounding mountains. He was very ready in mathematics.[10]

Kosciuszko's practiced eye saw the advantages of the terrain, and he incorporated the rugged mountains into his design. He agreed with the American generals that each completed phase of the defense offered at once a measure of resistance to the enemy and steadily increased as the construction went on. He labored assiduously to reach a confident level of defensive capability. "With each new fort, battery, and redoubt, the possibility of taking the Hudson became increasingly more remote to the British," West Point historians concluded. Soon the defensive features became noticeable. Governor Clinton informed General Gates on 8 April 1778: "The works calculated for the Defense & Obstruction of the Hudson's River are now carried on with a Degree of Spirit that promises their speedy Completion." Ten days later Colonel Robert Troup echoed the same optimism to Gates. While passing through Fishkill, he learned of the tempo of activity at West Point. He wrote that the works are in a great state of forwardness:

> Kosciuszko has made many alterations which are universally approved of; & I am happy to find he is esteemed as an able Engineer. This week the chain will be put across the river, & if the Enemy let us alone two weeks longer, we shall have Reason to rejoice at their moving this way.

By June 1778, the construction of the fort at the northeast corner of the plateau was sufficiently advanced for it to take a permanent garrison. McDougall had named it Fort Arnold, in honor of the hero of Saratoga, Benedict Arnold (to spite General Gates, it is believed). McDougall should have called the fort after James Clinton, following the practice of naming the forts and redoubts after the commanders whose troops constructed the works. When Arnold committed treachery in September 1780, the fort was renamed properly.[11]

General McDougall lost his command of the Highlands when Congress assigned Gates to that command on 15 April 1778. McDougall had no love for Gates or Congress. His ill-will found expression in a gratuitous remark about Kosciuszko's competence. He wrote Governor Clinton on 11 May 1778: "I am far from being pleased with Mr. Korsuaso's constructing the Batteries, and Carrying on the works, and I fear they will not answer the expectations of the Country." His statement was without foundation. He was upset at losing his command and revealed his resentment: "General Gates is not yet arrived, nor do I learn when tis likely he will. I think I am not well treated by him and Congress." Clearly he transferred his animosity for Gates to Kosciuszko by association. Shortly, on 19 May 1778, McDougall led Gates and his staff to West Point where Kosciuszko met his friend again and escorted him on a tour of the fortifications under construction. Gates made no changes, being well-satisfied with what he saw and having full confidence in Kosciuszko's ability. Indeed, much progress was being made, but the heat in June slowed down the work. For several days the temperature rose above 100 degrees Fahrenheit, and the humidity became so unbearably high that General John Glover, who replaced Parsons, ordered a five-hour break for the soldiers over the noon hour, from 10:00 A.M. to 3:00 P.M. The soldiers were also relieved of the worry of an enemy attack, for Washington marched his army to positions between West Point and New York. He always followed this strategy of protecting West Point from the British in New York.[12]

On 16 July 1778, General Washington visited West Point for the first time. Kosciuszko had the honor of escorting the commander-in-chief around the elements of the defense. He described the purpose of each fort and redoubt, and brought out its weaknesses as well as strengths. Because of the urgency of erecting the fortifications quickly, no masonry work had been attempted, as yet; the forts were built with dirt and wood. The four shore batteries around the point had eleven cannon between them. The battery on Constitution Island, where the chain was anchored, bristled with six cannon. The shore batteries were reinforced with the nine cannon of Fort Arnold and the five of Sherburne's Redoubt. Standing guard over the plain rose the lofty Fort Putnam with five cannon. Fort Putnam also supported Forts Meigs, Webb, and Wyllys with their total of four guns. Fifteen more pieces were ready to be emplaced, bringing the total to nearly sixty guns. Most of these had been captured at Fort Ticonderoga. Satisfied with the design and progress of construction, Washington made no changes.[13]

General Glover commanded at West Point for only a month. He was eager to return with his brigade to the main army, and Washington ordered him to join General John Sullivan in Rhode Island. Washington replaced Glover with Colonel William Malcolm, who was devastated by the assignment since West Point was the last place on earth he wanted to be. He wrote General Parsons: "Here I am holding committee with spades and shovels. Why was I banished?" In a disgruntled frame of mind, he made a quick inspection of the fortifications, and just as quickly condemned the works as "not worth a farthing." What struck him was the great amount of labor that remained to be done. He complained to Parsons, "The more we do the more we find we have to do. Why did you not begin to move the mountain rather than add to its magnitude?" Malcolm also complained to Washington about Kosciuszko in a letter of 26 July 1778, but the commander-in-chief rejected Malcolm's complaint. He told the discontented colonel, "Colo. Kosciusko was left at the Fort as acting Engineer and I have always understood is fully competent to the Business. I do not therefore see why another is necessary."[14]

Although Kosciuszko's design for West Point was practically completed by the summer of 1778, the building of the forts and redoubts proceeded only as fast as the officers and soldiers could carry on the work. He needed a thousand men, but the available number was much less. Units ordered to West Point arrived much under strength. The militia left promptly on the expiration of their short enlistments, and replacements were habitually delayed. Artificers were always in short supply. Kosciuszko prepared a list of manpower needs for Colonel Malcolm, who included it in a letter to Congress, 1 August 1778:

The Engineer estimates that it will require:

300 men	to finish Putnam's Redoubt	one month
200	Webb	3 weeks
300	Wyllys, Meigs & Sherburne	2 weeks
<u>300</u>	Constitution (East side the River)	3 weeks
1100		

The work tempo improved noticeably when Washington involved himself in the affairs of West Point. He now required commanders to report their needs to him directly. Malcolm could no longer lament his assignment. Command interest at the highest level spurred him on. Governor Clinton offered Tory prisoners for the construction work, and Malcolm gladly accepted his help. At this time Kosciuszko began a bombproof shelter in the interior of Fort Arnold for the storage of powder that had been kept in sheds outdoors. Duportail's inspection of West Point in September 1778 resulted advantageously for Kosciuszko. True, Duportail's flawed assessment and disapproval of the need for Redoubt No. 4 was temporarily sustained by Washington. Kosciuszko did not complain; he had much work to do. Fortunately, Washington reversed himself and ordered Kosciuszko to build the redoubt that insured the central role of Fort Putnam. The episode of the inspection proved the Pole's military and engineering superiority over the Frenchman.[15]

In the summer of 1778, Kosciuszko sought to join General Gates for a proposed invasion of Canada. The conquest of the former French possession became feasible again with the help of French forces when Admiral D'Estaing sailed his fleet to the shores of America in early July 1778. General Washington charged Gates to develop a plan of invasion. He then submitted Gates's plan to Congress. Meanwhile, D'Estaing attempted to attack the British fleet in New York harbor. However, his heavy ships could not pass over the sand bar, and he sailed for Newport, Rhode Island, where Washington planned a joint American-French attack on the British garrison. D'Estaing had some 4000 soldiers available for the assault, and General Sullivan commanded 10,000 American troops, mostly militia. The target, Newport, stood at the southern end of a long, narrow island between Seaconnet and Middle Passages, and it was guarded by entrenchments north of the town. As planned, French troops were to land on the west shore of the island. Before they did, however, Sullivan ferried his army to the east shore a day early. Thus, the American major general upstaged a senior lieutenant general and a Frenchman. D'Estaing became incensed. The surprised American pleaded with D'Estaing to carry out the joint attack. The admiral refused, and the expedition failed. Sullivan became angry, openly criticizing D'Estaing. Fearful of damage to the American-French relationship, Washington entered the fray. He silenced Sullivan and mollified D'Estaing, who sailed his fleet to Boston for refitting.[16]

Shortly thereafter, Washington grew suspicious over sizable movements of the British in New York. He suspected that the enemy would transport the whole or the greatest part of its forces eastward and combine one great land and sea operation against the French Squadron in Boston harbor. Accordingly, he relocated the army units so as to be better able to respond to events in Boston. He kept a portion in the Highlands and moved the remainder toward the Connecticut River so that, if necessary, the two wings might form a junction to defend either the Hudson or the French Squadron and town of Boston. Washington assigned Gates the left wing of the army based on Danbury, Connecticut.[17]

Kosciuszko saw Gates's new command as an opportunity to join him. He much preferred active campaigning to stationary duty. Life at West Point was isolated and monotonous. One lived there as if in a vacuum. He echoed the complaints of Parsons and Malcolm, when he wrote Gates, "West Point is as barren of news as the mountains that surround it." He probably discussed the assignment with Gates at White Plains, when he testified there at the court martial of General St. Clair, September 7 and 8. Three days later Gates wrote Washington:

> I earnestly entreat your Excellency will be pleased to permit
> Col. Kuscuiusco to be The Engineer to serve with the troops

marching under my command. If I had not an affectionate regard for this Amiable Foreigner, I should upon no account have made this my request. The out Works at West Point are in a manner finished & the Body of the place in such forwardness as to put it in the power of the Two Engineers now There to compleat the whole with the utmost Facility.[18]

Washington at once rejected Gates's request. The control of the Hudson River was of utmost importance to the commander-in-chief. He stressed to Gates, "If they were able to possess themselves of the Highland passes and interrupt the navigation of the River, the consequences on the score of subsistence would be terrible as well to the fleet as the army." Washington was not convinced that the works were in a state of great forwardness, and he insisted on continuity of effort. Above all, he was well satisfied with Kosciuszko's work. As he explained to Gates:

> Colo. Kosciusko has had the chief direction and superintendence of the Works at West point, and it is my desire, that he should remain to carry them on. New plans and alterations at this time, would be attended with many inconveniences, and protract the defences of the River. These possibly in some degree, might take place in case of his absence, under the management of Another Engineer.[19]

Kosciuszko naturally was deeply disappointed by Washington's refusal. The engineer wrote Gates, "You cannot Concive in what passion I am having not plaisure to be under your Command, my happiness is lost, but I hope you will help me to recover it soon as possible." To Colonel John Taylor of Albany, New York, Kosciuszko revealed his feelings more openly:

> I am the most unhappy man in the World, because all my Yankees the best friends is gone to White Plains or to Eastern and left me with the Skotches or Irishes impolites as the Saviges. The satisfaction that I have at present only is this to go all day upon the Works and the Night to go to bed with the Cross Idea of lost of good Compani. I should go to the Eastern with General Gates but Gl. Washington was obstacle of going me ther, and I am very sorry of it.[20]

Washington was right to keep Kosciuszko at West Point. He, therefore, maintained the army's best engineering skill at that critical site. Perhaps unconsciously to both men at the time, Washington gained a greater objective—that of allowing Kosciuszko to complete the building of West Point into a remarkable and impregnable fortress.

In late November 1778, General Burgoyne's demoralized British Army was ferried across the Hudson just above West Point. The soldiers were marching to prisoner-of-war camps in Virginia after Congress reversed Gates on his agreement with Burgoyne to allow the captured soldiers to return to Great Britain. A tradition lives on that Kosciuszko fed British prisoners from his own meager allowances. Haiman writes that several decades later "a Polish traveler in Australia would have died of yellow fever were it not for a local merchant who took the best possible care of him, explaining that he thus wished to repay the kindness of Kosciuszko who fed his grandfather, a hungry prisoner at West Point, with his own bread."[21]

In early December 1778, Washington ordered General McDougall to take command of the Highlands again and to place a brigade at West Point. McDougall set up his headquarters at Peekskill, a village of about twenty homes placed fairly close to each other and located on the Hudson River. Washington, as always, stressed the key role of West Point: "I need not observe to you that West Point is to be considered as the first and principal object of your attention." McDougall ordered Brigadier General John Paterson to march his brigade there and assume command of the site. Colonel Malcolm became upset. In the four months at West Point he had come to like the assignment, and he opposed giving up the command. He wrote an angry letter to the commander-in-chief and several to Governor Clinton. Washington was forced to explain that the post needed more soldiers and, therefore, a general officer. As for Kosciuszko, he was pleased to greet Paterson, one of his Yankee friends. Perhaps the presence of Paterson would temper the impolite atmosphere of the Scotch and Irish.[22]

Kosciuszko knew Paterson from the days of Fort Ticonderoga

and Saratoga. Paterson's great grandson, Thomas Egleston, wrote that the general had formed a close relationship with Kosciuszko, and often from the necessity of war, sleeping in the same bed. Egleston described both men as spirited and sprightly. Kosciuszko was full of fun and sometimes played practical jokes on the general. Kosciuszko's quarters were located on the bend of the river, where his monument at West Point now stands. General Paterson's were opposite, at the base of the hill. The general owned a slave, Agrippa Hull, who claimed to be the son of an African prince. Called Grippy, he became a great favorite of the officers, especially Kosciuszko. Paterson gave him Grippy. The Pole became embarrassed; he had never owned another individual. Kosciuszko hired Agrippa and treated him as a free man. He made Grippy his confidential and head servant, and put him in charge of his wardrobe. Soon a hilarious incident occurred. Kosciuszko planned to inspect construction work on the east side of the Hudson for two or three days. When he left, Grippy threw a big party and invited all the black servants. He put on Kosciuszko's formal uniform from Poland. The uniform was brilliantly adorned. Grippy added a crown-shaped cap set off with ostrich plumes. As the wine flowed freely, the voices grew exuberant. Meanwhile, Kosciuszko, not able to cross the river for some reason, returned to the plain. Before he reached his quarters, he was told about the loud party. He came up undetected and surprised the revelers, who scurried to safety, while Grippy prostrated himself and begged forgiveness. The scene was so ludicrous that Kosciuszko burst into laughter, and he continued the charade. Taking hold of Grippy's hand and with ostentatious formality, he said, "Rise, Prince, it is beneath the dignity of an African prince to prostrate himself at the feet of any one." Next, Kosciuszko led Grippy across the plain to General Paterson's quarters. Seeing the gaudily-dressed servant, officers and soldiers joined the entourage. After the "prince" was toasted a few times, the charade ended. Grippy never forgot the episode. When he grew old, he delighted in telling the story himself. For more than four years, Agrippa Hull served Kosciuszko with great devotion.[23]

When General McDougall assumed command of the Highlands again, he brought along a French engineer, Lieutenant Colonel Jean Baptiste de Gouvion, who had come to America with Duportail. Gouvion became an assistant to Kosciuszko. In contrast to Duportail and La Radiere, Gouvion was a personable as well as capable individual. He and Kosciuszko got along well. The chief engineer assigned him duties, principally on fortifications down river from West Point.[24]

At the end of 1778, a new problem confronted Generals McDougall and Paterson—that of picking up the chain and boom from the river before the ice formed. The ice floes could damage and even destroy the chain. Removing the chain before the first cold snap, storing it for the winter, and again placing it across the river in the spring became an annual and time-consuming responsibility. Washington anticipated the requirement, advising Colonel Malcolm in early November to "put all things in readiness to take up the Chain and Boom" with the advent of the cold weather that would remove the risk of an enemy attack. Unfortunately, the change in command caused a loss of coordination. General Paterson did not show any concern over the chain until McDougall's visit in early December. Noticing the chain still in the water, McDougall ordered its immediate removal, and he gave Kosciuszko detailed instructions on the method to be employed. In response, Paterson ordered two sloops from New Windsor to assist in the removal set for December 21, but the boats failed to show up. A sudden drop in temperature caused ice to begin forming along the banks and between the chain links. To save the chain before the river froze solid, Paterson ordered the chain unhooked from its anchor on Constitution Island and swung over to the West Point side. The work was difficult and dangerous. As the ice in the river grew solid, the chain snapped in two or three places, but, for the time being, it was safe. While waiting for a thaw, Kosciuszko designed a machine for hoisting the chain aboard boats as soon as it should be freed from the ice. Kosciuszko assured General McDougall that the chain was safe and could be picked up when the cold weather moderated. The thaw occurred on December 29. Kosciuszko now extricated about seventy-five links a day. By 2 January 1779, his soldiers had piled up some 400 links and their supporting logs at the Moore House. A big task subsequently faced Kosciuszko. Inspecting the float logs, he found that more than half were ruined from the long immersion in the water. He sent crews into the woods to cut down pine trees. After the trees were cut to size and shaped, he coated them with pitch and painstakingly reassembled the chain. Meanwhile, McDougall became impatient. Rather than call on the commander, General Paterson, for a report, McDougall on 18 March 1779, asked Kosciuszko directly to explain the delay and inform him of impediments preventing the placing of the chain. In a matter of a few days, Kosciuszko was ready. He stretched the chain across the river again, carrying out the work competently. He would do the same the following year.[25]

The episode of the Great Chain disclosed General McDougall's ill-will and lack of confidence in Kosciuszko. Discovering in early December that the chain had not been picked up, he turned his anger on Kosciuszko. He gave him detailed instructions on what he should do, perhaps lecturing him like a second lieutenant. Kosciuszko's immediate reaction was correct, telling the general, "I shall perfectly acquiesce in and execute your Commands." Nevertheless, he frankly informed McDougall of problems at West Point—the lack of discipline and confusion he faced in working with the artificers and fatigue men (and indirectly reminding the general of his command responsibilities). At Fort Arnold, on 28 December 1778, Kosciuszko wrote McDougall: "As confusion has taken place respecting the Artificers since Col. Malcolm took the Command of this Post, I should be glad your Honor would regulate those Matters that each one may [know] what to depend on in prosecuting the Business carrying on here." Kosciuszko objected to the practice of the Quartermaster to move artificers from one site to another indiscriminately and without coordination with the chief engineer. He was also appalled by the undisciplined behavior of a unit, whose captain granted a furlough to his soldiers without notifying Kosciuszko or even gaining permission of the garrison commander. Clearly there had to be some order, and Kosciuszko asked McDougall, "I should be very glad if I might have a daily report made me that I may know how many I can have to employ on the Works." As McDougall expected Kosciuszko to do his utmost, and the engineer was most willing, he still needed the general's support. On 6 February 1779, he wrote McDougall: "I am in great Want of a Whipsaw and cannot get it from Fishkill. Should beg the favor of having one from Maj. Campbell." About two weeks later, he informed McDougall: "I have no more Intrenching Tools but twenty spades and twenty-five Pickakes. Som[e] is in the Regiments but very few." Subsequently, with General Paterson in command, conditions at West Point improved. From his position of commander-in-chief, Washington understood the manner of executing a task efficiently. Whenever he ordered units to furnish artificers for West Point, he stressed that the soldiers must be under Kosciuszko's supervision.[26]

General McDougall revealed his resentment and anger at Gates and Congress at the beginning of his second tour in the Highlands. He wrote a long letter to Washington on 10 December 1778, in which he accused the members of Congress of "many instances of Indelicacy towards me." He pointed to his unceremonious relief from command in favor of General Gates earlier in the spring. McDougall complained: "Congress without any Charge of Mal Conduct, or Misfortune happening to the Post, from Motives of more than Athenian Caprice (for I know not by what Name to call it) superseded me in command." McDougall also deeply resented the appointing by Congress of "six Gentlemen over my Head, since 1776." Perhaps McDougall's ill-will toward Congress and Gates extended by association to Kosciuszko. No doubt, McDougall was bitter, and the feeling undoubtedly caused him to be suspicious of others. He saw his current command as a possible occasion for his downfall. He admitted that much labor and expense had been bestowed on the works at West Point, and in case of misfortune or even a critical inspection the public outcry could be indignant. "It is a capricious, censorious and perilous Hour for General Officers," he noted. Considering his situation to be very serious, he wrote, "I am determined not to be made a Scape Goat of any Ignorant, wicked, or inattentive Servant of the Country, appointed by the Cabals or Intrigues of any Set of men." Having stated his determination to protect his reputation, McDougall told Washington how he planned to accomplish his objective: "I have directed Lieutenant Colonel Gouvion the Engineer to repair to West Point with me to make an accurate Report of the present State of the works." He specified the works to be inspected, whether properly constructed, others to be erected, the suitability of the materials, and the like. Once he completed the inspection, he said he would report to Congress and Washington "and order the Engineer on the ground to keep a Journal of my orders directing the works, the Strength and Materials he shall have, and the Progress of the work from Day to Day." In his letter, McDougall identifies Gouvion by name but refers to Kosciuszko only as "the Engineer on the ground."[27]

A week later, December 17, General McDougall issued detailed written instructions to Gouvion. Although he told Washington that he would make the inspection, with Gouvion in attendance, he now instructed the Frenchman to make the inspection himself: "You will on the first fair day repair to West Point and Inspect the works there erected...and report to me the result." McDougall demonstrated a lack of leadership when he directed Gouvion a junior to inspect Kosciuszko a senior. Had McDougall been that distrustful of Kosciuszko's competence, the general should have asked Washington for the engineer's removal. Otherwise, he would subject the chief engineer to uncalled for embarrassment. There was a proper way for McDougall—direct one of his brigadier generals to conduct the inspection and assign Gouvion as technical assistant. McDougall had every right to have the inspection made, as part of his responsibility to know the condition of his command. Washington knew the proper method. In August 1779, he ordered a team of generals to evaluate the required number of cannon at West Point and their proposed employment. McDougall headed the team, along with Duportail for engineering matters, and Brigadier General Henry Knox, chief of artillery.

With respect to Gouvion and his instructions of 17 December 1778, McDougall assigned him another mission, a tactical one. He ordered Gouvion to make a reconnaissance of the area of West Point in the role of a British general, possessing an assumed army of 7000 soldiers and with a supporting fleet on the Hudson River. He posed this question to Gouvion: "What would be your plan of operation to reduce the works or to remove or to pass the chain?" Before Gouvion could make the analysis, McDougall apparently had a change of heart. Three days later he sent Gouvion on a task, assigned by Washington, to Haverstraw and King's Ferry, where he stayed during the winter. McDougall's manner of employing Gouvion came to the attention of Washington, who undoubtedly did not approve of McDougall's handling of his engineers. Washington expressed concern over the whereabouts of Kosciuszko and reiterated his leading role at West Point. On 9 February 1779, he wrote McDougall: "From the manner in which you speak of employing Mr. Gouvion in this business, I am in doubt whether Col. Koshiosko still remains at West Point, or not. As he has not been removed by my order or permission, I should imagine he is still there." The commander-in-chief again stressed Kosciuszko's senior position: "If Koshiosko be still at West Point, as he is a senior officer, he must of necessity have the chief direction." McDougall allayed Washington's concern, replying tersely that "Colo. Kusiasco has been undisturbed in his Line at West Point." Thus Kosciuszko remained in a senior role at West Point as Washington insisted.[28]

In the spring of 1779, Congress considered a proposal to organize all the engineers into a separate corps under an appointed commandant. Congress designated Brigadier General Duportail the head of the Corps of Engineers, but it delayed his formal appointment. Becoming impatient, the Frenchman urged John Jay, President of Congress, to confirm the appointment without further delay, and Duportail fabricated a reason to justify the urgency. He pointed to West Point, which he called "Key to the North River." He lamented that "unhappily I have lately heard that *almost nothing has been done.*" Even though the statement

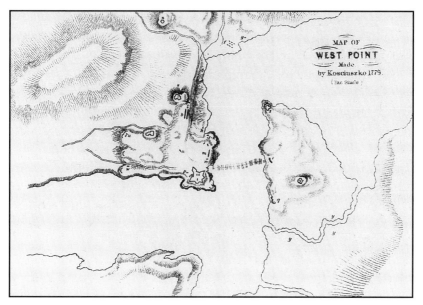

Colonel Thaddeus Kosciuszko drew the map for Major General Alexander McDougall, commander in the Hudson Highlands, in April 1779. Sketch shows Fort Arnold at the bend of the Hudson River, and Constitution Island to the right. The Great Chain floats on rafts of logs across the river. Fortifications, top down: Redoubt No. 4, Fort Putnam, Fort Webb, and three redoubts to the left. (Collection of the New-York Historical Society).

was false, Duportail did not hesitate to snipe at Kosciuszko's reputation. He also worried about being blamed for the loss of West Point, should the enemy capture the site. Therefore, he claimed the need to have control over the engineers and the construction at that key post.[29]

No one blamed Duportail for anything relating to the fortifications at West Point. Washington repeatedly said he was well satisfied with Kosciuszko's design and progress. On 28 May 1779, Washington told McDougall: "The completion of the works at West point has prudently [been] made a principal part in our system, and I am persuaded everything has been done by you for this purpose." However, as the British began to stir in New York, Washington ordered Duportail on June 2 to make a second inspection of West Point, and he told McDougall: "It gives me pleasure that the forts at this critical moment are in the hands [Kosciuszko's] where they may be safely trusted."[30]

Washington received intelligence reports that the British at New York planned to conduct a strike up river, probably West Point. He alerted McDougall and deployed the army for the protection of the site. On June 8, he visited West Point to assure himself of its security. Kosciuszko escorted the commander-in-chief, who left reassured. In view of the British threat, the garrison worked feverishly night and day. All approaches to the forts were blocked with felled trees. An American deserter reported this activity to the British, and Major General James Pattison wrote to Viscount Townshend: "This Place is a great Object of their Jealousy & Attention, and they have been long labouring to render it as strong as Art can make it."[31]

During the British threat to the Highlands, General Washington made his headquarters at New Windsor, a short distance above West Point. Issuing an order for artificers to be employed at West Point, he ruled that "All those Soldiers who are Masons by Trade in the Line are immediately to be drawn out and sent to the Fort for a special and temporary Service. They are to take their orders from Col. Kosciuszko." Despite the order, Kosciuszko did not get more needed craftsmen. Kosciuszko explained his troubles to Washington, when he moved his headquarters to West Point on 19 July 1779:

> I have only two Masons as yet come from the Main Army, and do not expect any more, the Officers being unwilling to part with them. I applied to the Detachments here who had a number of them, wrote to the officers in the most pressing terms shewing the necessity of it but got none. I am out of lime, it is true I have a promise of having some more but when I cannot tell.

Kosciuszko's pleas to the detachment commanders gained scant support. "Col. Stewart was so good as to let me have a Stone Cutter from his Regiment for one Week," the engineer wrote, "I wish to have him for a Month, having much to do and know not where to find another." He also reported twenty carpenters sick from drinking water in the hot, summer weather, but the carpenters hinted that perhaps "one Half Gill added to their Daily allowance would remedy the Evil." Washington's reaction was swift and positive. He impressed soldiers to work under Kosciuszko, and he ordered the Commissary General to obtain a supply of rum for the carpenters. He told Kosciuszko, "They must be paid in Rum (if that was the agreement) or an equivalent in Money when they do not get Rum. They must not at any Rate think of returning to their Regiments while their services are waiting."[32]

In addition to his military qualities, Washington excelled as a diplomat, and he received foreign visitors with a gracious air gained from the congenial life of a Southern planter. He had the honor to greet the Chevalier de la Luzerne, newly-arrived French Minister to the United States, on 15 September 1779. The American chief met the minister and his entourage upriver at Fishkill, New York. La Luzerne's secretary wrote that Washington "received us with a noble, modest, and gentle urbanity and with that graciousness which seems to be the basis of his character." The secretary, Marquis de Barbe-Marbois, studied Washington and noted his friendly behavior toward his officers and soldiers alike. Washington's sterling character impressed the Frenchman. "If you like historical parallels," he wrote, "I might compare him to Timoleon who freed the Sicilians from the tyranny of the Carthaginians." Washington himself took the tiller of the vessel that the party boarded on the Hudson, and he sailed it with the tide to West Point. Army chefs served dinner under a huge tent specially erected for the occasion on the shores of the river. Barbe-Marbois found the site fascinating. "The river was being driven back by the tide," he recorded, "and the waves came right up to the tent-pins, where they broke with a solemn roar." Nearby, musicians played military and French airs; cannon shots reverberated in the hills as they accompanied toasts to the health of the King and Queen; and bon fires lit up the opposite shore of the river. Kosciuszko attended the dinner in honor of the French guests. Barbe-Marbois wrote, "All the generals and the higher officers were there."[33]

A cannon shot at four o'clock in the morning startled the guests. Immediately the fife and drum corps beat their drums and shrilled the air with fifes as they marched around the tents. The guests were thoroughly aroused. At nine o'clock La Luzerne and his party mounted horses; and, led by Washington, they looked over the principal fortifications of West Point. Apparently Barbe-Marbois was not aware of La Radiere's objection to the choice of West Point by the American generals, for he wrote favorably, "The river narrows at that spot, and since it curves on itself, the headway of a ship which arrives with full sail, or pushed by the tide, is almost destroyed." Following the tour, La Luzerne and Washington and their aides held a long conference on the strategy of the war (Washington sent a report to Congress). At about four o'clock in the afternoon, the Americans and French crossed the Hudson to dine at Brigadier General Duportail's quarters. The French engineer had set up a similar tent for his guests at the Bay of the Assassins, today the site of the village of Cold Spring. Barbe-Marbois said nothing about the identity of guests in his written account. Undoubtedly Duportail did not invite Kosciuszko. The next day La Luzerne and his party departed West Point, and Washington escorted the minister as far as New Bethune.[34]

The French secretary offered some comments on the fortifications of West Point:

> The fort on the right [Arnold] is commanded by a hill, and other heights to the number of four command it, rising up as if in stories. They have felt obliged to fortify all these heights to protect the principal fort from being regularly attacked. We visited them in order, in spite of the steepness of the cliffs.

He made a telling statement when he continued, "Perhaps it is unfortunate that they have had to multiply these works and complicate the defense in that way, but at the price of this inconvenience the position has been put in a respectable condition." Like Duportail and La Radiere, Barbe-Marbois revealed again the French fascination for the massive, Vauban-style forts.

The are impressive-looking, like medieval castles, but of little value in the geographical environment of America. General Burgoyne proved their ineffectiveness when he captured Fort Ticonderoga without the Americans firing a single shot in defense.[35]

Washington was proud to show La Luzerne the state of construction at West Point. More than anyone else, the commander -in-chief considered West Point his project. He had conceived it, spurred it, protected it against possible British attacks, approved Kosciuszko's design and tolerated no changes to it, and kept Kosciuszko at his post in order to insure continuity of effort. When La Luzerne came, Washington had something to show him. Indeed, the works began to stand out, especially to an outsider. On 28 November 1779, Colonel Israel Angell of the Second Rhode Island Regiment passed through West Point. Writing that he saw "a fort on Every Eminence Some Distance round," he was struck by the sight of Fort Putnam, which he called "the American Gibraltar."[36]

General Washington departed West Point for Morristown, New Jersey, on 30 November 1779. He seemingly took the good weather with him, for winter shortly struck in all its fury. The winter of 1779 – 1780 was the most severe in memory. Heavy snowstorms blanketed the Northeast in early January. Snow and ice blocked the roads for nearly six weeks. The supply of provisions for the army was cut, causing hunger and suffering among the soldiers, and the garrison at West Point was especially affected. A worried Major General William Heath, who replaced the ailing McDougall on 28 November 1779, reported to Governor Clinton, "The situation of the army at this instance is truly alarming. The garrison of West Point have during the winter been at a scanty allowance of Bread, and often without any at all…Some of the troops are yet in Tents, and during the winter hitherto have been obliged to encounter hunger and cold." Palmer vividly describes the misery:

> Subzero temperatures, howling winds, and blinding snow paralyzed the post at West Point. Men struggled only to survive. They

pooled what wood was available, crowded into a few huts, selected to have fires, and huddled close together for warmth. Every stitch of clothing was worn and blankets were draped around shoulders, and still they were miserably cold.[37]

The bad weather had actually begun in mid-November and presaged a hard winter. Still in command and responding to Washington's order of 21 November 1779, McDougall bent every effort to complete the barracks already begun. He placed every soldier with experience as a mason under Kosciuszko's supervision for the construction of the barracks. The scarcity of lumber slowed the work, and the severe storms stopped it. McDougall took extraordinary measures to house his soldiers. He ordered them to occupy shelters at the forts and redoubts, like the bombproofs of Forts Arnold and Putnam. Still, some men were left with only tents. Already heavy snowstorms appeared in December, and food ran out. On Christmas Day the soldiers went hungry. Morale dropped, even before the worst storms struck in January. At the redoubts, a high incidence of fires occurred. Although arson was suspected, it could not be proven. The garrison hung on, but General Heath had to leave because of impaired health. Major General Robert Howe of North Carolina took his place. He promptly moved into Beverly Robinson's warm house on the east bank of the Hudson and did not venture out for two weeks. When the weather turned somewhat warmer, he visited his exhausted garrison at West Point. On 22 February 1780, a warm rain fell, melting the snow and ice. And on March 1, the thick ice on the river began to crack and rumble. The hard winter was over.[38]

During the frigid temperatures and blizzards of winter, Kosciuszko drew plans of the forts for General Washington. The engineer wanted a senior officer to review them, and he turned to General Nathanael Greene. He wrote him on 28 January 1780:

> I have sent the Commander in Chief the Plans of Fort Putnam and at the Point [Fort Arnold] with their respective profiles as I propose them to be when finished. I beg you would see and give me your opinion. Conscious of your Extensive abilities, I am

certain will afford as well as to the public good, as to my own improvement.

Two months later, Kosciuszko alerted Colonel Richard Kidder Meade, Washington's Assistant Adjutant General: "I wrote you the 11th of this instant and sent three more Sketches of Plans. I do not know if they are come to hand. I delivered them to General Howe, who promised to forward them." Kosciuszko asked Meade to inform the commander-in-chief of the continual scarcity of construction workers. "I beg you would inform him I have but Eighty fatigue men for all the works at West Point, " he wrote, " and I expect less and less every day." Kosciuszko also wrote to Governor Clinton for help and asked General Howe to do likewise. Whenever he found skilled soldiers, he held on to them tenaciously. As he told Meade, "I have three Masons from the Virginia Line. They are best Masons of the few number that I have. I should beg to keep them." Kosciuszko looked after the basic needs of soldiers under his supervision, and in the same letter to Meade pointed out, "As they are in Great want of shoes, I will thank you to procure an order for three pairs of shoes on the Commissary of Clothing at Newburgh." Meade answered on 30 March 1780, saying that the maps had not reached Washington, as yet. As for more fatigue men, Washington was instructing General Howe on the matter of augmentation.[39]

The severity of the winter and deep snow delayed the replacement of the float logs that had become waterlogged. Because it was also a time-consuming task, Kosciuszko was not able to place the chain across the river until April 5. Turning his attention to the continuing construction, he was dismayed to find the forts and redoubts heavily damaged, both by the weather and the soldiers. In their desperation to gather fire wood for warmth, the men had stripped the fortifications of wood used in construction. Kosciuszko's first job was to rebuild the damage. With so much work remaining, the engineer became frustrated, expending time and energy on construction previously done. The work seemed endless. As Palmer writes, "Building West Point was like running on a treadmill. Frustration was a constant companion.

The entire garrison shared Kosciuszko's mood of utter discouragement." Nonetheless, Kosciuszko persevered, and, at times, sought the peace and solitude of his garden, located down the slope on a bluff overlooking the Hudson River. He had cleared a small area of weeds and dead branches and beautified the site with flowers and ferns. The only sound was that of the musical flow of water from a spring. Dr. James Thacher, surgeon of the Continental Army, recorded a visit to West Point on 28 July 1778: "Here I had the pleasure of being introduced to Col. Thaddeus Kosciuszko, a gentleman of distinction from Poland." Thacher saw the engineer's garden hideaway and wrote, "He has amused himself while stationed at this point in laying out a curious garden in a deep valley, abounding more in rocks than soil. I was gratified in viewing his curious water fountain, with spouting jets and cascades." With occasional renovation, Kosciuszko's Garden has survived to the present. It is found on the bluff below Cullum Hall.[40]

The great hunger that afflicted the army during the winter persisted into the spring of 1780. Washington reported the hardship to Congress and could only repeat his plea for help. Lack of clothing for the soldiers was a perennial problem and distressed Kosciuszko profoundly. He did an extraordinary deed. He wrote General Philip Schuyler, then a member of Congress. Kosciuszko acted not only on behalf of his own men at West Point but also for the Corps of Engineers, in the absence of General Duportail, who with the Southern Army was besieged and captured by the British at Charleston, South Carolina. The letter to Schuyler was the only time Kosciuszko assumed the role of senior engineer of the Continental Army. Kosciuszko wrote:

> As you are the only Person in Congress with whom I have the Honor to be acquainted, that knows the system of the whole Army and its several Departments, you will forgive me the trouble I am about to give you in favour of the Corps of Engineers.
>
> We beg that the Honourable Congress would grant us Cloathing in Apointed manner as for the Army. Why should all Departments receive and we be excluded? Justice speaks for its self without any

KOSCIUSZKO GARDEN
(Renovated).

Rock stairwell (at bottom) leads down to the garden. Descending cat-walk opens to the garden (out of view) and continues to Flirtation Walk, West Point, New York. (Photo by the author, 25 September 1996)

further request from us. If Cloathing could be purchased very easy in this Country and without injuring the Public service in the Time which must be necessarily employed for that purpose, we should not solicit, but you know how Difficult it is to get at, and what inconsistancies it would be for us to be absent often from camp.

Your remonstrating to Congress in our behalf will I am sure bare great weight, which favour will always be greatfully acknowledged, with the greatest Sincerity from us.[41]

In the spring of 1780, Kosciuszko began his third year as chief engineer at West Point. His defense design, approved by General Washington, had been built up to near completion, in spite of shortages of artisans and workers. At the same time, these men had been subjected to the same hardships that afflicted the Continental Army—lack of food and clothing, and inadequate housing. Kosciuszko showed much patience and perseverance. Had it not been for the keen interest and unfailing attention of Washington, who exercised his authority to overcome problems, the construction would have been seriously delayed. Still, duty at West Point was becoming monotonous. An engineer at the fortress would always be engaged in "continual improvement of position," repairing damage caused by rain and snow, and in the annual and time-consuming requirement of lifting the chain in early winter, renovating it, and stretching it across the river in the spring. Nevertheless, Kosciuszko was eager for active campaigning, and he got his chance from the fortunes of war. On 12 May 1780, the British forced the surrender of General Benjamin Lincoln and his Southern Army of 5500 soldiers. The Americans suffered a crushing defeat. Notwithstanding, Congress vowed to continue the war in the South and sought to raise another army. Washington intended to give General Nathanael Greene the Southern command, but Congress appointed its favorite, General Horatio Gates.[42]

Gates planned to bring together the same staff that served him so well at Saratoga. He wrote to Major John Armstrong:

I am destined by Congress to command in the South. In entering on this new and (as Lee says) most difficult theatre of the war, my first thoughts have been turned to the selections of an Engineer, an Adjutant General and a Quarter-Master-General. Kosciuszko, Hay, and yourself, if I can prevail upon you all, are to fill these offices, and will fill them well. The *excellent qualities* of the Pole, which no one knows better than yourself, are acknowledged at head-quarters, and may induce others to prevent his joining us. But his promise once given, we are sure of him.[43]

Gates immediately asked Washington for the assignment of Kosciuszko to the Southern Army. On 21 June 1780, he wrote:

I could wish your Excellency would somewhat Brighten the Scene by indulging me in my request to obtain Colonel Kuscuiusco for my Chief engineer. His services with me in the Campaign of 77, and the High opinion I entertain of his Talents, and his Honour, induce me to be thus importunate with your Excellency, to let me have the Colonel for my Chief Engineer.

Meanwhile, Kosciuszko worked vigorously to repair the damage of the hard winter and to finish up construction. He made a critical estimate of the number of men needed to complete the construction of the forts and redoubts in two additional months. He personally examined Redoubt No. 4, Fort Putnam, Wyllys Redoubt and two batteries, a battery at Fort Arnold, and the remaining work on redoubts at Constitution Island. He assigned Redoubts 1, 2, and 3 to Gouvion. From the results, Kosciuszko concluded that a two-month effort would require at least 600 fatigue men, 160 carpenters, twenty masons, twelve miners, and ten teams. He submitted the two estimates to General McDougall, who then forwarded them to General Howe two days later. McDougall pointed out in his cover letter that he had only 200 men for all the works. Unless he received additional manpower, his current work force would need a period of six months to complete the construction.[44]

Kosciuszko was stalled temporarily when all his artificers were ordered across the river to work on a project under Gouvion's supervision. Hearing nothing of his anticipated reassignment, he wrote Washington on 30 July 1780:

To this day I have not received your Excellencys order respecting my destination, having nothing to do at present as all the artificers are directed to receive Liut. Colo. Gouvions orders. I beg your Excellency to give me permission to leave the Engineer Department and direct me a Command in the light Infantry in the Army under your immediate Command or the Army at the Southward agreeable to my rank I now hold. Your Excellency may be certain that I am acquiented with the Tactic & discipline and my Conduct joined with a small share of ambition to distinguish myself, I hope will prove not the Contrary.

From his headquarters in nearby Peekskill, Washington answered immediately. He explained that the artificers were diverted from West Point for a special but temporary project. He emphasized his conviction that an engineer must be at the fortress continually and "as you have from your long residence there are particularly acquainted with the nature of the Works and the plans for their completion, it was my intent that you should continue." Washington further explained that the "arrangement" of the Infantry Corps had been completed before the receipt of Kosciuszko's letter. And now Washington came to the interesting part of his letter: "The southern Army, by the captivity of Genl. du portail and the other Gentlemen in that branch, is without an Engineer, and as you seem to express a wish of going there rather than remaining at West point, I shall, if you prefer it to your present appointment, have no objection to your going."[45]

Kosciuszko was delighted with Washington's decision, and the next day he thanked the commander-in-chief for the opportunity to serve in the Southern Army. Wishing to take his servant, Agrippa Hull, with him, he asked permission of Washington:

I beg your Excellency would grant me a request to Carry my boy with me, who since three years wait on me. I have no other at present, and I Cannot get one to go with me so far off. Colo. [Ebenezer] Sprout is willing if your Excellency will give order for it.

Washington had no objection: "It is perfectly agreeable to me that you should carry your Servant with you and so You will inform Colo. Sprout." On 3 August 1780, when Washington had already given Kosciuszko permission to leave West Point, the commander-in-chief received Gates's letter of June 21. He answered Gates: "A few days since upon Col. Koscuisco's application for leave to serve to the Southward, he obtained my permission, and I suppose designs setting out immediately. Capt. Dalzien accompanies him." Kosciuszko's replacement at West Point, Major Villefranche, reported to General Benedict Arnold, the new commander who had persuaded Washington to give him the command of West Point. Washington informed Arnold that Kosciuszko had permission to join the Southern Army and that Villefranche (who lived with Kosciuszko in his quarters) would assume the duties of engineer.[46]

Kosciuszko's twenty-eight months of dedicated service at West Point resulted in the construction of a remarkable and typically American fortification. Perhaps the assessment of historian Palmer best describes Kosciuszko's masterpiece. Palmer writes, "Sixteen enclosed positions and ten major battery sites formed three roughly concentric defensive rings around the great chain. Each fort was capable both of defending itself and providing support by fire to its neighbors." Palmer further stresses: "No more formidable a position had ever been seen in the New World. As it had evolved, West Point was a fortress far ahead of its time." It was "Yankee ingenuity—abetted admittedly by Continental poverty and a Polish engineer" that devised and constructed a uniquely-suited fortress. Kosciuszko and the Americans built the fortress in spite of strong protests of the French engineers. "But it is not at all surprising that the Frenchmen protested," Palmer states, "for they were looking backward to the seventeenth century."

Palmer becomes more specific when he describes the quality of design and workmanship. The many positions revealed similarities, although no two were identical. "The practical Pole shaped each stronghold to conform best to its nearby terrain," Palmer says, "using wherever he could nature's sheer walls and

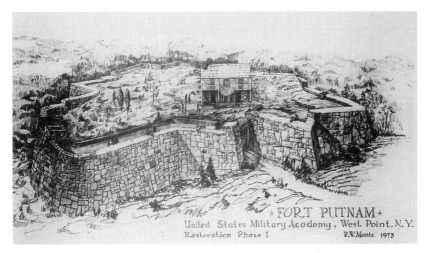

FORT PUTNAM, key fortification of Fortress West Point, designed and built by Colonel Thaddeus Kosciuszko, chief engineer. Photo shows the first phase of restoration in 1973. (Courtesy of the Library of the U.S. Military Academy, West Point, New York).

rocky obstacles." But, for the actual construction, Kosciuszko set up careful criteria for the work crews to follow. Palmer continues with a host of engineering measures of Kosciuszko:

• Batteries were built by raising an exterior stone scarp wall that varied in height as necessary to provide a level firing platform on the spot chosen.

• The stonework was all dry masonry with an inward talus. Capping the scarp wall stood a parapet fabricated of fascines or timber, or perhaps of soil held in place by fascines and logs. Thickness and height differed according to the degree of danger from enemy artillery.

• Gun platforms were elevated on stone piers or placed upon timber sleepers sunk in the earth. Redoubts were formed in the same manner, except for the scarp wall which was raised enough above the terrain to afford control of the surrounding area. Inner revetment walls on all redoubts were also of dry masonry.

• Many of the redoubts were bolstered by a detached battery located just outside the walls.

• Banquettes were provided for the troops, and, in most instances, bombproofs were built.

• Shielding all redoubts were various combinations of palisades, pickets, *chevaux de-frise,* and moats. Abatis encircled batteries and redoubts alike.

Palmer concludes: "All in all, the separate works constituting Fortress West Point displayed a remarkable level of engineering sophistication. Observers were invariably impressed."[47]

And Palmer is so right. On 21 November 1780, less than four months after Kosciuszko's departure for the South, the Marquis de Chastellux visited West Point during his travels in America, 1780–1782. Reaching the east bank of the Hudson River, he saw a magnificent view of the fortress and the river. "On lifting your eyes," he wrote, "you behold on every side lofty summits, all bristling with redoubts and batteries." Crossing the river in a barge to its west side, Chastellux was greeted first by General Heath's aides and then by the general. Heath led the Marquis on a tour of the fortifications. The Frenchman recorded his impressions:

> The first fort we met with above West Point, on the declivity of the mountain, has been named for General Putnam. It is placed on a rock very steep on every side; the ramparts were at first constructed with trunks of trees; they are being rebuilt of stone and are not yet entirely finished. There is a bombproof, powder magazine, a large cistern, and a souterrain for the garrison. Above this fort, and on reaching the highest peak, you can still see, on three other summits, three strong redoubts lined with cannon, each of which would require a formal siege. The day being nearly spent, I contented myself with judging by the eye of the very intelligent manner in which they are calculated for mutual protection.

Chastellux also commented on Fort Wyllys and two batteries down river. He expressed surprise that a young nation would have expended in two years upwards of twelve million *livres,* but a Frenchman "would doubtless feel some satisfaction," Chastellux boasted, "upon hearing that these beautiful and well-contrived works were planned and executed by two French engineers, M. Duportail and M. de Gouvion."[!][48]

CHAPTER SIX

Kosciuszko Joins the Southern Army

General Nathanael Greene's Engineer

OSCIUSZKO DEPARTED WEST POINT for the South about 7 August 1780. He could feel well satisfied with his effort in the cause of American Independence. At Saratoga, his strong fortifications on Bemis Heights blocked General Burgoyne's advance on Albany and thus destroyed the British Grand Strategy. At West Point, he designed and built the inter-locking defenses that created an impregnable fortress, and this bastion insured the American control of the Hudson River. In his current assignment, he would contribute his engineering skill and flexible capabilities to Greene's successful mobile cam-paign and carry out the only Vauban system of siegecraft of the Revolutionary War. This latter operation occurred at Ninety-Six, South Carolina, in the spring of 1781.

Kosciuszko missed the scandal at West Point caused by the treachery of General Benedict Arnold, who arrived two days before the Pole's departure. Arnold's attempt to turn West Point over to the British failed when American partisans captured the British agent, Major John Andre. Documents on his person revealed Arnold to be a traitor, but Arnold escaped capture by fleeing West Point. Unfortunately, the dastardly act affected

Kosciuszko, too. A trunkful of his engineering drawings and plans was destroyed. The loss became known when General Washington directed General William Heath, Arnold's replacement, to safeguard Kosciuzko's invaluable documents. In his letter of 31 October 1780, Washington wrote:

> There is I am informed by General [William] Irvine, a Chest belonging to Colonel Kosciuszko, containing principally Papers of a public nature; which General Greene had determined to have removed from Mrs. Warrens to a place of more security; but in the hurry of business might have omitted. If the chest still remains at West Point, you will be pleased to take it into your charge, or have it removed to a place of safety. As the Drafts and Papers are of service to the Public.[1]

Unfortunately, the confusion at West Point resulting from Arnold's treachery also caused the destruction of Kosciuszko's military papers. General Heath answered Washington on 6 November 1780, "I shall take immediate measures for the security of Colonel Kosciuszko's chest; it shall be lodged at my own quarters." At the same time Heath ordered an immediate search that disclosed the loss. Before dispatching his letter, he added a postscript:

> P.S. I have just sent for Colo. Kosciuszko's chest; it was left without a lock. Mrs. Warren saies upon the detection of Arnold she burnt the plans lest their being found with her should raise a suspicion to her disadvantage.[2]

Along the way south, Kosciuszko first stopped at army headquarters at Orange Town, New Jersey, to pay a courtesy call on General Washington. Kosciuszko again expressed his appreciation for the assignment to the Southern Army. The commander-in-chief commended the engineer for his highly satisfactory work at West Point. Washington had been reluctant to see Kosciuszko leave West Point, for he told General Gates, "I have experienced great satisfaction from his general conduct, and particularly from the attention and zeal with which he has prosecuted the Works committed to his charge at West Point."[3]

At Philadelphia, Kosciuszko tarried there for several days while visiting friends. William Clajon, former personal secretary to Gates,

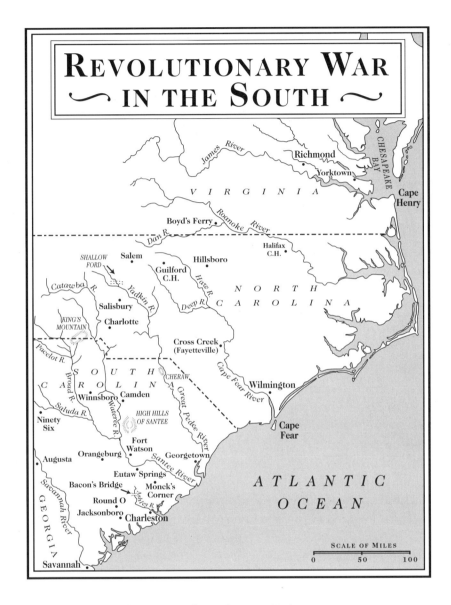

REVOLUTIONARY WAR IN THE SOUTH

told him that the general's only son Robert, twenty-two, was gravely ill at the family estate of Traveler's Rest. Even though the residence in Berkeley County, Virginia, was out of his way, Kosciuszko decided he must travel there. He knew Mrs. Gates and Robert well and valued their friendship. In addition, he could

later inform the general of conditions at home. Clajon wrote
Gates of Kosciuszko's decision on 20 August 1780. Clajon said
he would have liked to accompany Kosciuszko to Traveler's
Rest, but he had no money for travel.[4] From Traveler's Rest,
Kosciuszko continued to Richmond and there called on Thomas
Jefferson, Governor of Virginia. Kosciuszko was eager to meet the
champion of liberty who had drafted the immortal Declaration
of Independence. Perhaps Jefferson appealed to the Pole as a
modern Timoleon. From that first meeting, a close and lasting
friendship developed.[5]

During Kosciuszko's journey, General Gates fought the enemy
at the Battle of Camden, South Carolina, on 16 August 1780.
The British Army under General Lord Cornwallis attacked the
Americans fiercely, and the inexperienced North Carolina and
Virginia militia regiments stampeded, throwing the Southern
Army into chaos. In fact, the commander lost his head, as well.
Gates mounted his horse and galloped from the battlefield. The
Continental regulars, however, stood their ground, but the de-
termined British attack overpowered them and killed their
commander, General Baron de Kalb. The Battle of Camden was
an unmitigated disaster. Shocked, Congress relieved Gates of
his command and asked Washington to name a replacement.
Washington appointed his favorite general, Nathanael Greene,
who had served as Quartermaster General of the Continental
Army. Although Greene preferred field command, he carried out
his quartermaster duties loyally and well.[6]

The remnants of Gates's Southern Army retreated to Hillsborough,
North Carolina, where Gates began to reorganize his broken force.
Kosciuszko joined Gates here prior to 20 October 1780. Undoubt-
edly, Kosciuszko felt sad over his commander's plight, for Gates
was devastated by the damage done to his military reputation.
He next received the worrisome news of the serious illness of his
son. Nevertheless, he did the best he could while awaiting the
arrival of General Greene. Meanwhile, Major General William
Smallwood, with part of the army encamped at Salisbury, asked
Gates to send him Kosciuszko for the purpose of constructing

defensive works. Before Kosciuszko departed, Gates called a Council of War to decide "if they should stay at this Post until further Intelligence from Virginia about the Enemy's being landing there." Brigadier Generals Isaac Huger and Edward Stevens, Kosciuszko, as well as several colonels and majors, unanimously recommended that Gates remain at Hillsborough and await further news from Virginia.

While at Hillsborough, Kosciuszko shared inadequate quarters for six weeks with Huger and Dr. William Read, chief of hospital service. Conditions in the army were so wretched that the three did not have a single blanket among them. They shared the general's cloak under which they slept occasionally. "The weather was in the meantime very cold," historian Robert W. Gibbes wrote, "but they bore it without a murmur." As for the soldiers, Colonel Otho Williams, adjutant general, described their plight: "Absolutely without pay; almost destitute of clothing; often with only a half ration, and never with a whole one (without substituting one article for another)." Nevertheless, he praised the fortitude of the men: "Not a soldier was heard to murmur, after the third or fourth day of being encamped." Kosciuszko was not unmindful of the basic needs of his black servant, Agrippa Hull, who desperately needed shoes. Not able to find any in the Hillsborough area, Kosciuszko turned to the North Carolina Board of War for help, and it responded with an order for a pair of shoes for "Colo. Cusiasko's Servant."[7]

General Greene had not yet arrived at headquarters by November 25 when Gates called another Council of War at New Providence, fourteen miles south of Charlotte. Due to a number of unfavorable conditions, the encampment at New Providence proved unsatisfactory. Valuing his engineer's advice, Gates again invited Kosciuszko to the meeting. When Greene took command of the Southern Army, he likewise trusted the chief engineer and developed a close-working relationship with him. At the second council, Gates posed the following question to his key officers, Generals Smallwood, Huger, Morgan, and William Davison, Colonels Kosciuszko and Abraham Buford, and Lieutenant Colonels

MAJOR GENERAL NATHANAEL GREENE
Commander of the Southern Army, 1781-1783
Greene admired Kosciuszko's character and abilities, and he developed a great friendship for his chief engineer. Portrait by Charles Willson Peale, c.1783. (Independence National Historical Park Collection).

126

John Eager Howard and William Washington: "What position the Troops ought to take? Whether at or near Charlotte, or at the Waxhaws or in that Neighborhood?" Smallwood alone recommended "the Army's moving to the Waxhaws [a district near the North Carolina southern border], "taking post there for Three weeks; and then returning to Charlotte." The remaining officers, however, recommended that the army march directly to Charlotte.[8]

It was at Charlotte that General Gates graciously welcomed Major General Nathanael Greene, 2 December 1780. The next day Gates issued a general order in which he announced Greene's arrival and appointment "by his Excellency General Washington, with the approbation of the honorable the Congress, to the command of the Southern Army." Gates sincerely thanked the officers and men "for their Perseverance, fortitude, and patient Endurance, of all the Hardships and Sufferings they had undergone while under his command." He hoped that their misfortunes would cease and that victory would crown the efforts of the Southern Army in the future. Two days later, December 5, Greene responded with his general order: "General Greene returns his thanks to the Hon'able Major General Gates for the polite Manner in which he has introduced him to his command and for his good Wishes for the Success of the Southern Army."[9]

General Gates departed Charlotte for Traveler's Rest on 8 December 1780. He felt dispirited by the loss of his command. But more tragic was the news of the death of his son Robert, who passed away on 4 October 1780. Dr. Robert Brown wrote the general on 16 November 1780. (It seems that family friends were reluctant to tell the general, who was weighed down with serious military problems). "He was all that you could wish for a son," Brown wrote. "I also must lament him; He was all that I could wish in a friend." The future of Gates looked very lonely, indeed.

Directed by Congress, General Washington ordered Greene to conduct a court of inquiry of Gates's conduct at the Battle of Camden. Washington ruled that "the inquiry should be conducted in the quarter in which he acted" due to the presence of witnesses. Washington appointed Major General Baron von Steuben president of the board. Von Steuben, however, was unable to call the board into session because he himself was engaged in military operations in Virginia. Meanwhile, Greene interceded in behalf of Gates. According to Colonel Williams, Greene gathered information relative to the circumstances of the Camden battle. He wrote letters to members of Congress, and this body finally rescinded its resolution against Gates on 14 August 1782. In the interim, Gates was left without a command until November 1782, when Washington ordered him to duty at army headquarters at Newburgh, New York.

General Washington was courteous and cooperative with Gates, notwithstanding allegations that the commander-in-chief harbored animosity toward Gates for his alleged participation in the Conway Cabal. Likewise, Washington was never cool toward Kosciuszko, as Elizabeth Kite alleges, because of Kosciuszko's friendship with Gates. Washington did not stoop to guilt by association. In fact, Washington thought well of Kosciuszko. For example, the general praised Kosciuszko and shielded him from the petty attacks of General Louis Duportail.[10]

Despite the departure of General Gates from Charlotte, Kosciuszko was pleased that he was still among old friends. He served again with Daniel Morgan, whom he first met at Saratoga three years earlier. Major John Armstrong, his constant companion at Fort Ticonderoga and Saratoga, had joined the Southern Army with Gates. There were also Lewis Morris and Dr. Robert Brown, both of whom had advised and assisted Kosciuszko during his controversy with John Carter at White Plains, New York, in 1778. As for General Greene, Kosciuszko knew of him from his reputation. Over the next two and a half years, they would work closely and develop mutual respect and friendship. However, it was with Greene's adjutant general, Colonel Otho Holland Williams, that a special friendship with Williams evolved. The adjutant general also became Greene's right-hand man. Today Williams would be called "chief of staff." As always, Kosciuszko was ready to serve the new commander and the cause of American independence.[11]

CHAPTER SEVEN

The Race to
the Dan River

Kosciuszko Builds an Amphibious Army

ENERAL GREENE did not command much of an army. His effective force consisted of fewer than 2000 soldiers, half of whom were Continentals. He was assisted by partisan militia units of Generals Francis Marion, Thomas Sumter, and Andrew Pickins. However, they were not under Greene's direct control and, at times, acted on their own. Less than half of the army was properly clothed and fed. Unfortunately, the Charlotte area had been stripped of foodstuffs and basic supplies. Greene's first act was to find a better campsite where the troops could renew their strength. He called on his engineer to reconnoiter the area of the Pedee River and make the selection. In this respect, Greene followed the lead of Generals Schuyler and Gates, who, likewise, had relied on Kosciuszko to choose well-suited encampments in the Northern Department. On 8 December 1780, Greene instructed Kosciuszko:

> You will go with Major Polk and examine the country from the mouth of Little River, twenty or thirty miles down the Pedee, and search for a good position for the army. You will report the make of the country, the nature of the soil, the quality of the water, quantity of produce, number of mills and the water transportation that

may be had up and down the River. You will also enquire respecting the creeks in the rear the fords. and the difficulty of passing them. All which you will report as soon as possible.

Kosciuszko found an excellent location on the east bank of the Pedee River and nearly opposite Cheraw Hill, just south of the border between the Carolinas. On December 28, Greene reported the movement of the army to Samuel Huntington, President of Congress: "I sent Col. Kosciuszko to see if a healthy camp and plenty of provisions could be had. His report being favorable, I put the troops in motion the 20th and arrived here the 26th instant." Clearly Greene trusted the military evaluation of Kosciuszko, and in the words of historian Ward, "upon whose judgment and engineering ability he greatly relied."[1]

Greene's opponent in the South was the experienced and aggressive General Lord Cornwallis, who commanded an army of some 4000 well-equipped regulars, not counting the British garrisons that occupied the principal towns in the Carolinas. Greene believed he could not risk open battle with the British with his own inferior and ill-equipped army. He needed to pursue a plan that would prevent Cornwallis from seizing control of the entire South. Greene decided on a bold and imaginative but risky strategy—to divide his army in two. The strategy ran counter to the principles of war. But it placed Cornwallis in a dilemma. Should he strike after one American force, the other was free to attack a critical target in his rear. Cornwallis felt compelled to divide his army, too, so as to deny the unopposed movement of the Americans. He actually divided his army into three forces, under Major General Alexander Leslie, Lieutenant Colonel Banastre Tarleton, and Lord Cornwallis himself. Greene, on the other hand, formed his army as follows: Brigadier General Daniel Morgan with some 600 soldiers and Brigadier General Isaac Huger with about 1100 Continentals and militia. Greene stayed with Huger's force.[2]

Greene's strategy could work, if each force marched rapidly to outdistance a superior enemy or reunited quickly for a major battle. Keys to this strategy were mobility and knowledge of the terrain. A study of the map of the Carolinas shows that several large rivers cut the country. Greene needed to know the location of roads, river fords, and ferries. He also sought to use the rivers for the easy transportation of supplies. He directed Brigadier General Edward Stevens to survey the Yadkin River and dispatched his quartermaster officer, Edward Carrington, to examine the Dan River in Virginia. To Kosciuszko, he gave the task to "explore the navigation of the Catawba river from mill creek below the forks up to Oliphant mill." All three officers had the added mission of collecting boats for the transportation of supplies and of flat-bottomed boats for the crossing of rivers by the troops. Greene's directive to Kosciuszko was specific:

> Report to me its particular situation as to the depth of water, the rapidity of the stream, the rocks, shoals or falls you may meet with and every other information necessary to enable me to form an accurate opinion of the transportation which may be made on the river in the different seasons of the year.

Greene also cautioned Kosciuszko: "It is of the utmost importance that your report to me should be very particular and as early as possible."[3]

Rapid and uninterrupted movement was fundamental to Greene's strategy of mobility, and the movements had to be done across rivers. On 1 January 1781, Greene ordered his chief engineer to Cross Creek (Fayetteville), North Carolina, to scour the surrounding area for carpenters and tools for "constructing a number of boats, the quantity and kind that will be wanted, you are perfectly acquainted with." The general expressed his reliance on Kosciuszko: "Confiding in your zeal and activity, I persuade myself you will make all the dispatch the business will admit as the safety & support of the Army depend upon your accomplishing this business." Greene informed Washington of his proposed means of mobility, telling him, "Kosciuszko is employed in building flat-bottomed boats to be transported with the army, if ever I shall be able to command the means of transporting them." Throughout January 1781, Kosciuszko built flat-bottomed boats.[4]

Earlier, in mid-December 1780, Greene had ordered Morgan to cross the Catawba River into South Carolina and operate in the region between the Catawba and Pacolet Rivers. For his part, General Cornwallis ordered Tarleton's Legion of 1100 troops at Ninety-Six to attack Morgan and defeat him. Cornwallis then planned to clean up the remnants of Morgan's force. The battle occurred at Cowpens, between the Pacolet and Catawba Rivers. Morgan's position was a most unlikely choice for a battlefield, but it suited his masterful plan. On 17 January 1781, Morgan shattered Tarleton's command. Nearly the entire British force was killed or captured, and the great victory lifted the spirits of the Southern Army and the country, as well.[5]

Still superior in number to the Southern Army, General Cornwallis determined on a strategy that would cut off Greene's communications with Virginia. The next campaign, therefore, became a test of skill and endurance between the opponents, and the race to the Dan River began. Equally determined to thwart the British effort at encirclement, Greene reunited his army. He ordered Huger with the main force at the Cheraw camp to march up the Yadkin River while he rode ahead to meet with Morgan. Greene planned a key role for Kosciuszko, and he summoned his engineer to his side. At Masks Ferry, Major Lewis Morris, aide-de-camp, wrote Kosciuszko on 1 February 1781: "Genl. Huger has just received a letter from Genl. Greene dated at Olyphant mill on the Catawba. He requests that you would join him there or where ever he may be as soon as possible." Although Kosciuszko was building boats, Morris explained Greene's instructions for preparing the army against the new danger from Cornwallis:

> You will order such of the boats as are finished to follow the army immediately and such as are not finished you will deliver to the charge of Colonel Wade. Let Captain Dellyenn [Dalzien] attend to this business. The artificers you will order to join the army as soon as possible, they are much wanted.[6]

Heavy rains during this winter season caused the rivers to run full and made most of the fords impassable. The troops and supply wagons had to be ferried across in boats. Greene had foreseen this need and had set his engineer to construct a flotilla of boats that were brought along with the troops. Greene thus insured his mobility. Cornwallis, too, was well aware of the flooded condition on the rivers. He planned to turn the weather to his advantage by attempting to pin his American opponent against one of the major rivers, Yadkin, Deep, or Dan in Virginia. However, Cornwallis apparently was not aware of Greene's brilliant idea of equipping his army with Kosciuszko's boats. Nevertheless, Cornwallis improved his chances of overtaking the Americans by removing and burning his wagons and heavy baggage that impeded fast movement. He made a risky decision. He had to bring Greene to battle quickly or lose his staying power.[7]

Greene instructed Huger and Morgan to march their separate forces to the designated reunion site of Salisbury. The wretched condition of the roads and other problems, however, slowed down Huger's troops, and Cornwallis was closing the gap. With Salisbury no longer a safe place, Greene changed the juncture of his two generals to Guilford Court House, some fifty miles northeast of Salisbury. In responding to the change, Morgan successfully eluded his British pursuers. Ward explains:

> Morgan had passed through Salisbury and reached Trading Ford on the Yadkin, about seven miles east of the town. It was usually a good fording place, but the long continued rains had raised it above fording depth. Boats were necessary, and by Greene's foresight and Kosciuszko's energy, they were there. In the night of the 2nd and 3rd of February, the cavalry swam their horses across, and the infantry took to the boats.

Left without means of crossing, British General Charles O'Hara and his mounted infantry looked helplessly at the Americans on the far bank of the swollen river.[8]

At Guilford Court House, Greene called a Council of War, attended by Generals Huger and Morgan, and Colonel Williams, 9 February 1781. Greene informed his key combat officers that the army consisted of only 1426 infantry, many of whom were poorly armed and lacked proper clothing. In addition, the available militia numbered 600 men, but they were poorly armed, too. Opposing them were between 2500 and 3000 enemy located at Shallow Ford on the Yadkin River, only forty miles away. Their proximity could bring on a battle. The general posed this question: "Whether we ought to risque an Action with the Enemy or not?" His subordinates expressed the unanimous recommendation of avoiding a general action and retreating at once over the Roanoke River in Virginia.[9]

Accepting the recommendation, General Greene decided to adopt a plan of deception that would lead Cornwallis to the passable fords on the upper Dan River, while the Americans crossed some distance down the river. Greene formed a light force of 700 soldiers composed of the cavalry and lightly equipped infantry. He gave the command of this special force to Colonel Williams, since General Morgan had left the army for reasons of poor health. Williams' mission was to lead Cornwallis to the upper fords, harassing his flanks but always staying in front, and avoiding anything more than light skirmishing. Williams carried out the feint with consummate skill, and Cornwallis took the bait. He continued to believe that Greene's escape door was the upper Dan, where the fords were passable. He aimed to beat Greene to the Dan, turn on him, and keeping him pinned to the river, crush the Southern Army once and for all. Greene knew that he must elude Cornwallis. The fate of the Revolution in the South hung in the balance.[10]

Greene chose Boyd's (Irwin's) Ferry on the Dan River as his marching objective. Because of the depth of the river at this location, it could be crossed only by boat. Greene, however, had Kosciuszko's flotilla ready. He ordered the boats transported as rapidly as possible to Boyd's Ferry under the supervision of his quartermaster officer, Lieutenant Colonel Carrington. He also directed Kosciuszko to throw up entrenchments at this site for the protection of the boats and the army, should the British be able to attack the American position. Historian William Johnson reaffirms Greene's thoughtful planning: "In the meantime, a proper party was pushed forward to collect the boats, and with

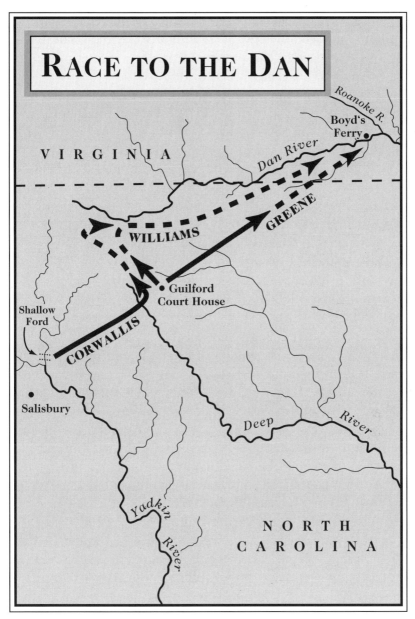

RACE TO THE DAN

General Nathanael Green's army eludes the pursuing British under General Lord Corwallis. Greene escapes across the Dan River at Boyd's Ferry on Kosciuszko's flotilla of boats, February 13 – 14, 1781.

them General Kosciusko, who had rejoined his commander at Guilford, and who now preceded him for the purpose of throwing up a breastwork at the ferry, for the double object of protecting the boats, and covering the passage of the army." Kosciuszko and Carrington executed their tasks with skill and alacrity.[11]

The distance from Guilford Court House to the Dan River is seventy miles, and Greene took a direct route to Boyd's Ferry. The march of the Americans was exhausting. It rained and snowed in February. By day the ground was a deep mud that clung to everything. By night the ground froze into a rough and broken surface. Greene reported the difficult march to Washington: "The miserable situation of the troops for want of clothing had rendered this march the most painful imaginable; several hundreds of Soldiers tracking the ground with their bloody feet." Although the main army marched unmolested, as Cornwallis thought mistakenly that Williams' harassing force was Greene's rear, it nevertheless moved as fast as humanly possible. Greene reached the Dan on February 13, welcomed by Kosciuszko and Carrington. The boats ferried the troops and stores to the north shore. Meanwhile, Williams approached the Dan River farther upstream from Greene. By now, February 13, Williams believed that Greene had had sufficient time to reach the ferry, and he suddenly veered east to join with Greene. He placed Lee's cavalry as the rear guard and strained to stay ahead of the British who, led by Tarleton's horsemen, pursued madly well into the night. After resting a few hours, Williams again rushed the troops along before daybreak. They reached Boyd's Ferry at sunset on February 14 and were ferried across in the waiting boats. Bringing up the rear, Lee's horsemen galloped up to the crossing site after dark. Their timing was perfect. The empty boats were being brought back to the south shore as Lee's cavalry appeared. The troopers piled into the boats, and the horses swam the river. Just as Lee's men reached the opposite shore, the pursuing British cavalry dashed up, too late. The Americans had all the boats. They were beyond immediate pursuit. Greene, indeed, had outmaneuvered and outdistanced a superior and determined foe. Elated over

Greene's performance, General Washington congratulated the commander of the Southern Army, but in his usual subdued manner: "You may be assured that your Retreat before Lord Cornwallis is highly applauded by all Ranks, and reflects much honor on your military Abilities."[12]

Lord Cornwallis was uncertain as to his next move. He had imposed British control over Georgia and South Carolina, thus far. North Carolina was still to be conquered before he could venture into Virginia. Anticipating the British general's next move, Greene concluded that Cornwallis would most likely march to Halifax on the Roanoke River and subdue North Carolina from that advantageous location. As Greene told Washington, "That position would greatly awe Virginia and almost totally subject North Carolina." However, Greene would not give the enemy Halifax without a fight. The day after crossing the Dan, he directed Kosciuszko to Halifax to select a good defensive site for the army, and, if practicable, to construct the fortifications quickly, as Lord Cornwallis's movements were rapid. Before Kosciuszko departed, Greene gave him two letters to carry to Halifax; one to the North Carolina Board of War and the second to General Richard Caswell, former governor and present commander of the North Carolina militia. Greene asked them to give his engineer all possible and prompt help. To Caswell, Greene wrote:

> It is more than probable that the enemy will file off towards Hillsborough and Halifax, the last of which places, I think they will endeavor to establish a post at, to prevent which I have sent Col. Kosciuszko to fortify it, providing that he finds its position and the circumstances favorable for the purpose. The work must be executed as fast as possible.

Greene considered Kosciuszko's mission essential to his strategy of disabling the enemy's effectiveness. Greene told Washington, "If we can prevent his taking post there and oblige him to fall down into the lower Country, he will reap little advantage from his movements.[13]

Traveling more than eighty miles along poor roads, Kosciuszko carefully avoided capture by Tories and reached Halifax safely on February 18. He reported to Greene that he had traveled slower than expected because he could not find horses on the way, being forced to go on foot part of the distance. The next morning, accompanied by Colonel Nicholas Young, deputy quartermaster of North Carolina, Kosciuszko examined several sites and concluded that the work of fortifying a site could not be done quickly. An adequate defense called for not less than six redoubts. In addition, the quartermaster department lacked intrenching tools, and those of the inhabitants were few. Negro workers were also few in number, and a ready militia was not available for work. Kosciuszko believed that the only reason for a British presence at Halifax would be the seizure of magazines and stores of provisions. He recommended that the stores be moved to the northern shore of the Roanoke River where a "thousand good militia" stationed at Taylor's Ferry would be sufficient to protect Halifax. While in Halifax, Kosciuszko informed the natives of the fierce race to the Dan, without the loss of soldiers or equipment. The patriots were elated with the news and credited Greene with the successful campaign.[14]

Halifax did not become the objective of Lord Cornwallis. He fell back into North Carolina and reached Hillsborough on 20 February 1781. With his presence and encouragement, he expected to rally loyalists to his army. However, Greene did not allow him a free hand. Greene recrossed the Dan river on February 23 and followed Cornwallis. By March 14 he marched into Guilford Court House, while Cornwallis encamped at New Garden. The two armies were only about twelve miles apart, and Greene's proximity was a challenge to a battle. Greene felt strong. His repeated pleas to the governors of Virginia and North Carolina for militia prompted them to send reinforcements. He now commanded 2600 militia and volunteer infantry. His Continentals numbered 1600. With the addition of the cavalry and artillery, Greene's Southern Army totaled more than 4400 soldiers. In contrast, Cornwallis could muster about 1900 rank and file. But they were all regulars, seasoned and disciplined.[15]

Cornwallis accepted Greene's challenge and marched to meet

him. Greene selected the battlefield in the area of the court house. He formed three lines of soldiers. On the first line he positioned the North Carolina militia commanded by Brigadier Generals John Butler and Pinkertham Easton. Virginia militia occupied the second line, 300 yards behind the first. Many of its officers, former Continentals, were veterans. The Virginians were commanded by Brigadier Generals Edward Stevens and Robert Lawson. Another 400 yards behind the second line, Greene placed his regular Continental troops. General Huger commanded the Virginia regiments and Colonel Williams, the Maryland regiments. The cavalry of Lieutenant Colonels William Washington and Henry Lee guarded the flanks.

On 15 March 1781, at about one in the afternoon, Cornwallis attacked the Americans with his entire force, leaving no reserves. He ordered his redcoats to rush the foe with the bayonet. The tactic worked. As the British charged the first line with naked steel, the militia fired once, broke ranks, and fled. The second line of Virginia militia stood somewhat more firmly, but they were pushed back. The redcoats kept coming. At the third line, Colonel Gunby's disciplined Marylanders charged the British with the bayonet and routed them. Meanwhile, British soldiers under Generals Leslie and O'Hara attacked the 5th Maryland, a new regiment, whose soldiers fled from their position. The veteran 1st Maryland Regiment rushed into the gap, and a fierce fight erupted. The veterans on both sides stood their ground and took heavy casualties. Observing the action, Cornwallis in desperation ordered his artillery to fire grapeshot into the melee, killing friend and foe. The shock to both sides brought the fighting to a standstill. Had Greene continued the battle, he might have won a clear victory, but he always sought to save his Continentals, the core of his army, for another day. He withdrew from the battlefield. Although Greene lost the battle, barely, he had inflicted severe casualties on Cornwallis. The significance of the battle was not immediately evident. In retrospect, however, the Battle of Guilford Court House became a turning point of the war in the South. Kosciuszko apparently took no active part in the battle. He may have thrown up some intrenchments, but no mention is made.[16]

Cornwallis kept retreating to the British base of Wilmington, North Carolina. Having burned his wagons and the heavier baggage when he attempted to intercept the Southern Army in the race to the Dan River, the British general needed to reequip his army. With Cornwallis at Wilmington, Greene had an open road into South Carolina. Here the enemy had a tight hold on the region, maintaining strong posts at Georgetown, Camden, and Ninety-Six. Greene marched his army for Camden, which he approached by 6 April 1781. Meanwhile, General Francis Marion with help from Lee's Legion attacked Fort Watson on the Wateree River below Camden and captured it. Greene found the position at Camden too strong to attack and fell back a mile to Hobkirk's Hill where his close presence challenged the aggressive Lord Rawdon.

Greene prepared for battle. Changing his deployment from that used at Guilford Court House, he placed his Continentals out front, on the first line. These were Huger's Virginia brigade and Williams' Maryland brigade. Greene deployed the North Carolina militia behind the Continentals, and Washington's cavalry on the left flank. As Lord Rawdon's forward elements approached the Americans, Greene noticed that they formed a narrow front. He determined to attack the British frontally and on both flanks simultaneously. The 5th Virginia and the 1st Maryland made the direct attack with the bayonet, but not before Greene had given them the order "No firing!" Notwithstanding, two companies on the flank of Colonel Gunby's 1st Maryland Regiment began to fire. Gunby, who had fought so well at Guilford Court House, became confused. Instead of pressing the attack, he ordered a retreat to a rear position where he sought to reform his troops. The delay was fatal. Observing the weakness of his own leading units, Lord Rawdon rushed up reinforcements. Charging, the British panicked the Marylanders into fleeing. Greene's opportunity for a smashing victory was lost, and he ordered a retreat. Greene had parried British attacks for several months. At Hobkirk's Hill, on 25 April 1781, Greene felt confident of victory, only to have that chance snatched away by the vicissitudes of battle.[17]

Despite his victory, Lord Rawdon considered Camden too exposed to continue defending it. He abandoned Camden on 10 May 1781, and fell back to Monck's Corner, about thirty miles from Charleston. Shortly thereafter, American militia forces captured the British post at Orangeburg and Forts Motte and Granby. Greene made the capture of Ninety-Six his objective and marched the army to this strongly-fortified post.[18]

CHAPTER EIGHT

Siege of Ninety-Six

Kosciuszko Carries Out
Vauban's Siegecraft

AN UNPRECEDENTED OPERATION of the American Revolutionary War occurred at Ninety-Six, South Carolina, where General Greene laid siege to a strongly-fortified British position. Here Kosciuszko executed an engineering plan of going over and under the fort. The siege failed, but a controversy developed when Lieutenant Colonel "Light-Horse Harry" Lee criticized Kosciuszko's engineering judgment and competence.

Greene's emaciated army of 1000 Continentals reached Ninety-Six on 22 May 1781. The unusual name originated from the number of miles from Keowee, the center of the Cherokee Indians in southwestern South Carolina. The British considered the region of Ninety-Six important to their plan of conquest. The fort offered security to the large loyalist element from which the British Army recruited soldiers. The possession of the area cowed the patriots into submission and insured contact with Indian allies.[1]

Lieutenant Colonel John Harris Cruger commanded the fort with an all-loyalist garrison of 550 men. He was an officer of unusual ability and courage and had acquired much fighting experience. Historian Joseph B. Mitchell writes that Cruger "conducted one of the most brilliant defensive operations of the entire war." Cruger's own 350 soldiers were mostly natives of New York and New Jersey. Under competent leadership, they developed into disciplined regulars. An additional force of 200 were local Tory militia. Opposed to their patriot neighbors, these loyalists waged partisan warfare against them. Attitudes hardened to the point where both sides practiced cruelty against each other.[2]

Ninety-Six had a stockade around it for many years. British Royal engineer, Lieutenant Henry Haldane, improved the defenses greatly by directing workers to dig a deep trench with abatis around the village and to throw up the earth in front to form a high bank. To the east of the village, Haldane erected an usually strong redoubt called Star Fort. He built it circular but punctuated the wall with sixteen salients and reinforced the redoubt with a circular ditch and abatis. The villagers and the garrison drew their water from a rivulet flowing in a shallow ravine west of the village. To protect the source of water from attack, Haldane erected a fort with two blockhouses on the western bank of the ravine. He also fortified a jail near the village. Indeed, Haldane made Ninety-Six into a formidable defensive site.[3]

On the first night at Ninety-Six, General Greene conducted a reconnaissance of the enemy fortifications, taking along his chief engineer, Kosciuszko, and his aide-de-camp, Captain Nathaniel Pendleton. They examined the strength of the fortifications, sometimes within hailing distance of the enemy sentries who fired upon them. Greene and Kosciuszko noted that the Star Fort on the east was the strongest and commanded the remaining fortified points. If the Star Fort were to fall, the rest of the defense would become untenable. Greene decided to launch his attack against the Star Fort. Kosciuszko offered his assessment and recommendation that the attack likewise be made against the Star Fort. Reporting the result of Greene's and his joint inspection, Kosciuszko noted, "We thought proper to begin against the Star redoubt."[4]

Material to the Kosciuszko-Lee controversy is Greene's decision to attack the Star Fort first. In his *Memoirs*, published in 1812, Lee failed to mention that Greene himself conducted the evaluation of the British fortifications. In fact, Lee implied that the commander directed his engineer (perhaps at army headquarters) to examine the British position and decide on the best course of action. Lee wrote: "To this officer General Greene committed the designation of the course and mode of approach." Greene's biographer, William Johnson, rebutted that "it was perfectly understood in camp that the General himself directed the operations of the engineer." As an experienced commander of his own partisan Legion, Lee should have known better. In military operations, staff officers, including engineers, offer recommendations, but the commander makes the decisions. Lee apparently questioned the leadership of General Greene, one of the foremost tacticians and strategists of the Continental Army.[5]

That a direct attack on the British fort would undoubtedly bring heavy casualties and result in failure seemed evident to Greene and Kosciuszko. The engineer, therefore, recommended the method of attack perfected by the eminent Frenchman Marquis de Vauban whose siegecraft Kosciuszko had studied in Europe. The essential feature of Vauban's system was the use of temporary fortifications, trenches, and earthworks for the protection of the advancing troops. Professor Henry Guerlac writes: "Vauban's system of attack, which was followed with but little variation during the eighteenth century, was a highly formalized and leisurely procedure." Guerlac explains the process as follows:

- The attackers gather their men and stores at a point beyond the range of the defending fire and adequately concealed.

- At this point the sappers dig a trench that moves slowly towards the fort. After the sappers progress some distance, a deep trench paralleling the point of future attack is flung out at right angles to the trench of approach. This is the so-called "first parallel."

- From the first parallel, the trench is moved forward again, zigzagging as it approaches the fort. After it progresses the desired distance, the second parallel is constructed.

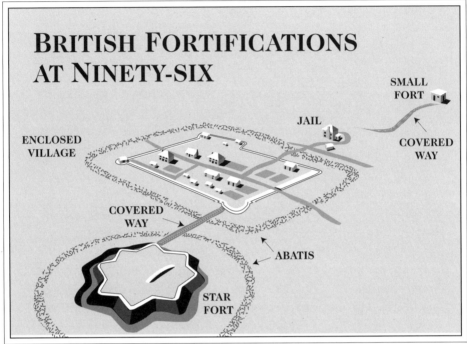

BRITISH FORTIFICATIONS AT NINETY-SIX

SMALL FORT

ENCLOSED VILLAGE

JAIL

COVERED WAY

COVERED WAY

ABATIS

STAR FORT

(Based on National Park Service sketch at Ninety-Six National Historic Site)

Major General Nathanael Greene with Colonel Thaddeus Kosciuszko, chief engineer, and the General's aide, Captain Nathaniel Pendleton, reconnoitered the British fortifications at Ninety-Six, South Carolina, during the night of 22-23 May 1781. Greene found the Star Fort to be the strongest element of the enemy defense. He decided to attack the Star Fort, believing that once it fell, the rest of the defensive complex was untenable for the British and would fall easily. Kosciuszko concurred with Greene.

- The trench is moved forward once more, until a third and usually final parallel is constructed, only a short distance from the foot of the glacis [outer rampart of the fort that slopes down to the level of the surrounding ground].

- The perilous task of advancing up the glacis, exposed to the enemy's raking fire, is accomplished by the aid of temporary high earthworks, from which the besiegers can fire upon the defenders. (For this purpose, Kosciuszko built a forty-foot high firing platform).[6]

Greene approved Kosciuszko's engineering method of building parallels. Hoping to score a quick victory, Greene directed Kosciuszko to begin excavations within seventy yards of the fort, but so close that Cruger found the work crews a tempting target. Cruger constructed a platform for his three artillery pieces at a position in the fort closest to the working Americans. He then opened fire with his cannon and muskets, followed by a surprise attack by thirty men who sallied out of the fort and bayoneted anyone who did not scurry to safety. Chastised by the experience, Kosciuszko started anew at a safer distance of 220 yards from the Star Fort. The regiments furnished working parties who toiled from dawn to dusk under Kosciuszko's supervision and that of his assistant engineer, Captain Joseph Dalzien. Colonel Otho Williams remarked that "the Americans, being unacquainted with the art of besieging, had difficulty in carrying out Kosciuszko's plans, but they were extraordinarily brave." The hard compact earth also impeded the work. Kosciuszko compared the soil to soft stone. Despite the difficulties, Kosciuszko completed the first parallel and a twenty-foot high battery at 140 yards from the fort on June 1. The parallel was dug four feet wide, three feet deep, and extended about 180 feet. In another three days the engineer completed the second parallel. He then began work on the third parallel just sixty yards from the fort. Worried, Cruger placed intense fire on the American crews, but they protected themselves behind a rolling wood shield. To counter the British fire, Greene directed Kosciuszko to erect

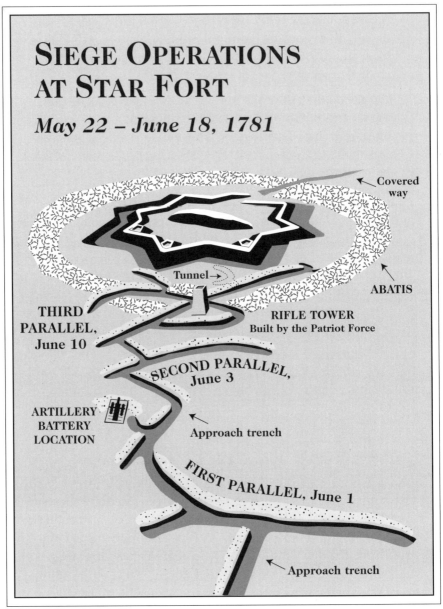

SIEGE OPERATIONS AT STAR FORT

May 22 – June 18, 1781

Covered way

THIRD PARALLEL, June 10

Tunnel→

ABATIS

RIFLE TOWER
Built by the Patriot Force

SECOND PARALLEL, June 3

ARTILLERY BATTERY LOCATION

Approach trench

FIRST PARALLEL, June 1

Approach trench

(Based on National Park Service sketch at Ninety-Six National Historic Site)

Kosciuszko plans and excavates series of trenches and parallels protecting the approach for the American assault.

a Maham Tower, that is, an elevated platform forty feet high. American riflemen were now able to shoot at any defender who lifted his head above the parapet. The resourceful Cruger, however, raised the level of the parapet three feet with sand bags, interspersed with loop holes for musket fire.[7]

At this stage General Greene demanded Cruger's surrender. Colonel Williams delivered the summons to the British commander, who rejected the demand. Thus far, Cruger felt confident, having lost only one officer killed and eight others wounded. Greene tried another tactic. He ordered selected men to shoot arrows tipped with burning pitch into the town to ignite the wooden dwellings. Cruger ordered immediately that the roofs of the houses be torn off. Meanwhile, Kosciuszko kept advancing the trenches toward the fort, and Cruger continued to send out parties of loyalists to make quick raids and then retreat, but American artillery silenced Cruger's cannon. Kosciuszko confirmed the effectiveness of American artillery: "The next day [June 5] upon our left we desmount the Canon in the star Redoubt from the battery and killed few men in it."[8]

On 9 June 1781, General Greene reported the difficult progress of the siege to the President of Congress:

> We have been prosecuting the Siege at this place with all possible diligence with our little force, but for want of more sustenance the approaches have gone on exceedingly slow, and our poor Fellows are worn out with fatigue, being constantly on duty every other Day and sometimes every Day. The Works are strong and extensive. The position difficult to approach and the ground extremely hard. The garrison numerous and formidable when compared to our little force. They have sallied more or less every night, but have been constantly driven in.[9]

General Greene received some help when Colonel Lee arrived at Ninety-Six with his Legion, 8 June 1781. He had been engaged with South Carolina militia in the capture of small enemy forts along the Savannah River near Augusta. Lee immediately differed with General Greene over the mode of approach to Ninety-Six, and Lee blamed the Pole. He explained, "Never regarding the importance which was attached to depriving the enemy of water, for which he depended on the rivulet to his left, Kosciuszko applied his undivided attention to the demolition of the star, the strongest point of the enemy's defense." Naturally Kosciuszko "applied his undivided attention" to the Star Fort because that is what his commander had directed him to do, and Kosciuszko concurred in Greene's decision. Still the commander saw an advantage in Lee's plan of attacking Cruger from the west, a course of action he could not have undertaken previously since he lacked a sufficient number of soldiers for attacking along two directions at once. The dual preparations would subject Cruger to greater stress and during the planned assault cause him to divide his forces. Lee began to build parallels along the rivulet toward the British stockade fort.[10]

Historian Charles Stedman explains that Lee's soldiers, within pistol shot of the rivulet, prevented the enemy garrison from obtaining water during daylight hours. At night Cruger sent out naked blacks to fetch a scanty supply. The garrison became distressed from an insufficient amount of water. Stedman states, "A well had been dug in the Star with great labour, but no water was to be found." Lee seized upon this disclosure, published thirteen years after the siege, to justify his choice of denying water to the British garrison rather than attacking the Star Fort. Lee conveniently had forgotten the situation at Fort Watson, South Carolina, two months earlier. His Legion joined Francis Marion's partisans for an attack on the British garrison that depended for water on nearby Scott's Lake. The Americans cut off the enemy's water supply. "But on the third day, " historian George W. Greene writes, "they found that the British commander had sunk a well within the stockade and obtained an abundant supply." Therefore, cutting off Cruger's water source at Ninety-Six did not seem to be a necessary course of action because a well anywhere in the area could undoubtedly provide water. As historian Miecislaus Haiman observes, "It was much easier for Lee to decide the question *post factum* than for Greene to weigh it accurately before the attack."[11]

During the night of June 9, Cruger sent out two strong assault groups from the fort. One group entered Kosciuszko's trenches and found the opening of a mine that the engineer was digging to the enemy fort. Kosciuszko planned to blow up the wall with gunpowder and open the way for an American assault. He was making a night inspection of the tunnel when the loyalists surprised and almost captured him. "The gallant Pole escaped but in his hurried departure received an 'inglorious wound'," Lumpkin writes, "that made it difficult for him to sit [on] a horse with ease during the next several weeks." Some Britishers took delight in playing up Kosciuszko's posterior wound. Undoubtedly the incident also made him the butt of some ribbing at army headquarters. When Colonel Williams submitted a list of early casualties at Ninety-Six to Congress, he reported that "Colonel Kosciuszko, Chief Engineer, was slightly wounded."[12]

The second British sortie on the same night of June 9 attacked Lee's trenches on the west where several of his soldiers were bayoneted and one officer captured. Lee became so upset that he committed a rash act. He decided to set fire to the stockade fort. A volunteer squad of a sergeant and nine soldiers dragged bundles of combustible material while crawling on the ground in broad daylight. As they neared the fort, enemy sentries saw them and opened fire, killing the sergeant and five soldiers. The remaining four escaped.[13]

Greene's troops worked relentlessly to ready themselves for the assault while the commander looked anxiously toward Charleston for any movement of Lord Rawdon. Earlier, Lord Rawdon had decided that the up-country fort of Ninety-Six could no longer be defended. He dispatched messages three times to Cruger to abandon the fort. However, all messages were intercepted by patriot partisans. Subsequently, Greene invested Ninety-Six, and Lord Rawdon determined to march to its relief, expecting reinforcements from overseas any day. When three regiments landed at Charleston on 3 June 1781, Rawdon marched off with these troops four days later to Monck's Corner where he picked up the rest of his command. With an army of 2000 regulars, he marched rapidly in summer heat for Ninety-Six. Partisan leader

Thomas Sumter informed Greene of Lord Rawdon's march. The British commander, too, wanted to inform Cruger that help was on the way. A local, unsuspected farmer managed to gallop past American sentries into the British fortification.[14]

As Lord Rawdon approached Ninety-Six, Greene weighed the choice of attacking him, but he gave up this option because of the greater strength of the British. With time running out, he decided to storm Ninety-Six with simultaneous attacks from the east and west. He was about ready. Kosciuszko had built the third parallel, and two trenches almost reached the ditch around Star Fort. The engineer could not use the mine to blow up the wall in the assault because it ended short of the wall. Preparing for the assault, Greene chose teams from Maryland and Virginia units commanded by Lieutenant Colonel Richard Campbell. The general planned that the first party of axmen would cut through the abatis, and the second party of hookmen would follow. Armed with long poles with iron hooks on the ends, they would pull down the sand bags from Cruger's parapet. The main force would then storm out of the trenches and over the parapet. On the west side, Greene assigned Lee the capture of the small stockade fort, followed by the village and the west side of Star Fort. Captain Mitchell Rudolph of the Legion led Lee's assault. At noon on June 18, the firing of a second cannon began the simultaneous attacks. Rudolph met with scanty opposition because the loyalists, after delivering some fire at the Americans, hastily abandoned the stockade. William Johnson writes that the British actually abandoned the stockade the previous evening, allowing Rudolph to walk into an empty fort. Indeed, Lee scored a quick victory. Still he halted the attack until he learned of Campbell's progress on the east, "before following up the blow by passing the rivulet, entering the town," as Ward writes, "and forcing the fortified prison which they intended to use as a base of operations that *would divide Cruger's efforts* to defend his post" (author's italics). Lee blundered by stopping the attack. He should have continued the momentum that he had gained. Consequently, he failed to divide Cruger's efforts, and Cruger was able to concentrate his entire attention and manpower against Campbell's assault.[15]

On the east, Campbell's axmen carved paths through the abatis, and the hookmen reached up to pull down sand bags from the parapet. From the tower platform and the third parallel, Greene's soldiers delivered a covering fire. The assault was beginning to succeed after three quarters of an hour of fighting. In desperation, Cruger resorted to a bold tactic—to attack Campbell's soldiers outside the fort. With Lee's guns silent, Cruger concentrated on Campbell. He ordered two parties of thirty men each to exit the Star Fort in the rear (and Lee could possibly have been in position to prevent their exit). Each loyalist party circled the fort in opposite directions. Silently, with complete surprise, and with fixed bayonets, they savagely attacked Campbell's men. The resulting carnage was swift and stunning. Some forty patriots were slain or wounded. The unexpected and devastating attack on the flanks broke the force of Campbell's assault. Recording the event, Kosciuszko described the storming of Star Fort in his Notes:

> ...at 9 clock in the morning the attack began. Blind fortune not always keep pace with Curage and Good Cause. Col. Lee upon our right took possession of the donut redoubt with very small loss, but Col. Campell upon our left was unsuccessful in this attack. Capt. Amstrong and 30 soldiers were killed of which Valor intrepidity let us Chearish their memory, regret the loss and bring Example to posterity.

General Greene had no time to regroup and mount another assault the following day. Lord Rawdon was very near. Greene broke off the siege on June 19 and marched his army away the next day, deeply disappointed to be forced to give up Ninety-Six on the eve of its surrender. Williams likewise regretted the escape of a resounding victory. He wrote brother Elie on June 23 that the capture of Ninety-Six, "if attained, would have added a lustre to our former services sufficiently brilliant to have thrown a proper light upon the Character of our Excellent General & reflected a ray of Glory upon the reputation of each inferior officer." With reference to the chief engineer,

Williams wrote of the siege of Ninety-Six in his Notes:

> Col. Kosciuszko, a young gentleman of distinction from Poland who left his native country to follow the banners of Liberty in america, superintended the operation, and by his Zeal, assiduity, perseverance and firmness promoted the business with such expedition that, tho' the ground was excessive hard and the situation unfavorable, by the 17th a third parallel was completed within 30 yards of the enemy's ditch & a rifle battery 30 feet high erected at the same distance…two trenches and a mine were extended to within six feet of their ditch and a few days more we'd have reduced the garrison to the necessity of surrendering.

The tantalizing result vanished, however, when the British Army relieved Cruger's garrison on June 21.[16]

After the Revolutionary War, Lee carried his criticism of Kosciuszko at Ninety-Six into his *Memoirs*. Although the Virginian admitted that the Pole was not deficient in his professional knowledge, still "he was very moderate in talent—not a spark of the ethereal in his composition. His blunders lost us Ninety-Six." It is evident that Lee either did not know or did not wish to acknowledge Greene's decision to attack the Star Fort. Lee found it easier to blame Kosciuszko.[17]

Historian Henry Lumpkin straddles the controversy. He states that Lee's "opinion is probably correct, but Colonel Kosciusko, a classically trained European military engineer, believed, in accordance with that training, that a fort must fall if its key defense work is taken." Lumpkin's explanation ignores Kosciuszko's proven skill and experience. The Pole was remarkably adaptable to military situations and the terrain, as he had demonstrated at Saratoga and West Point. Certainly he was a product of the best engineering schools of Europe. At the same time, he was refreshingly flexible, like the typical American, and in sharp contrast to the rigid Duportail and La Radiere.[18]

William Johnson, Associate Justice of the United States Supreme Court (1804–1834), defended Kosciuszko. "This chief engineer was no other than the celebrated Kosciusko," Johnson wrote, "between whom and Colonel Lee the world will decide, whether

AMERICANS ASSAULT THE BRITISH STAR FORT AT NINETY-SIX, 18 June 1781. Painting by Robert Wilson in the Town Hall of Ninety-Six, South Carolina. Courtesy of the Ninety-Six Chamber of Commerce. (Photo by the author, 7 May 1996).

the following note of the former"[very moderate talent and not a spark of the ethereal] "is conspicuous for modesty or correctness." Lee became downright derogatory when he rejected Johnson's statement:"We are confidently assured, by a member of the general's family" [staff] "at the time that it was perfectly understood in camp, that the general himself directed the operations of the engineer." Lee derided Johnson: "It is obvious, that the *member of the family* here relied on, must have been the cook or the groom." Although Lee was caustic of Johnson, Lee also lauded Kosciuszko as a brave and enthusiastic patriot. "The cause of liberty," Lee wrote, "is deeply indebted to him, for the courage and ardour with which he espoused it in our country; and Poland will long remember, with sorrow, but with pride, the gallantry and devotion with which he fought and failed, in defending her own." Nevertheless, Lee would not concede that

Kosciuszko's fame depended on the gift of genius.[19]

Despite Lee's exclaiming that "there exists no monuments of his extraordinary talents, no evidence of his genius," three of Kosciuszko's great achievements in the American Revolution support a claim to genius: Saratoga, Fortress West Point, and the engineering contribution to General Greene's mobile and successful Southern campaign. Lee, a dynamic commander who helped bring about victory, was nevertheless rash at times, opinionated, arrogant, and quick to criticize others. South Carolina officers disliked him. Doctor Joseph Johnson of Charleston said: "Lee was accustomed to live among and act like the higher orders of Virginia gentlemen." William Johnson likewise criticized Lee's arrogance: "Lee produced embarrassment by the assertion of rights, which were, at least, doubtful; and seldom failed to disgust the state and militia officers, whenever he was called upon to serve with them."[20]

George Washington Greene, whose three-volume biography of his grandfather, General Nathanael Greene, is very detailed, remained strangely silent about Kosciuszko's important role at the siege of Ninety-Six. Very partial to Lieutenant Colonel Henry Lee, Jr., G.W. Greene perhaps wished to avoid the controversy that Lee caused. Even indirectly, Lee questioned the generalship of Nathanael Greene. Nevertheless, G.W. Greene credits the general with all command decisions. He writes that after the general examined the fortifications, "Greene resolved, therefore, to begin with the star redoubt, as the chief point of defense, and which could be held independently of the others." With respect to Kosciuszko's role, G.W. Greene mentions only that the general inspected the fortifications, accompanied by Kosciuszko and Pendleton. After this brief statement, he says nothing further of Kosciuszko's siege operations. However, he quotes Greene's Order of the Day in which the general commends Kosciuszko and several other officers. The praise seems out of place, if indeed Kosciuszko had not been at the center of the siege. George W. Greene never explains why he omits Kosciuszko's key role at Ninety-Six.[21]

Lee seemed to be obsessed with the siege of Ninety-Six. His unfair criticism of Kosciuszko influenced several historians of the nineteenth century, such as Alexander Garden and Cecil B. Hartley. Garden speculated about the outcome of Ninety-Six. Writing in 1822, Garden said,"Had he [Lee] directed the operations of the besiegers at Ninety-Six, instead of *Kosciuszko,* different indeed would have been the result." Understandably Garden was partial to Lee, having served in Lee's Legion as cornet, a cavalry officer carrying the colors. Nevertheless, Garden was prejudiced against Kosciuszko. In his *Anecdotes of the Revolutionary War,* he lists eleven subordinates who assisted General Greene in an outstanding manner, but he pointedly omits Kosciuszko. Garden writes: "Aided by the zeal, activity, enterprise, and varied talents of Huger, Morgan, Williams, Carrington, Howard, Washington, and Lee in the regular Line, and of Sumter, Marion, Pickens, and Davie, the Partisan Commanders of the militia, he looked forward, with no presumptuous hope, to the certainty of success." Hartley likewise writes disparagingly of Kosciuszko: "On commencing the siege General Greene had entrusted the engineering operation to Colonel Kosciusko, the Polish officer who subsequently became so famous, but who on the present occasion showed utter incapacity, and by his blunders caused the failure of the siege."[22]

Even in the twentieth century, some historians repeated Lee's unfair criticism of Kosciuszko. Noel B. Gerson wrote in 1966 that when Lee asked Greene for permission to cut off the fort's water supply, "Kosciuszko was dubious." It is difficult to imagine that Kosciuszko would interfere with Greene's orders to a subordinate commander. Lee's activities on the west would have little, if any, effect on Kosciuszko's siege operations on the east, and the engineer had been pursuing them effectively in the absence of Lee. Nevertheless, Gerson makes an assertion without quoting an eyewitness. In fact, he offers no evidence. Apparently Gerson wrote his biography of Lee much like a work of fiction, a mode with which he was very familiar, having penned twenty-one books of fiction. In his *Encyclopedia of the American*

Revolution, Colonel Mark Mayo Boatner also imitates Lee's shortsightedness. "In the Siege of Ninety-Six, S. C., 22 May –19 June '81, Kosciuszko got a costly lesson in the art of practical military engineering," Boatner writes, "making two mistakes that may well have caused this operation to fail." As a West Point-trained officer, Boatner had the capability of evaluating the Siege of Ninety-Six. He apparently did not, finding it easier to repeat Lee's criticism.[23]

Lee's ill-tempered criticism turned the siege into a blunder for a few historians. Other historians, however, have rejected or ignored Lee's tantrum, like William Johnson, Benson J. Lossing, Christopher Ward, and Lynn Montross. The one person who had the most to lose or gain from Kosciuszko's engineering performance was General Greene. On 20 June 1781, Greene issued an Order of the Day, in which he praised the chief engineer:

> The General presents his thanks to Colonel Kosciuszko Chief Engineer, for his assiduity, perseverance and indefatigable exertions in planning and prosecuting the approaches, which he is persuaded were judiciously design'd and would have infallibly gained Success if time had admitted of their being Compleated... The General also presents his thanks to...Captain Dalzien, the assistant engineer.[24]

WHO BLUNDERED AT NINETY-SIX, GREENE OR LEE?

An Evaluation

The issue of Colonel Cruger's water supply is only a peripheral matter. The blunder that lost Ninety-Six for the Americans occurred during the dual assault on 18 June 1781.

The plans of attack from the east and the west of Star Fort are presented earlier in this chapter. Let us examine more closely the execution of the plans. On the west, Lee prepared the details of the attack for his Legion, and he was responsible for the execution. The start for both assaults was timed to twelve noon, when a second cannon shot was fired. Greene had ordered simultaneous attacks so as to divide Cruger's defense capabilities. Lee began his attack against the stockade fort, which Christopher Ward called Holmes' Fort, and his troops walked practically unopposed into the stockade. Having scored an easy victory, Lee halted the attack. Why? Ward says that Holmes' Fort was Lee's first objective. True, but it was also an intermediate objective. For Lee, the main objective was the west side of Star Fort, and Ward almost says so. But Lee stopped his attack because, as he explained, he wanted to learn of the progress of Greene's assault before continuing his. Lee's reasoning is hard to accept. If Lee had to know the status of Greene's attack for reasons of his own, he could have dispatched a rider to get it. Meanwhile, he should have carried on the attack vigorously and without interruption.

George W. Greene writes that following the capture of the stockade after a short struggle, "Lee instantly prepared to follow his success and support the attack on the left." Author Greene's statement is astounding. He strongly suggests that Lee's planning did not extend beyond the capture of the stockade when, in fact, it was only an intermediate objective. In military operations, a planner prepares an attack that focuses on the main objective, setting up, if necessary, one or more intermediate objectives that lead the attacking force to the main objective. The actions of the enemy may cause the commander to make adjustments. Nevertheless, his subordinates and he pursue the plan to the final objective. Lossing clearly states Lee's mission. After Captain Rudolph captured the stockade fort quickly, Lossing writes: "The advantage Lee intended to follow up by entering the town, assailing the fortified jail, and then to assist in reducing the star redoubt."

If Lee had planned properly and fully, and executed vigorously, he could have captured the stockade, forced his way into the village, bypassing the fortified jail but leaving a small encircling party to keep the defenders occupied, and advanced through the village to the west side of Star Fort. Had he been able to reach the Star Fort, he could have prevented the exit of Cruger's two bayonet parties that devastated Greene's attack. Greene's assault lasted nearly an hour. Meanwhile, Lee did nothing for nearly an hour.

Colonel Boatner offers the same incomplete assessment as George W. Greene: "Rudolph fought [!] his way into Fort Holmes, which was now lightly held; the rest of the Legion infantry and Kirkwood's Co. followed. Lee then awaited the outcome of Campbell's attack and prepared to attack across the stream." After the easy capture of Holmes' Fort, Boatner never questions Lee's inaction. To repeat, the purpose of the coordinated dual attack was to divide Cruger's attention and manpower. Lee failed to carry out his mission. In sum, Lee's poor planning and weak leadership on this occasion caused the dual assaults to fail. Lee's blunder lost the siege of Ninety-Six.[25]

CHAPTER NINE

Eutaw Springs:
Greene's Last Major Battle

Kosciuszko: Master of His Profession

FTER REACHING NINETY-SIX, Lord Rawdon attempted to pursue Greene, but he gave up the effort. The
summer heat had been unbearable for the heavily-clad British
troops, and his army became exhausted by the forced march from
Charleston. Rawdon ordered Cruger to abandon Ninety-Six and
withdraw to Charleston. Thus, Greene won the strategic objective of regaining control of the upper country of South Carolina.[1]

The Southern Army needed rest, too. It had been drained of
strength by incessant maneuvering and the long siege operation
at Ninety-Six. The hot summer sun was no less kind to the Americans than to the British. Greene encamped his army on the High
Hills of the Santee, located on the east bank of the Wateree River
near Stateburg and north of its junction with the Congeree (here
the two rivers form the Santee). Elevated some 200 feet above
the Wateree, the area forms a chain of sandy hills about twenty-
four miles long. In contrast to the noxious swamps that the
soldiers had been exposed to, the hills offered pure and breezy
air, clear water, fruit trees, and a verdant green landscape. The
Southern Army rested in this idyllic setting for six weeks. Whether
Kosciuszko recommended the selection of the High Hills to

Greene is not known. Certainly the area was known to South Carolina officers.[2]

From the High Hills on 29 July 1781, Kosciuszko wrote General Gates about the siege of Ninety-Six and the fighting at Monck's Corner. "Part of our Troops with the Militia," he said, "attacked Monks Corner 22 mill from Charles Town, killed about one Hundred and took one Hundred fifty Prisoners, some of the same party [came] six mill near Charles town and caught twenty Prisoners, in all this Col. Lee's Legion bear the greatest Share." Commenting on the advantages of the army camp on the High Hills, Kosciuszko added, "We took at Present this position, very healthy and expect to be reinforced by North Carolina and Pennsylvania Brygades who are in their march."[3]

On 12 August 1781, Greene answered North Carolina Governor Thomas Burke's letter of 30 July, in which Burke requested engineering help for erecting defenses against enemy raids on military stores. The British still occupied Wilmington, and their strong presence in Virginia also posed a constant threat to North Carolina. Greene told Burke: "I will send to your assistance Colo. Kosciuszko, our principal Engineer who is Master of his profession, and will afford you every aid you can wish." Greene's letter reaffirmed his high regard for the engineer with the term "Master of his profession." Greene advised Burke to build small fortifications "just sufficient to secure the Stores against Parties of Horse who can perform rapid marches." He pointed out that large works would be expensive to erect and to garrison. In addition, large stores would tempt the enemy to attack. Passing on the thoughts of General Washington, Greene added, "A number of small Posts judiciously dispersed in different parts of the State will accommodate the service more effectually than one or two large Posts."[4]

Kosciuszko did not have the time to build fortified posts in North Carolina because the military situation in Virginia rapidly neared a climax. Count De Grasse sailed his French Fleet into Chesapeake Bay, and the combined American and French Armies closed in on Lord Cornwallis at Yorktown. Governor Burke became less concerned with protecting stores than the possible escape of Cornwallis into North Carolina. Burke determined to block avenues of escape. He called large numbers of militia into service. He ordered boats on the rivers to be seized or destroyed, and placed every river crossing under guard and fortified them with abatis. Kosciuszko had a new mission. However, what blocking positions he may have erected were never tested since Washington and De Grasse trapped Cornwallis at Yorktown and forced the surrender of his British Army, 19 October 1781.[5]

The Yorktown campaign affected Greene only to a minimum extent. He apparently was not aware of Washington's plans in August 1781, and Greene resumed operations in pursuit of his strategic objective—to wrest control of the South from the British. With colors flying, Greene's rested army departed the High Hills of the Santee on 22 August 1781. Greene's foe now was Lieutenant Colonel Alexander Stuart who replaced the ailing Lord Rawdon. As for Lord Cornwallis, after he had re-equipped his army at Wilmington, North Carolina, he marched into Virginia, where Washington bagged his entire army. No doubt, during the Yorktown campaign, Washington wished to prevent reinforcements from South Carolina from reaching Cornwallis. The Daughters of the American Revolution maintain that Washington's concern caused General Greene to resume campaigning and to fight the Battle of Eutaw Springs, South Carolina. Although pinning down British forces in South Carolina was logical, and Greene knew this fact intuitively, being the strategist that he was, historians offer no proof that Greene left the High Hills in response to an order from Washington. In fact, Greene was unaware in August 1781 that Washington planned a brilliant stroke to capture the army of Lord Cornwallis. Letters between Washington and Greene were often intercepted by the enemy, and Washington would not reveal sensitive matters, especially his planned Yorktown campaign. Greene admitted his lack of knowledge of operations elsewhere. Writing to Washington on 26 August 1781, he said, "I am much at a loss what are Lord Cornwallis' intentions in Virginia...I am also totally ignorant what is going on at New York, having heard nothing from your Excellency since June, which induces me to believe that your dispatches are intercepted." Nevertheless, Greene understood the necessity for cooperation with Washington. "If things are flattering in the North," he wrote, "I will hazard less in the South; but if otherwise there we must risk more here."[6]

When Greene descended from the High Hills, his army consisted of 2600 soldiers, of which the effective strength was 1600. Greene's intelligence reports placed Stuart at Eutaw Springs, some forty-five miles above Charleston. In contrast, British intelligence attempts failed to gain information as American reconnaissance parties intercepted and turned them back. Consequently, Stuart did not know of Greene's movements. At Eutaw Springs, Stuart occupied a good position. His right rested on Eutaw Creek and the Santee River; the center covered open ground that had been cleared of trees on both sides of a road; and the left ended on woods. The British had pitched their tents in the cleared area. Behind them stood a strong brick house, two stories high, whose thick walls could withstand the impact of light artillery rounds of the Americans. Greene had less strength than Stuart, who commanded a force of 2300 trained and disciplined soldiers. When the battle began on 8 September 1781, the redcoats were eating breakfast.[7]

The advance of Greene's army first met groups of British soldiers digging for potatoes, and Stuart reacted swiftly to the news. He deployed his redcoats in a single line, barely in front of the camp. Greene marched toward the British in two columns, each ready to spread out into two lines of battle. The first column consisted of militia—two small battalions of North Carolina and two of South Carolina. In the second column marched the Continentals—three small brigades of Maryland, Virginia, and North Carolina troops. Lee's Legion covered the right flank, and Lieutenant Colonel John Henderson's South Carolina soldiers protected the left flank. Lieutenant Colonel Washington's cavalry and Captain Robert Kirkwood's Delaware soldiers formed the reserve. At eight o'clock in the morning, the American advance

BATTLEFIELD OF EUTAW SPRINGS, SOUTH CAROLINA. The Americans fought the British here, the last major battle of the American Revolution in the South, 8 September 1781. Except for the monument erected by the Daughters of the American Revolution in 1912, the battleground is hardly noticeable. (Photo by the author, 10 May 1996).

met a body of the enemy whom they charged and dispersed. Soon they approached the main force of the British. Stuart, seeing militia in front of him, ordered an attack. Contrary to expectations, however, the militia stood its ground, engaging the redcoats in a fierce battle. The relentless pressure of the disciplined British in the center forced the militia back, but the Americans recoiled. Throwing in his reserve, Stuart again attacked the center and again made the militia pull back. At this stage, Greene committed his Continentals. Attacking with the bayonet, they routed the British, who fled through their camp to the safety of the brick stronghold. British soldiers on the flanks, protected by natural terrain features, stood their ground. The American momentum in the center sputtered to a halt when the soldiers saw food and drink in the abandoned camp. The hungry

Americans broke ranks and scattered through the camp in pursuit of food and rum. The unexpected behavior of the Americans gave the British commander an opportunity to fight back. But Greene now called off the attack. He had inflicted heavy casualties on the enemy, and he believed that Stuart would retreat to Charleston. Greene marched his army to the encampment of the previous day, the nearest point of water. The battle had lasted four hours, and Greene was satisfied with the losses that his army had inflicted on the British. He reported the results: "We have taken 500 Prisoners, including the Wounded the Enemy left behind; and I think they cannot have suffered less than 600 more men in killed and Wounded."American losses were severe, too: 114 killed and 340 either wounded or missing.[8]

In his report of the Battle of Eutaw Springs to the President of Congress, Greene praised the gallantry of his army and, in particular, the officers. "Our loss in officers," he wrote, "is considerably more from their value than their number, for never did either Men or Officers offer their blood more willingly in the Service of their Country." He also complimented his four aides-de-camp and singled out Colonel Williams. "I cannot help acknowledging my obligation to Col. Williams for his great activity on this and many other occasions in forming the Army, and for his uncommon intrepidity in leading on the Maryland troops to the charge, which exceeded anything I ever saw."[9]

Kosciuszko was not present at Eutaw Springs. Most probably he was still in North Carolina assisting Governor Burke in his efforts to block Cornwallis's routes of escape. Kosciuszko undoubtedly learned of the battle upon his return to army headquarters and from Colonel Williams, in particular. From his long service under Greene, Kosciuszko had the opportunity to observe and assess Greene's generalship in the South. Writing to Molineri in France in 1809, Kosciuszko said that Greene expelled the British from the Southern states in the time period of three years. "Fifteen combats have taken place," he said, "among which the hardest and the most murderous were that of Guilfort Court House with Lord Cornwallis and that of Youtaha [Eutaw] Springs with Lord Gordon [Rawdon] where they fell twice upon the enemy with bayonets." Kosciuszko praised Greene as "one of the best generals of America," and the Pole described him (as translated from the French): "He had a profound penetration, a just judgment, a firmness, an energy, and an activity necessary, his mind was ingenious in difficulties, his glance precise— nevertheless, simple in his manners, affable and polite."[10]

CHAPTER TEN

The War Subsides

Kosciuszko Fights the Last Battle

EUTAW SPRINGS and the siege of Lord Cornwallis at Yorktown were the final major battles of the American Revolution, although this fact was not apparent at the time. In the face of large British forces at New York and Charleston, the Americans had to maintain their vigilance. From Eutaw Springs Greene marched his army back to the High Hills of the Santee. He was encumbered with hundreds of wounded soldiers. Their condition became the more aggravated when hospital supplies from the North, destined for Greene's command, were captured by the British in Virginia.[1]

General Greene strongly recommended to Washington that, following Yorktown, Charleston should be wrested from the British with the current powerful American and French forces. Washington agreed and pressured Count de Grasse to continue his cooperation with the American Army. But the French Admiral begged off on the grounds of other requirements of the French Court and sailed to the West Indies. Consequently, Washington broke up the army at Yorktown: the French troops under General Rochambeau wintered in Virginia; the major portion of the Americans under General Benjamin Lincoln returned to the New York area; and General Arthur St. Clair, commanding Maryland

and Pennsylvania troops, marched to reinforce Greene near Charleston. Greatly disappointed by the dissolution of Washington's combined force of land and sea power, Greene departed the High Hills for the low country where he planned to contain the British in Charleston. At Dorchester, he fought with British units. His bold tactics awed the enemy who retreated to the safety of Charleston.[2]

At Riddlesperger's Plantation in early December 1781, Greene directed Kosciuszko to find a suitable encampment for the army. Although the engineer suffered with a painful inflammation in the face, he left immediately on a reconnaissance and selected Colonel Saunders' Plantation at the Round O, located between the Edisto and Ashepoo Rivers, some forty miles northwest of Charleston. Kosciuszko chose an admirable site, for it lay in a fertile land of rice farms and an abundance of wild game and domestic animals. The area boasted beautiful homes, gardens, and a cultured life. The change from many previous miserable conditions struck the soldiers very favorably. Here the Southern Army occupied the site on 9 December 1781. For security, the general fanned out his partisan units and Lee's Legion some thirty miles to his front. At this time Greene could muster only 800 effective men. On 4 January 1782, St. Clair arrived from Yorktown with reinforcements of some 2000 Pennsylvania and Delaware Continentals. Along the 500-mile march, St. Clair steadily lost soldiers so that the reinforcements barely brought up the army to the strength it had at the Battle of Eutaw Springs.[3]

In mid-January 1782, Greene attempted to seize St. John's Island, lying off Charleston. The plan miscarried, however, and Greene gave up the attempt. He then marched the army to Skirving's Plantation on the Pon-Pon where he shielded the legislature at Jacksonboro from the British at Charleston. While on the Pon-Pon, Kosciuszko and Williams shared quarters at the home of Mrs. Susan Hayne, but not for long. Williams' health failed him. The hardships of the campaign sapped his strength and reduced him to the level of an invalid. Greene released Williams from the army, and the colonel returned to Baltimore. He took with him Susan Hayne's son William, aged sixteen, whom he planned to educate. Following the departure of Williams, Kosciuszko wrote him several letters about the military activities and news of friends and acquaintances.[4]

On 22 March 1782, Greene relocated the Southern Army to Bacon's Bridge on the Ashley River. Only twenty miles from Charleston, the general continued to keep the British bottled up there. In a few days, on March 28, Mrs. Greene arrived from Rhode Island to join her husband. Johnson writes that "the attention lavished on the lady of the man whom all wished to honour, contributed greatly to enliven the monotonous scenery of an army in a state of inactivity." Kosciuszko noted her charm and gracious manners. Taking a liking to the modest Pole, Mrs. Greene brought him into her circle of friends. She also cultivated pleasant relations with members of the South Carolina society. Among close friends, Mrs. Greene was known as "Kitty." Although Kosciuszko found the relaxed atmosphere in camp pleasant, he chafed from the lack of engineering work, and he nurtured a long-held wish to serve as a line officer. Unexpectedly, he got his chance when Lieutenant Colonel John Laurens was killed in a clash with British forces on the Combahee River in late August 1782. This much admired and respected patriot had joined the Southern Army after returning from a successful mission to France where he obtained a massive aid package from the King. On the death of Laurens, Greene gave Kosciuszko the sensitive and very responsible post at Ashley's Ferry, some fifteen miles above Charleston. The forward base served as a listening and intelligence-gathering operation on the British, who possessed the strength of breaking out of Charleston and resuming campaigning. Greene had originally assigned Laurens the mission of opening up secret communications with patriots in Charleston, and Kosciuszko continued this vital function. His carefully selected command consisted of two squads of cavalry of the former Lee's Legion (Colonel Lee having retired) and a number of infantry from the Delaware and Pennsylvania Continentals. Lieutenant John Markland, who had fought at Yorktown, commanded one platoon of Pennsylvanians. He had come with the reinforcements under General St. Clair. Kosciuszko welcomed the command assignment. Johnson writes that Kosciuszko's "innumerable communications exhibit the industry and intelligence with which he discharged that service."[5]

The constant patrolling and skirmishing stimulated Kosciuszko. On one occasion he directed Markland to punish a party of British dragoons who were causing trouble in the vicinity. Markland set an ambush near the Quarter House, four miles outside Charleston. The trap was so complete that the Americans killed eight to ten dragoons, captured most of their horses, and took two prisoners. Markland succeeded without the loss of a man. Kosciuszko also made daring incursions on James Island, harassing the British and reminding them of the ever-present and vigilant patriots. In early October 1782, Kosciuszko carried off some sixty excellent cavalry horses that he turned over to the quartermaster general, in accordance with regulations of Congress. His seizure of the horses precipitated a crisis between the Southern Army and the Governor of South Carolina. Among the captured animals were a number that were claimed by South Carolinians, having been confiscated earlier by the British. A state law required that property belonging to citizens must be returned to them. The State Council called on the Governor to demand the return of all horses claimed by the residents. "It was obviously a struggle between state and United States' powers," Johnson writes. General Greene called a Council of War, attended by Kosciuszko and eight other officers. Greene asked for their opinion as to:

> ...whether he can consistently with the duty he owes the U. States restore all movable property taken in the enemy's possession to their original owners upon the unlimited scale on which the Council have demanded it; and whether this demand will not militate directly against the 20th Article of the 13th Section of the rules and articles of War.

Greene also asked his officers to determine whether the rights of citizens to recovered property (postliminy) is not reserved to Congress. After deliberating on October 16 and 19, all officers ruled in favor of Congress and Greene's responsibility to that body. Colonel Thomas Cotesworth Pinckney, a prominent lawyer of South Carolina, dissented and gave Greene a minority opinion.[6]

Greene informed Governor John Matthews of the results of the Council of War, along with the sentiments of Pinckney. However, the general decided to refer the dispute to Congress for final determination. "I would propose to your Excellency, therefore," Greene wrote, "to refer the matter to Congress for their determination, as it is a question between this State and the United States." Meanwhile, in a gesture of respect for the citizens and cooperation with the Governor, Greene ordered quartermaster Carrington to impose firm conditions on the public sale of the horses. Should Congress rule in favor of the original owners, purchasers must give up the horses and public agents must return the purchase price. On 23 December 1782, a committee of Congress, composed of James Madison, Alexander Hamilton, and Thomas McKean, decided the question in favor of the original owners.[7]

At Ashley's Ferry, Kosciuszko had the added responsibility of suppressing contraband trade with Charleston. The American Army was practically starving while the British were able to buy food and other products that the merchants of Charleston smuggled in. He intercepted boat loads of food for Charleston, only to be frustrated by discovering that the persons in charge possessed passes issued by General Anthony Wayne. Kosciuszko complained to Greene that Wayne's passes caused him embarrassment. Civilians, too, began to resent him for "meddling" in their activities. However, Wayne was to blame for not being careful in his dealings with merchants, who often abused his waivers. A serious case of smuggling arose over a shipment of beef from the American camp to Charleston. Kosciuszko suspected an American officer in the quartermaster department, but the suspicion fell on Wayne. In answer to Greene's investigation, Wayne denied any guilt. "I was not a little astonished," he protested, "at a charge you mention against the Army supplying the Enemy with Provisions, a charge which, I believe, to be false, however, for my part I declare upon the honor of a gentleman and soldier." Nevertheless, according to biographer Harry Emerson Wildes, "Greene warned Wayne that no more passes must be given and that every food boat going down the river would be confiscated."[8]

As the commander of an elite unit, Kosciuszko has the distinction of engaging the British in the last fight of the Revolutionary War. He planned and executed an attack on a British party cutting wood on James Island, 14 November 1782. His scouts reported that a work party cut wood during the day and withdrew to near Fort Johnson during the night. With a force of some sixty soldiers, Kosciuszko planned to surprise them. The Americans crept up to the working area at 2 A.M. and remained hidden until morning. They saw British dragoons lead the party. Kosciuszko ordered a volley that forced the dragoons back. He formed his soldiers and charged the British infantry who retreated before his determined attack. As the British fell back, they were reinforced by other troops behind them, until they numbered some 300 redcoats and were armed with a field piece. The superior enemy strength prompted Kosciuszko to call off the attack and retreat in good order, bringing off one prisoner. The fight had been hot and bloody. British losses are unknown, but Kosciuszko lost Captain William Wilmot of Maryland and his second-in-command, Lieutenant Moore. Three soldiers of Lieutenant John Markland's platoon were also killed. The intensity of Kosciuszko's attack placed him in great personal danger. His coat was pierced by four bullets and a weapon (spontoon) was shattered in his hand. In the thick of the fight, an enemy dragoon was about to cut down Kosciuszko with a saber when William Fuller leapt to his commander's aid and killed the dragoon. Fuller was a young civilian volunteer who joined the operation.[9]

Although the attack on James Island demonstrated Kosciuszko's fearless leadership, nineteenth century historian Alexander Garden criticized Kosciuszko's decision to attack as "very rash." Garden's claim that the British were prepared for the attack and ambushed the Americans differs markedly from the account of a participant, Lieutenant John Markland. Furthermore, Garden's comment prompted historian Edward McGrady to accuse Kosciuszko of being eager for enterprises that spilled blood, perhaps behaving like a soldier of fortune. McGrady makes the same accusation against John Laurens, one of the great patriots of the American Revolution. "Upon Colonel Lauren's death," McGrady writes, "the confidential services upon the lines were committed to Count Kosciuszko, who was scarcely less eager for enterprises than Laurens himself had been." McGrady continues in a jaundiced manner against Kosciuszko's seizure of British horses and Greene's failure to release the horses immediately to South Carolina's original owners. McGrady then brings up another "enterprise" of Kosciuszko's—"the last bloodshed of the Revolution." McGrady's remarks are derogatory and naive. Fighting usually results in bloodshed. Clearly he did not understand Kosciuszko's character nor his purpose for joining the American fight for independence.[10]

Although the British first showed signs of evacuating Charleston as early as August 1782, they delayed the move for four more months, until December 14. Meanwhile, Americans eagerly awaited the evacuation and engaged in daily speculation. From his advanced command post at Ashley's Ferry, Kosciuszko scouted the British for the least signs of movement, and, like others, he grew impatient. Finally, the British Army embarked on ships and sailed for New York. On the heels of the enemy, American troops, including Kosciuszko at the head of his elite unit, followed General Anthony Wayne into the city. The people of Charleston joyfully welcomed them. Later on the same day, Governor John Matthews and General Greene, escorted by 200 cavalry and the Governor's Council and other leading citizens, rode into Charleston. Johnson writes, "Arrived at the centre of the city, the governor, the commander, and their retinue alighted to exchange congratulations." The victory celebration closed with a grand ball organized by Mrs. Greene. At her request Kosciuszko decorated the ballroom with magnolia leaves displayed in festoons, along with pieces of paper cut in the shape of flowers. The war in the South was over.[11]

With the end of hostilities, the American populace grew indifferent toward the army. During the fighting the people found the army a heavy burden because Congress provided Greene little, if any, money and supplies. Now support became an obnoxious burden. The soldiers were hungry and half-naked, and the residents looked upon them as a menace. Johnson observes, "The army had now become very unpopular. The people regarded them as little else than the last enemy to get rid of." Kosciuszko noticed the ill-will first hand, for General Greene had directed him to organize an armed expedition by water for the transportation of rice for the army. Attempting to find boats, Kosciuszko met with hostility from the civilians and indifference of state officials. He reported the problem to Greene: "The former not willing to go, and the latter not taken proper measures for it."[12]

The abject condition of his army tried Greene's soul. After exhausting his pleas with Congress, he resorted to desperate measures. He pledged his reputation and modest fortune to enter into an agreement with a speculator, John Banks. Greene agreed to Banks' hard terms for supplies of food and clothing. As a result Greene would experience personal financial loss and innuendoes of corruption. Nevertheless, his soldiers benefited greatly. Soon conditions in camp were noticeably better. The officers and men wore proper uniforms, and they looked like soldiers. Kosciuszko wrote Brigadier General Otho Williams in Baltimore: "The Army is in camp upon James Island, a beautiful and healthy place." In Charleston, Greene accepted the generous offer of John Rutledge to make his elegant house on Broad Street the army headquarters. Here the vivacious Kitty Greene entertained her numerous friends. The General and Mrs. Greene also invited the officers, and Kosciuszko enjoyed their hospitality, as well.[13]

In the spring of 1783, Kosciuszko became sick with fever. A kindly couple, Mr. and Mrs. Scott, took him into their home on James Island and nursed him to health. He always remembered with affection their kindness and friendship. General and Mrs. Greene became concerned for their friend's health. They wrote him words of sympathy and encouragement. Affected by their anxiety, Kosciuszko, who was almost recovered, answered immediately. He joked about his health with Mrs. Greene, saying, "I hope you'll be well tomorrow and expect to Breakfast with you in Town." To General Greene, he wrote, "I am sorry I was the object of uneasiness in your breast, your generous attention to your Friends health, make me more alarming of yours, of which all care ought to be taken. I had fears of the fever, but today I am prety well and expect to come over tomorrow very early."[14]

On 11 April 1783, Kosciuszko accompanied Greene on an inspection of Fort Moultrie. It was his last official duty in the South. Five days later, Charleston received the news of the preliminary peace agreement, and the rejoicing was enthusiastic. Greene staged a review. Kosciuszko put on a fireworks display in the city. In camp on James island, the ladies and gentlemen of Charleston enjoyed a *feu de joie* with the army. Greene now released the soldiers to their homes. The Virginia and Maryland troops marched overland while those of Pennsylvania and Delaware traveled by ship to Philadelphia. A brig from New England transported two companies. Many of the officers had left the army, and Kosciuszko was one of the last. He bade farewell to General Greene and other officers and friends. He sailed for Philadelphia aboard that New England brig on 8 June 1783. Mrs. Greene boarded the same ship. Because she was pregnant, the general detailed one of his aides, Major William Pierce, to escort her. Another passenger was Major Alexander Garden of Lee's Legion. On June 15, Kosciuszko debarked in Philadelphia, and three days later he wrote General Greene for help in settling his back pay with the financier and President of Congress. Greene answered immediately, July 10. "I was happy to hear from you by your letter of the 18th of June," Greene said. "Mrs. Greene says you had an agreeable passage and pleasing society. Pierce also says all your healths except Gardens is bettered by the voyage." Telling Kosciuszko that he wrote to the financier and the president, he enclosed copies of the correspondence. "I expect to be in Philadelphia in six or eight weeks," Greene added, "and if I can render you any further service should you not have succeeded before my arrival, it will afford me the greatest pleasure." General Greene departed Charleston for Rhode Island on 11 August 1783. Accompanied by two aides, he traveled overland, and along the way the people greeted him joyfully.[15]

CHAPTER ELEVEN

Kosciuszko Prepares to Depart America

Joins Society of the Cincinnati

AVING LANDED IN PHILADELPHIA in June 1783, Kosciuszko prepared to leave the United States. He had two objectives to carry out first: settle his financial accounts with Congress and seek promotion to brigadier general. Knowing that officers had not been paid for months on end and that Congress struggled to meet its obligations, Kosciuszko had sought the help of General Greene on June 18, when he wrote:

> In setling my accounts I forsee and aprehend will be tedious and difficult mater without your recomendation to the Financier and President of Congress wich I would beg you was of such nature that they could be setled with me the Pay what is due, and what Congress resolv'd for half pay wich is five years pay in ready money if possible.

Despite his own preparations for departure for the North, the general immediately wrote letters of support to the President of Congress and to Robert Morris, Superintendent of Finance. Because of Kosciuszko's modesty and reluctance to agitate his case, Greene offered him some advice:

> I know your modesty and feel your difficulty on this head; but

unless you persist I am apprehensive nothing will be done in the matter. For once you must force nature and get the better of that independent pride which is our best support in many Situations; and urge your suit from the necessity of the case which may accomplish this business; and without which I have too much reason to apprehend a disappointment.

Greene closed his letter with "My warmest approbation is due you as an officer and my particular acknowledgement as a friend."[1]

In supporting Kosciuszko's request for back pay to the President of Congress, Greene lauded the Pole's performance as one "whose zeal & activity have been equaled by few & exceeded by none." Aware that he might be intruding in matters reserved to Congress, Greene conceded: "My friendship for the Colonel must apologize for the singularity of this recommendation. My feelings are warmly interested in his favor." The President of Congress referred Greene's letter to the Superintendent of Finance, Robert Morris, but he faced a dilemma. Congress had little money, and many other officers in Kosciuszko's situation demanded their pay. However, Morris recognized Kosciuszko's outstanding service in his report to Congress, 31 July 1783:

> That the merit of Col. Kosciusko is great and acknowledged, his Talents brilliant, his zeal unquestionable, and of Consequence his application must be placed among those which are not to be declined unless for the most cogent Reasons and even insurmountable obstacles. But that if it be complied with, other officers of Merit Talents and Zeal will doubtless make similar applications.

The next day, August 1, Morris wrote Greene to confirm the general's endorsement of Kosciuszko's application: "That young Gentleman's acknowledged Merit and Service joined to your warm Interposition in his favor excite my sincerest Wish to render the adjustment of his affairs equal to his most sanguine Expectations." Nevertheless, Morris pointed out the "Danger of excepting Individuals out of the general Rules," for only Congress could make exceptions. And Congress did, when Major General Duportail requested the immediate settling of accounts of Laumoy, Gouvion, and himself on 6 October 1783. Within four days of the application, 10 October 1783, Congress acted swiftly, instructing the Superintendent of Finance to adjust the accounts of the three French officers and to advance them money. In addition, Congress provided them free passage to France on the ship *Washington*. Congress acted from political expediency rather than merit. Understandably, Congress was under pressure from France, having their minister to the United States, the very influential Chevalier de la Luzerne, at the elbow of Congress. Then, too, France had provided material support and loaned the infant country large sums of money for the prosecution of the war. The French Foreign Minister, Comte de Vergennes, grumbled in Paris about the crushing debt that France had incurred. Therefore, to have pushed Duportail's request for payment aside, as it did Kosciuszko's, was not politically advantageous, and Congress rushed to accommodate Duportail. In the process, however, Congress did Kosciuszko and all American officers a grave disservice.[2]

The plight of the officers of the Continental Army was well known to Congress. While General Washington and his soldiers were encamped at Newburgh, New York, in December 1782, fourteen officers of the Line, headed by Major General Henry Knox and Brigadier General John Paterson, dispatched an "address and petition of the officers of the army of the United States." Informing Congress of "the great distress under which we labor," the petition was frank and heartrending. One paragraph, in particular, painted an exceedingly bleak picture:

> Our distresses are now brought to a point. We have borne all that men can bear—our property is expended—our private resources are at an end, and our friends are wearied out and disgusted with our incessant applications. We, therefore, most sincerely and earnestly beg, that a supply of money may be forwarded to the army as soon as possible. The uneasiness of the soldiers, for want of pay, is great and dangerous; any further experiments on their patience may have fatal effects.

The committee of officers also suggested: "We are willing to commute the half-pay pledged for full pay for a certain number of years, or for a sum in gross." The force of the petition prompted

Congress on 22 March 1783 to offer the officers the amount of five years full pay in money or securities, on interest of six percent per annum. This proposed settlement in lieu of half-pay is the one Kosciuszko referred to in his letter to Greene on 18 June 1783. Nevertheless, the resolution of Congress was only a promise to pay at a future date, and it did not solve Kosciuszko's need for cash for travel. In his seven years of service, he seldom got paid. Major John Armstrong said that Kosciuszko declined to draw his monthly pay, undoubtedly from patriotic motives. In common with other officers, he drew rations, but all other expenses were paid from personal funds. Friends helped him from time to time. Aware of Kosciuszko's acute hardship, Morris wrote Greene on 19 December 1783: "I suppose Col. Kosciusko informed you how desirous I was to comply with your request in his behalf. I wish you have interest sufficient to induce your little state to join in measures for the relief of him and all other public Creditors."[3]

Though advised by General Greene to press Congress for his pay, Kosciuszko found the situation tense in Philadelphia. Congress faced mutinous Pennsylvania troops who threatened that body unless they were paid. The indignant President of Congress issued a proclamation in which he accused the troops of renouncing obedience to their officers and, under the direction of sergeants, surrounding and threatening the members on 21 June 1783. He also accused them of grossly insulting the authority of the United States. Congress escaped the rebellious soldiers by relocating to Princeton on 30 June 1783. Kosciuszko traveled to Princeton, too. Meanwhile, he planned to meet his friend Otho Williams, now a brigadier general, at Elizabethtown, New Jersey, on July 4. To Kosciuszko's regret, Congress tasked the engineer to prepare and carry out a display of fireworks, marking the seventh anniversary of the Declaration of Independence. He wrote Williams of the unexpected requirement on July 2 and lamented the irony of fate that prevented the meeting of two old friends.[4]

General Greene, who had departed Charleston for the North by land, reached Philadelphia in late September. Here Kosciuszko greeted his commander joyously, and, undoubtedly, the two traveled together to Trenton. Unexpectedly they met General Washington, and the trio continued to Princeton and Congress. President Elias Boudinot entertained the two commanders and their staffs at a dinner. Major Alexander Garden, an eyewitness, described the slight that Kosciuszko received from Congress on this occasion. When dinner was announced, Boudinot placed himself between Washington and Greene and led them to the dining room. Whereupon a member of Congress, a Mr. H_____, called each member by name and invited him to proceed into the dining room one at a time. As Garden writes, "Thus he went on, till all the gentlemen in the Civil Department had gone forward; and then (being a Member of Congress himself) quitted the room, leaving General Kosciusko, Colonel Maitland, Major Edwards, the Adjutant General of the Southern Army, and the Aides-de-Camp of General Greene, to find their own way to the table." Garden observes that such discourteous conduct is no novelty. During the war soldiers are esteemed and valued, but with the fighting over, they are frequently forgotten.[5]

Kosciuszko's effort to obtain the pay due him ended with a promise of a future payment. Meanwhile, he sought to carry out his second goal of promotion to brigadier general. He met with General Benjamin Lincoln, Secretary of War, who agreed to recommend him to Congress. On 8 August 1783, Lincoln penned a favorable letter to the President of Congress, pointing out the earlier promotions granted to the French engineers:

> At the close of the Campaign of 1781, Congress from a conviction of the services and merits of General Du Portail, and of other Gentlemen, officers in the Engineering department, gave them promotions in the army of the United States. At that time, Colonel Kosciuszko, who is among the oldest Colonels in our service (his Commission is dated 18 October 1776) was with General Greene, who has made the most honorable mention of his service to Congress, they have been such from his first entering into our service, as to gain the notice and applause of all under whom he has served.—I beg leave therefore to mention him to Congress as a highly deserving officer and hope that the same regard to merit which procured the promotion of the greatest part, if not all, of

his brother officers in the Engineering department will operate in his favor so far that he may be promoted to the rank of Brigadier General.

Congress referred Lincoln's letter to a committee consisting of Richard Peters, James McHenry, and James Duane. The committee pigeon-holed the recommendation. Despite Greene's admonition to keep pressing Congress, Kosciuszko maintained a quiet dignity. He would not beg. Perhaps he wished he had the support now of General Gates. However, his friend was experiencing serious problems of his own. Gates left the army at Newburgh in March 1783 and returned home to Traveler's Rest, where his wife lay dying. Elizabeth Gates passed away on June 1. Gates was left a tragically broken man. His wife and only son were deceased, his military service ended, and personal funds exhausted.[6]

Not hearing from Congress about his promotion in seven weeks, Kosciuszko asked General Washington for help on 26 September 1783. He wrote the commander-in-chief, "Your Excellency will forgive me the Liberty I take in troubling you in this affair—unacquainted as Congress may be of my Services." He said he feared that Congress would place him on the "oblivion List of a General promotion," undoubtedly having heard of the proposal of Congress to give a merit promotion by brevet to all officers who had not been advanced since January 1777. "One word from your Excellency to Congress in my favor (if I can flatter myself to obtain it)," Kosciuszko concluded, "will clear the doubt and rase my hope to certainty." Kosciuszko's letter reached Washington when he, too, was busily occupied with settling his accounts with Congress. Notwithstanding, he immediately wrote the President, enclosing Kosciuszko's letter of September 26:

> I do myself the honor to transmit to your Excellency copy of a letter I received from Colonel Kosciuszko on the subject of his promotion.
> The General promotion now before Congress, should it take place, would have included him—but this does not seem to be his wish—as a Foreigner I suppose a particular promotion would be

more consonant to his views and interest and from my knowledge of his merit and service, and the concurrent testimony of all who know him, I cannot but recommend him as deserving the favor of Congress.[7]

Washington's endorsement of Kosciuszko's promotion was not particularly vigorous, but the general expressed himself in his usual restrained manner. Unfortunately, Washington's letter of October 2 reached Congress too late, for on September 30 Congress resolved to advance all officers one grade by brevet on the "oblivion list," which included Kosciuszko. The committee of Jacob Read, Richard Peters, and James Duane, charged with the promotion of Kosciuszko, reported that "nothing further on that subject can with propriety be done at this time." Nevertheless, Washington's support may have prodded the trio to accord Kosciuszko an additional measure of recognition by a special tribute and handling through the Secretary of War. On their motion, Congress passed the following resolution:

> RESOLVED, That the Secretary of War transmit to Colonel Kosciosko the brevet commission of brigadier general; and signify to that officer, that Congress entertain an high sense of his long, faithful, and meritorious services.[8]

Kosciuszko accepted the brevet promotion quietly. In his modest way he undoubtedly understood that America would not remember the rank he gained as much as his significant contribution to its freedom.

The independence of the United States finally was acknowledged by Great Britain on 3 September 1783. Representatives of the United States and Great Britain met at Paris on this date and signed the Treaty of Peace. And Washington proceeded to end his long service as commander-in-chief. He issued his Farewell Orders on 2 November 1783, calling attention to the great achievement of American independence. "A contemplation of the compleat attainment (at a period earlier than could have been expected) of the object for which we contended against so formidable a power," he said, "cannot but inspire us with astonishment and gratitude." Cautioning his soldiers to show a conciliating disposition in their civilian communities to which they were about to return, Washington advised them to "prove themselves not less virtuous and useful as Citizens, than they have been persevering and victorious as Soldiers." The commander-in-chief thanked his generals, commandants of regiments and corps, staff, and "the Non Commissioned Officers and private Soldiers for their extraordinary patience in suffering as well as their invincible fortitude in Action."[9]

Kosciuszko was in New York for General Washington's triumphal entry on 25 November 1783. The British Army had evacuated the city, and General Knox commanding units of American troops took possession of the long-held British stronghold. In turn, Washington and Governor George Clinton and their staffs rode in on horseback. Other civilian officials and army officers followed. The Governor hosted a public dinner that Washington and the officers attended.

The gathering of his generals in New York gave Washington the opportunity to bid farewell to his comrades-in-arms. He met them at Fraunces Tavern in lower Manhattan on December 4. In a voice choked with emotion, Washington said, "With a heart full of love and gratitude, I now take leave of you. I most devoutly wish that your latter days may be as prosperous and happy as your former ones have been glorious and honorable." He invited each officer to come up and take his hand. General Knox, standing nearest him, was the first. In silence and with tears in his eyes, the grateful commander grasped Knox's hand, embraced and kissed him. In the same affectionate manner, Washington parted with Kosciuszko and the other generals.[10]

As Kosciuszko began the year of 1784 in America, he was not ready to sail for Europe. Congress had not settled his outstanding pay, as yet, although it struggled to do so. In January, Congress acknowledged that the foreign officers in the service of the United States, not attached to the line of any particular state, complained of great and singular hardships under which they labored. Their pay in depreciated Continental money failed to meet actual expenses, and they could not turn to a state for the balance of their pay. Consequently, foreign officers depended on the generosity of friends or incurred considerable debt. Congress, therefore, resolved on 22 January 1784:

> That the superintendent of finance take order for paying the foreign officers...such sums on account of their pay as may be necessary to relieve them from their present embarrassments, and enable those in America to return to their native country.

Following the resolution, Congress considered the letter of 26 January 1784 of Brigadier General Charles Armand (who had succeeded to the command of the Pulaski Legion), requesting that Congress set up measures for the prompt payment of the interest arising from the balances of their pay due to them. Congress resolved to do so on February 3. In due time, Kosciuszko received a certificate for $12,280.49, bearing interest at six percent from 1 January 1784. The interest was to be paid to him by drafts in Paris.[11]

While Congress wrestled with the difficult problem of pay for the army, Kosciuszko visited friends. General and Elizabeth Greene cordially invited him to their home at the Gibbs Mansion in Newport, Rhode Island. The Greenes were happy to meet with and entertain old friends, including Kosciuszko, Lafayette, Von Steuben, and the Reverend William Gordon. Kosciuszko planned a short visit, but the Greenes persuaded him to prolong his stay. The Reverend Gordon took a liking to Kosciuszko. Writing to Greene on 5 April 1784, Gordon mentioned Kosciuszko alone of all his guests and asked the general to pass on "my best regards" to Kosciuszko. George Champlin Mason wrote that during Kosciuszko's visit with the Greenes, the Pole presented Mason's grandmother with a beautifully carved ivory box, which the family has cherished and preserved. While in Newport, Kosciuszko probably visited other friends in the area, including Colonel Jeremiah Wadsworth at Hartford, Connecticut. Wadsworth had served as Commissary General in Gates's Northern Army.[12]

Kosciuszko journeyed to Philadelphia for the general meeting of the Society of the Cincinnati called by General Washington, 1–18 May 1784. Several of Kosciuszko's friends were there: Generals Otho Williams and Anthony Walton White, and Lieutenant Colonel Lewis Morris, who had served with Kosciuszko in the South. General Nathanael Greene was absent, although he was elected a state delegate from Rhode Island. The occasion was probably the last time that Washington and Kosciuszko saw each other.[13]

The formation of the Society of the Cincinnati occurred in 1783 while the Continental Army camped at Newburgh, New York. Washington encouraged the organization of a society of officers for the purpose of perpetuating the friendships formed during a time of common danger and distress. On 10 May 1783, Generals Henry Knox, Baron von Steuben, and several others began the organizing effort. They named the association after the Roman general Lucius Quintus Cincinnatus. When the general was called to duty in 485 B.C., he left his farm and led the armies of Rome to victory. He then returned to his plow, while refusing the honors offered him by a grateful Senate. Cincinnatus became the ideal of Roman simplicity and a model for his countrymen. Kosciuszko easily identified himself with Cincinnatus, who was much like the later Timoleon. Kosciuszko joined the Society as a charter member. His signature appears on the Parchment Roll with a group of officers of the Corps of Engineers—Duportail and seven other French officers. Kosciuszko contributed the required one month's pay to the Society. Very likely Lafayette encouraged him to join, since Washington asked the Marquis to invite the foreign officers. As a souvenir of the Society, Washington presented Kosciuszko with an antique cameo mounted in a ring. Kosciuszko later gave it to Baron de Gerardot, who served in the National Guard of Poland. In turn, Gerardot left the ring to his son. About the time of the General Meeting, Washington presented Kosciuszko with two other gifts, a sword and a pair of pistols, which are preserved today in National Museums in Poland.[14]

From Philadelphia Kosciuszko traveled to New York. His departure for Europe was imminent. Although the certificate of pay provided no money for travel, and neither the grant of 500 acres of public land in Ohio, still he received some cash from Robert Morris. Prior to sailing, Kosciuszko thanked the Superintendent of Finance:

> Your generous behavior towards me, so intirely took hold of my heart, that forgeting your uncomon delicat feelings, I am forced by a great uneasiness of my mind, to present my warmest thanks to you, before I quit this Country; and to assure you that your kindness will be always fresh in my memory with the gratitude I owe you, and shall endeavor to put in practice what susceptibility now sugest the means to adopt.[15]

Kosciuszko wrote several letters of farewell. He could not forget his great friend General Otho Williams. He told him how he regretted leaving the United States: "At last the necessity force me to quit this Country, you may be sure with great reluctance, as I have so many acquaintances amongst the number, some are very valuable friends, for whom no boundary can be afixed to my affection." He expressed special esteem for Williams, "I would be happy to convince you of one thing, that your friendship and kindness for me, never shall be vipe of [wiped off] out of my memory, by any circumstance whatsoever." Although Kosciuszko was departing the United States, he still hoped to return to his adopted country and serve in the American Army again. He asked Williams for help: "You have in your power to oblige me and I ask you with the same confidence that I expect you will act with me, and this is—if Congress should make a pease establishment that you would interest your self with the delegates of your state to appoint me a Chief engineer with the rank of Brygadier General." In addition to Williams there was their common friend General Nathanael Greene, for whom Kosciuszko had developed a great affection: "Farewell my dear General, once more farewell," he wrote. "Be as happy as my bosoom will augur for you. Let me Shook here by the hand by my delusive Imagination, as you should be present in Person, and seal our friendship for each other for ever."[16]

Kosciuszko sailed for L'Orient, France, aboard the *Courier de l'Europe,* 15 July 1784. Colonel David Humphreys, who had served as Washington's aide-de-camp, was his companion. Humphreys was going to France as secretary of a commission for negotiating commercial treaties with European countries. The two arrived at their destination on 8 August 1784, after a pleasant voyage of twenty-four days. Humphreys described the trip in a letter to Washington, August 12, adding that "General Kosciusko & myself are to set off in a Carriage together for Paris tomorrow," and in a postscript: "Gen'l Kosciusko desires his best respects may be presented to your Ex'y." Kosciuszko was returning to Poland with significant military experience and a wealth of new political and social philosophy.[17]

During his eight years in America, three of Kosciuszko's achievements in the fight for independence can be singled out. First, at Saratoga, where his brilliantly designed fortifications blocked General Burgoyne's advance on Albany and led to the destruction of the British Grand Strategy. Second, at West Point, where his imaginative plan of fortified sites, blending with the rugged terrain, resulted in an impregnable fortress. The British never dared to attack. Third, in the South with General Greene, where Kosciuszko's flexible skills as an engineer and soldier helped Greene's mobile strategy to succeed against the British. Influenced by the Coudray affair, Greene initially became biased against foreign officers. In time, however, he came to appreciate the great value of a few, like Lafayette, Von Steuben, and Kosciuszko. For the Pole, Greene developed great admiration and friendship. When Kosciuszko departed the Southern Army for the North, Greene praised his outstanding service in a letter to General William Irvine:

> Among the most useful and agreeable of my companions in the army was Colonel Kosciuszko. Nothing could exceed his zeal for the public service, nor in the prosecution of the various objects that presented themselves in our small but active warfare, could anything be more useful than his attention, vigilance and industry. In promoting my views to whatever department of the service directed, he was at all times, a ready and able assistant. One in a word whom no pleasure could seduce, no labor fatigue

and no danger deter. What besides greatly distinguished him was an unparalleled modesty and entire unconsciousness of having done anything extraordinary. Never making a claim or pretension for himself and never omitting to distinguish and commend the merits of others. This able and gallant soldier has now left us for the North, intending to return directly to his own country, where he cannot fail to be soon and greatly distinguished.[18]

No finer tribute of Thaddeus Kosciuszko's service in the American Revolution can surpass General Nathanael Greene's praise of this Polish Timoleon.

CHAPTER TWELVE

Kosciuszko in Europe

Performs Secret Mission for Jefferson

HADDEUS KOSCIUSZKO returned to an unhappy Poland threatened by its predatory neighbors. He lived quietly in his ancestral home in Siechnowicze, but he was constantly plagued with financial problems. He had not received any interest payments from his Revolutionary War certificate. In 1787, he reminded Congress, and it responded with a single payment of $700 for the year of 1784. Meanwhile, his sister Anna Estko helped him and buoyed his spirits.[1]

Kosciuszko found life boring. He turned to his friend Nathanael Greene and wrote him on 20 January 1786: "Do write me my dear General of the Situation in your Country because I heard many bad things; however, when our king have asked me, I gave him the best description I could." As well as mentioning his own conditions in Poland, Kosciuszko pleaded for a word from Greene:

> Write me of yourself, of your family, and of my friends. As to myself am in good health, something richer, but very unhappy of the situation of my Country which I believe *nullo redemptio* and well as I am, so much am attached to your Country, that I would leave every thing behind, and would fly this very moment even in the Baloon to embrace you, Could I obtain an honorable rank in your Country's Army.

Probably Kosciuszko's letter did not reach Greene by 19 June 1786, when the general died unexpectedly at his Mulberry Grove Plantation in Georgia. Kosciuszko heard nothing about Greene until Major Elnathan Haskell of Massachusetts wrote from France in 1788 and informed him of Greene's death. Kosciuszko was devastated. He answered Haskell to an address in Paris, "He is gone, my good friend Greene," Kosciuszko exclaimed. "Rain begins to fall heavy from my eyes whenever I think of. You ought to make a statue or Mausolium for his memory." And Kosciuszko believed that Congress should recognize Greene's contribution to American independence. "I knew his merit perhaps better than anyone," he continued, "and shall think always a very ungrateful Country if she will not Crown him with a title of a great General and Citizen." Kosciuszko, too, wished to honor Greene. He ordered an engraving of General Greene struck in Paris and, with the help of David Humphreys, sent copies to friends in the United States. Serving as American Minister at Lisbon, Portugal, Humphreys wrote Kosciuszko:

> I hope you received the Engravings of your good friend Gen Greene, which were put into the train of transmission at Paris, which you directed...It is a fortunate circumstance, that the Print which you caused to be taken of him, is the best likeness now existing of that excellent Man. Indeed it is pronounced to be a perfect resemblance by all his friends in America.[2]

In 1789, Kosciuszko's life took on new vigor, springing from the reforms of the Great Diet (*Sejm*) in Warsaw. Among the many progressive measures, the *Sejm* voted to increase the military strength. King Stanislaw August appointed Kosciuszko a major general in the Polish Army, 12 October 1789. He was stationed with forces in the Eastern region, where he assisted the young commander-in-chief, Prince Jozef Poniatowski, the King's nephew. Kosciuszko worked energetically to transform the new and ill-equipped army into a fighting force. In 1791, the Great Diet enacted the Constitution of the Third of May that, after the United States Constitution, became the second written constitution in the world. The Constitution established new rights for the people and imbued the nation with moral strength. The Constitution abolished the infamous *Liberum Veto,* which had given each magnate in the Diet the ability to paralyze the government. President George Washington hailed Poland and its King for making "large and unexpected strides towards liberty." Together with the soldiers of his division, Kosciuszko was one of the first to swear allegiance to the Constitution. The strength of its provisions would lead to the emancipation of Poland from foreign domination, especially that of Russia.[3]

Empress Catherine II, fearing that her goal of destroying Poland would be thwarted, gave the Polish nation no time to gain strength. She bought off a few Polish magnates who were dissatisfied with the Constitution because it had stripped them of extensive privileges. These traitors formed the Confederation of Targowica and invited Catherine to invade Poland. Just as France had reneged on its military alliance with Poland in World War II, so too Prussia in 1792 callously betrayed Poland and trampled on its alliance and pledges of help. Alone, Poland faced the overwhelming odds of Russia and Prussia. At first, the Polish Army scored a few victories in which Kosciuszko's division performed well. The King decorated him with the Cross of Virtuti Militari and promoted him to lieutenant general. Nevertheless, King Stanislaw August wavered between fighting and negotiating. He realized that the Russian and Prussian armies could overwhelm the Poles. Believing that Catherine would live up to her promise of maintaining the integrity of Poland, he gave in to her harsh demands. But Catherine deceived him. She was bent on destroying Poland, a policy of aggression that Russia has pursued to the present day. As demanded, the King reluctantly joined the Targowica faction and ordered the army to cease further resistance. Prince Poniatowski, Kosciuszko, and many other officers resigned in protest. The reforms of the Great Diet, including the King's greatest achievement, the Constitution of the Third of May, were abolished. The Second Partition followed in 1793.[4]

Kosciuszko left Poland for Austrian Poland, annexed in the

Partition of 1772, but he continued to Leipzig, Saxony, where he met many Polish patriotic leaders. He tried to enlist the help of France for a planned uprising in Poland. However, Robespierre, Danton, Marat, and other French leaders at the time turned him down. He now realized that the Poles would have to regain independence on their own. On 16 March 1794, Kosciuszko secretly crossed the border into Poland and entered Krakow. There on March 24 he issued his famous Act of Insurrection and proclaimed himself the Commander-in-Chief of the Insurrection. Modeled after the Declaration of Independence, the Act provided the framework for a new government. In subsequent actions, Kosciuszko freed the serfs and invited them to join the national army. He ruled like a dictator, but, like Timoleon, he would give up his power at the successful end of the revolution.[5]

The nation answered Kosciuszko's appeal for salvation from European despots. Poles flocked to the army. Kosciuszko scored a grand victory during the repulse of combined Russian-Prussian armies besieging Warsaw. The enemy commander was none other than King Frederick William II. Notwithstanding, the enemy strength was too great. At the bloody Battle of Maciejowice, overwhelming Russian numbers crushed the Polish Army, 10 October 1794. Leading the soldiers in person, Kosciuszko was seriously wounded, taken prisoner, and carted off to prison in St. Petersburg. With no one to take Kosciuszko's place, all resistance was crushed. The calculating Catherine achieved her dastardly goal. Russia and Prussia carved up the remaining territory of the nation in the Third Partition of 1795, and Poland was erased from the map of Europe.[6]

> *Hope, for a season, bade the world farewell,*
> *And Freedom shriek'd—as Kosciusko fell.*
>
> —THOMAS CAMPBELL

Americans followed the progress of Kosciuszko's Insurrection. David Humphreys reported to President George Washington on 28 June 1794: "Kosciuszko is by the last accounts going on well.

I dread, however, the result from the formidable force that will be opposed to the Poles." With the destruction of Poland came an outpouring of sympathy in the American press and among American leaders. Noah Webster exclaimed, "With what emotions of joy did we hear the intelligence of *Poland in arms!* Kosciuszko was hailed as the deliverer of his country and numbered with the Washingtons of the age!" But Webster lamented the unhappy ending: "What pleasure was inspired in our bosoms, when he was successful...How short the delusion! No sooner did the irresistible veterans of the Savage North appear in Poland, than Kosciusko was defeated, his troops dispersed and the hero himself a prisoner in chains." The Republican John Dickinson deeply regretted the aggression of Russia, Austria, and Prussia "by which a noble nation was despoiled of liberty." He lashed out at these three powers for perpetrating "a deed, as base and as cruel as any, the records ancient and modern of tyrannical hostilities against the human race, can supply." The infamous deed against Poland, occurring during the presidency of George Washington, made a lasting impression on him. He wrote Kosciuszko's friend Julian Ursyn Niemcewicz: "That your country is not happy as your struggle to make it so, was Patriotic and Noble, is a matter which all lovers of national Liberty and the Rights of Man, have sorely lamented." Thomas Jefferson, too, was indignant. He regretted the decline of political morality among nations. Some years later, writing to John Adams, January 11, 1816, he pointed to the baseness of certain European countries that led to the partition of Poland. "A wound indeed was inflicted on this character of honor in the eighteenth century by the partition of Poland," he said. He labeled it an "atrocity of a barbarous government chiefly" [Russia] in conjunction "with a smaller one still scrambling to become great" [Prussia]. He also condemned France, England, and Spain "inasmuch as they stood aloof and permitted its perpetration."[7]

Duke de Rochefoucault-Liancourt, former President of the National Assembly of France, condemned the cruel treatment of Kosciuszko, "whose imprisonment and barbarous treatment made every generous mind condemn Catherine, if the whole life of that infamous woman, blackened with crimes and vices, could be sullied by additional crime!" Fortunately for Kosciuszko, Catherine II soon died and was succeeded by son Paul I on 17 November 1796. He did not possess the cruelty of his mother and released Kosciuszko from prison immediately. Kosciuszko's wounds had not healed, and he could not walk. Accounts tell of Tsar Paul's visit to the prisoner's cell. Kosciuszko attempted to rise to his feet but was unable to. The Tsar sat for half an hour and conversed with the crippled general, offering to free him. But Kosciuszko thought of the thousands of his soldiers who were imprisoned in Siberia. To gain their release, too, he had to make a distasteful concession—take an oath of allegiance to the Tsar.[8]

Kosciuszko's one thought now was to come to America, his adopted country. At age fifty and an invalid, he departed St. Petersburg on 19 December 1796 in the company of his adjutant Julian Ursyn Niemcewicz and a former Polish officer named Libiszewski. Being strong and rugged, Libiszewski's duty was to carry the crippled Kosciuszko from his bed or couch to his carriage. The trio traveled through Finland and Sweden to England. Along the way Kosciuszko was hailed and feted. In England, the Tories treated the Pole with reserve, but the Whigs greeted him with enthusiasm. General Banastre Tarleton, President of the Whig Club, and the members entertained Kosciuszko. They presented him with an expensive sword "as a public testimony of their sense of his excellent virtues and of his gallant, generous, and exemplary efforts to defend and save his country." Kosciuszko and Tarleton had been adversaries during the American Revolution in the South. On the order of Tsar Paul, the Russian minister in London arranged for three prominent British physicians to examine Kosciuszko's wounds. They concluded that the pain in the head was the result of a stroke of a blunt sabre that severed a nerve in the lower part of the rear head. The paralysis of his legs was due to a wound in the hip with a Cossack pike which injured the sciatic nerve. The three doctors were optimistic about Kosciuszko's improvement in the future. They gave him their report and recommended that he seek the help of Dr. Benjamin Rush in Philadelphia.[9]

During Kosciuszko's two-week stay in London, American Minister Rufus King called on the Pole and offered him help. King arranged for Kosciuszko's passage to America and alerted the Secretary of State, Colonel Timothy Pickering. Departing London, Kosciuszko reached the seaport of Bristol on the west coast of England on June 14. He was again greeted enthusiastically by officials and the people. The American Consul in Bristol, Elias Vanderhost, invited Kosciuszko to his home. On 19 June 1797, Kosciuszko boarded the *Adriana,* Captain Frederick Lee commanding, and sailed for America. He experienced a rough passage during sixty-one days of sailing and arrived in Philadelphia on August 18.[10]

As the *Adriana* sailed up the Delaware River and approached Fort Mifflin, the commander greeted Kosciuszko with a salute of thirteen guns. The sound of the cannonade prompted the citizens to turn out into the streets in droves and move to the landing. John Lockwood, sailing master of the new frigate *United States,* provided a barge to carry the general ashore. Eight masters of vessels in the harbor manned the honorary barge. To the cheers of the citizens, Kosciuszko replied, "I consider America my second country and feel very happy on returning to her." The exuberant people unharnessed the horses from Kosciuszko's carriage and pulled it to his lodgings at the boarding house of Mrs. Loveson on Second Street.[11]

Kosciuszko found the United States of 1797 a changed country from that which he had left in 1784. The political atmosphere had become highly polarized between the Republicans of Thomas Jefferson and the Federalists of Alexander Hamilton and John Adams. Although the Republicans showered Kosciuszko with praise, the Federalists maintained a polite and courteous attitude toward the Pole. Kosciuszko had to be careful not to favor or offend either side. Nevertheless, Kosciuszko escaped the politics at the seat of the government upon the insistence of Dr. Rush. Philadelphia was plagued by an epidemic of yellow fever, and thousands of residents were deserting the city. Before he left, however, Kosciuszko carried out a mission for Sir John Sinclair, President of the Board of Agriculture in Great Britain. Sinclair had asked Kosciuszko to carry notes and packages for Washington and President John Adams. On 23 August 1797, Kosciuszko wrote the former President: "By sending a Packet delivered to me by John Sinclair for you, I have the honor to pay my respects not only to my chief Commander, but to a great man whose eminent virtues to his country rendered him dear to every breast." Kosciuszko asked Secretary of State, Timothy Pickering, to forward the packet to Mount Vernon. Since Attorney General Charles Lee was about to depart for Virginia, Pickering entrusted the correspondence to Lee. Upon receipt, Washington answered Kosciuszko immediately and invited him to Mount Vernon in his letter of 31 August 1797:

> Having been just informed of your safe arrival in America, I was on the point of writing you a congratulatory letter on the occasion, welcoming you to the land whose liberties you have been so instrumental in establishing, when I received your favour of the 23^d instant from Philadelphia; for which, and the Packet you had the goodness to bear from Sir John Sinclair, I offer you my thanks.
>
> I beg you to be assured, that no one has a higher respect and veneration for your character than I have; or one who more sincerely wished, during your arduous struggle in the cause of liberty and your country, that it might be crowned with Success. But the ways of Providence are inscrutable, and Mortals must submit.
>
> I pray you to believe, that at all times, and under any circumstances, it would make me happy to see you at my last retreat; from which I never expect to be more than twenty miles again.

President John Adams also thanked Kosciuszko for the package from Sinclair and welcomed him to America in a letter from Quincy, Massachusetts, 4 September 1797:

> Give me leave, Sir, to congratulate you on your arrival in America, where, I hope, You will find all the consolation, tranquility and satisfaction you desire after the glorious efforts you

have made on a greater Theater. On my arrival in Philadelphia I
hope to have pleasure to receive you....[12]

Having accomplished his mission for the two Presidents,
Kosciuszko departed from the epidemic-ravaged city. He planned
to visit friends, General Anthony Walton White in New Brunswick,
New Jersey, and General Horatio Gates in New York. With
Niemcewicz and a servant, Kosciuszko set off in a two-horse
carriage on August 30. He left in such haste that he did not notify
White and Gates before his departure. However, at the Whites
two days later, he alerted Gates with a short letter. Meanwhile,
Dr. Rush also wrote Gates on September 3: "Our illustrious friend
Kusiosco left this city a few days ago & is now pleasantly & hos-
pitably accommodated at General White's at Brunswick. His
wounds are all healed. One of them on his hip has left his thigh
& leg in a paralytic State. Time has done a little towards restor-
ing it. I do not despair of his being yet able to walk."[13]

On the first day of the journey, Kosciuszko passed through
Princeton, where Elias Boudinot entertained him and his companions. Boudinot had served as President of Congress for a term
during the Revolution and now held the post of Director of the
Mint. The next day Kosciuszko arrived at the White's residence
and spent a week with the general, wife Margaret, and sister-in-
law Mary Ellis. White had been a comrade-in-arms in the Southern
Army. Kosciuszko had met the two women in Charleston, where
White married Margaret Ellis. Following the war, General White
experienced heavy financial losses so that Margaret and he were
forced to live with Mary Ellis on her farm. During his visit
with the Whites, Kosciuszko renewed his acquaintance with
other friends, Colonel John B. Bayard and William Patterson,
Associate Justice of the U.S. Supreme Court. At the Whites
Kosciuszko exchanged his medal, Eagle of the Cincinnati, with
General White, who also was an original member of the Society
of the Cincinnati of New Jersey. Thus, Kosciuszko's medal remained in the White family for generations. In the 1930 decade,
the Kosciuszko medal was the possession of Walton White Evans

von Henert of Wassenaar, The Netherlands. The owner was the great-great-grandson of General White.

On Saturday September 9, Kosciuszko continued his journey to Hoboken, New Jersey. The next day he arrived at Rose Hill, the estate of General and the second Mrs. Gates, Mary Vallance, a wealthy spinster whom he married in 1786. The reunion was joyful, and the visit lasted three weeks, becoming a continual run of social events. Gates invited prominent members of New York society, among them former Governor George Clinton, a dozen Livingstons, and Marinus Willett, who had served with Kosciuszko in the Northern Campaign of 1777. Janet Montgomery, widow of General Richard Montgomery who had led the American invasion of Canada in 1775, protested to Gates for keeping Kosciuszko all to himself. A frequent visitor was French nobleman Duke de la Rochefoucault-Liancourt. Kosciuszko impressed him, and the Duke praised Kosciuszko in his *Travels through the United States of North America.* On September 29, Kosciuszko left the hospitable home of General and Mrs. Gates. Niemcewicz recorded the departure: "We left the house of Gl.[General] Gates and his kind wife with much regret. After embarking Gl. Kosci [uszko] with much difficulty, we once again embraced Gl. Gates, who had come to escort us to the bank of the North River, and crossed successfully to the other side." Passing through Newark, Kosciuszko reached Elizabeth and remained there for three weeks, taking lodging at the well-known Indian Queen Tavern. Many friends came to see him here. On October 20, he resumed the journey to New Brunswick and again visited the Whites. The appearance of colder weather began to subdue the epidemic of yellow fever, and by November 27 Kosciuszko prepared to return to Philadelphia. Niemcewicz went ahead alone to find lodging for the general. With the help of Dr. Rush, Niemcewicz rented a modest apartment on Third Street South.[14]

The apartment in a small boarding house consisted of two small rooms. Kosciuszko's could not hold more than four persons. The second room occupied by Niemcewicz was even smaller. Lying in bed or sitting in a large chair, Kosciuszko greeted visitors. His head was always bandaged. Republican member of Congress Senator Stevens Thomson Mason of Virginia and other prominent citizens called on Kosciuszko. His most frequent visitor was Vice President Thomas Jefferson. As Jefferson told Gates, "I see him often, and with great pleasure mixed with commiseration."[15]

Having returned to his adopted country, Kosciuszko thought about buying property and settling down. John Armstrong, residing on the Hudson River at Red Hook, New York, invited his friend to visit and explore the possibility of buying property near Saratoga, the scene of his military exploit in the Revolutionary War. Kosciuszko disclosed to Gates that "Genl Armstrong wrote me of a Farme in his neighborhood. I answered him, that in my way to Saratoga Springs I would be glad to see it." Jefferson also attempted to influence Kosciuszko to settle in Virginia. However, Kosciuszko could not buy any property unless the United States made good on its long overdue obligation to him. He had been waiting for payment for nearly fourteen years. The annual interest payments, too, were either not paid or were lost in financial channels. He turned to Washington for help:

> Formerly I was independent, but now my only resource is in the Justice of Congress, having lost my Certificate and wyth my Country lost my all—I must Request Sir, You will be so kind to mention my situation to that August Body and entreat, that I may be paid my Just demand; without the trouble of making another Application.

In the same letter Kosciuszko expressed his wish to visit Mount Vernon. "If the situation of my health would admit of my traveling so far, I would immediately pay you my Respects and my personal Homage; it was my first intention, and I hope I shall at last accomplish it." Washington answered with some feeling:

> I am sorry that the state of your health should deprive me of the pleasure of your company at this place, and I regret still more that the pain you feel from the wounds you have received, though glorious for your reputation, is the occasion of it.

Washington assured Kosciuszko that he would do all he could

as a private citizen, but that appropriations must originate with the Legislature. He felt confident that Kosciuszko's "claim upon the justice and feelings of this country will meet no delay." He added that the loss of the original certificate issued to Kosciuszko in 1784 would not prevent payment, offering the following opinion: "Your rank and services in the American Army are too well known to require that testimony of your claim, and the Books of the Treasury will shew that you have received nothing in discharge of it, or if any part, to what amount." As Washington had predicted, the arrears of Kosciuszko's payment were taken up by the House of Representatives. John L. Dawson introduced legislation to settle the claim. After some discussions and coordination with the Department of the Treasury, Secretary Oliver Wolcott reported that Kosciuszko was entitled to receive without any further action by Congress the sum of $12,280.54, the amount of his lost certificate, and $2,947.33 in interest for the years of 1785 to 1788. As for the interest in subsequent years, both Houses authorized the payment of $3,684.16 in interest for the period of 1 January 1793 to 31 December 1797. The principal and interest gave Kosciuszko a total of $18,912.03.[16]

Although Kosciuszko rejoiced in his new found freedom in America, still he could not forget the terrible fate that befell his beloved Poland. He hoped for its resurrection and sought to add his spirit of resistance to the Polish exiles who were forming Polish Legions in France. The exiles urged Kosciuszko to join them and take command of the Legions. The ruling group in France, the Directory, also invited him to come to Paris, hoping to capitalize on his reputation. Meanwhile, relations between the United States and France worsened. Both England and France treated the infant republic with contempt. In a move to negotiate away the English abuses of American trade and the Treaty of Paris of 1783, President Washington had sent John Jay to London in the summer of 1794. Jay agreed to a treaty, signed on 19 November 1794, that the Republicans attacked as "the most humiliating treaty in the entire history of the country." They were outraged, and the French, too, became incensed over unfavorable provisions to France. War with France loomed as a distinct possibility, but the Republicans under Thomas Jefferson sought to lessen the tension.[17]

In addition to official diplomatic overtures, Vice President Jefferson proposed a secret mission for Kosciuszko—go to France and exert whatever persuasion was possible with the French leaders for a lessening of tension. No documents exist to prove the mission, except Jefferson's role in arranging for Kosciuszko's abrupt and clandestine departure and the Pole's subsequent revelation. Kosciuszko disclosed that "Jefferson considered that I would be the most effective intermediary in bringing accord with France, so I accepted the mission even if without official authorization." Kosciuszko prepared to leave at once. He maintained the utmost secrecy because of political tensions in America where some Federalists might label him a spy. He also wished to avoid being seized at sea by the British. Jefferson made the arrangements for his passage and the procuring of passports. Kosciuszko assumed the name of Mr. Kann, but Jefferson changed it to Thomas Kanberg. As another ruse to confuse possible pursuers, Jefferson decided that Kosciuszko should travel via Lisbon and remain there for a few days. Kosciuszko revealed some details of the preparation in his letter to Jefferson (undated but probably March 1798):

> I must know six to ten days before I go to prepare the things and in the maner that nobody should know it.—it is requisit that I should have passports on the name of Mr. Kann from Ministers English, Portugal, Span, French...recommend me I beg you to your friend at Lisbon to help me in everything and as I am a Stranger and will stay few days I would wish if possible that he should take me to his house upon any Condition—not forget to recommend me to the care of the Capitain in whose ship I will go....

Jefferson applied personally and without delay to the ministers in Philadelphia for the passports. He said that they were needed for "his friend Thomas Kanberg...native to the north of Europe ...has been known to Thomas Jefferson these twenty years in America, is of the most excellent character, stands in no relation whatever to any of the belligerent powers, as to whom Thomas

Jefferson is not afraid to be responsible for his political innocence, as he goes merely for his private affairs. He will sail from Baltimore, if he finds there is a good opportunity for France; and if not he will come on here." (Dated March 27, 1798).[18]

Kosciuszko's imminent departure prompted him to settle two personal matters: finances and last will and testament. He converted part of his back pay into drafts on banks in Amsterdam, and the greater part he left in America under the management of John Barnes, whom Jefferson had recommended. Barnes placed the money in safe investments to the end of Kosciuszko's life. The Pole's second matter pertained to bequeathing his money in America for the benefit of the enslaved blacks. He wished that they be bought out of bondage, educated, and guided to becoming useful citizens. He wrote his will and named Jefferson executor. The document was attested to by John Barnes and John Dawson on 5 May 1798. Kosciuszko's will stands as a noble deed that proclaimed his unshakable conviction in the right of all individuals to be free of enslavement and oppression.[19]

Kosciuszko did not tell his close friend Niemcewicz of his secret plan to leave America until the night before departure. On the evening of 4 May 1798, Niemcewicz attended a meeting of the Philosophical Society, presided over by Jefferson. At about 10:30 P.M. he returned to the apartment, where Kosciuszko startled him with the news of his departure the next morning.

> "Mr. Niemcewicz," Kosciuszko said, "you must give me your word of honor that you will tell no one what I am about to confide in you. And that you will do what I ask of you."

Niemcewicz was astonished by Kosciuszko's secretive behavior, but having confidence in the general, he agreed.

> "I leave this night for Europe," Kosciuszko explained. "I leave alone."

Niemcewicz was dumbfounded. He could not understand how the crippled general could travel without his servant and without the presence and help of his friend. Kosciuszko would not reveal the reason for the journey nor the destination.

THOMAS JEFFERSON

Portrait by Rembrandt Peale in 1805. Jefferson wears the rich fur coat given to the then Vice President by Thaddeus Kosciuszko in March 1798, prior to the General's secret mission to France. Kosciuszko wrote, " I take the liberty to send you a Bear Skin as a Token of my veneration, respect, and Esteem for you forever."[18] (Collection of the New-York Historical Society)

"I beseech you to tell everyone," Kosciuszko continued, "that I have gone to take the waters in Virginia. You will leave Philadelphia in three days and you will go in that direction, saying it is to rejoin me."

Niemcewicz felt betrayed. "You give me then a fine commission," the distraught friend exclaimed. "I must tell lies here. I must run about the country in order to tell more lies. Ah! In what embarrassment you have placed me! Alone, without friends, and without means."

At one o'clock in the morning, Niemcewicz left the apartment and roamed the streets, weighed down with grief and torn with doubts about the uncertainties of the future.[20]

At 4 o'clock a covered carriage arrived at the dwelling. Jefferson was inside, and Kosciuszko got in without embracing Niemcewicz. The general showed more agility than in the past. Still Niemcewicz worried about the general's safety. "With my eyes I followed the carriage as far as I could," he recorded. "They took a route completely opposite from that to the harbor. I do not know for whom this precaution was taken for all the world still slept. I learned later that they had gone by land up to New Castel, where a boat awaited them." Three days later Niemcewicz departed Philadelphia, according to plan, traveling first to Baltimore and then Federal City. He wrote Jefferson, "I do not know how I have acquitted myself; I only know that the profession of a liar (to him who is not used to it) is as difficult as it is humiliating." The deception continued. On 1 June 1798, Jefferson informed Kosciuszko: "Your departure is not yet known, or even suspected." Two weeks later, the Vice President reaffirmed the secret: "Not a doubt is entertained here but that you are gone to the springs."[21]

The absence of Kosciuszko from the public eye sparked speculation and gossip. By September, however, the truth became known. The press learned of Kosciuszko's arrival in France, and Federalist papers sniped at his mission and alleged criticism of the Federal government. The editor of *Gazette of the United States* denounced Kosciuszko's motives and accused him of deception, "... exciting from our government a liberal mark of its munificence, he has returned to Europe, and early commenced the honest work of calumniating his benefactors!" In France, Kosciuszko plunged into his work with a vigor that he gained from the benefit of Dr. Rush's treatments and the gravity of his mission. He held secret meetings with members of the French Directory in an effort to lessen the tension between France and the United States, and he had some success. About the same time, President John Adams had sent two special commissioners to France, Federalist John Marshall of Virginia and Republican Elbridge Gerry of Massachusetts. Kosciuszko met with Gerry, and the two undoubtedly coordinated their activities. Nathaniel Cutting, American diplomatic agent in Paris, informed Jefferson of the intercession of Victor Dupont, former French consul at Charleston. Cutting also praised Jefferson's special envoy: "General Kosciuszko likewise has, I am persuaded, improved every opportunity of pleading our cause at the Fountain-head of Power in this Country, & with good effect." Kosciuszko also assisted Dr. John Logan, who had come to France on a mission of peace. The combined American effort achieved its goal. The Directory gave up its insistence on the payment of money, revoked its unfavorable edicts, released imprisoned American seamen, and promised to receive an American envoy. Richard Codman, a Federalist and an eyewitness in Paris, stated: "The Directory have been induced to make this essential alteration in their conduct from representations made to them by Dupont, Kosciuszko, Volney & others lately from America." French historian Antoine Jullien wrote that "Kosciuszko's remonstrances and friendly steps in the Executive Directory contributed much to bringing France and the United States closer." Kosciuszko wrote Jefferson of the change of attitude of France toward America: "The Amicable disposition of the Government of France are realy favorable to the interest of the United States by the recent prouves they give, you ought not to doubt that they choose to be in peace and in perfect harmonie with America...."[22]

American historians have paid little, if any, attention to Koscisuzko's secret mission to France on behalf of the United

States. Admittedly, the action was unofficial, but one that was conceived and arranged by Vice President Jefferson. The political tension between Federalists and Republicans did not allow Jefferson to act openly. The Federalists favored Great Britain and grew increasingly angry at France for its violations of American sovereignty—the seizure of American vessels trading with Great Britain and the imprisonment of the seamen, and the expulsion of the American minister to France, Charles C. Pinckney. As historian Asa Earl Martin concludes: "The Federalist leaders in the cabinet and in Congress appeared to be possessed with a grim determination to force war with France." Jefferson sought to prevent the drift into war with a nation that had materially aided the independence of the United States a short time earlier. From 1785 to 1789, he served as United States Minister to France and came to admire the people and their culture. Jefferson believed that the radical French Directory, although conditioned in the excesses of the violent French Revolution, could nevertheless be persuaded to moderate its conduct through quiet diplomacy. Hence Jefferson chose Kosciuszko as a voice of American moderation. Jefferson had implicit faith and trust in Kosciuszko, and the Pole's reputation as a freedom fighter made him amenable to the French leaders. Kosciuszko did not act alone, but, with several other like minds, he earnestly sought the lessening of tension and succeeded. A likely but unnecessary war with France was avoided, as Kosciuszko performed another great service for America.[23]

With his unofficial diplomatic mission accomplished, Kosciuszko continued to live in France and maintain a close association with Americans. He was a welcome visitor at the residence of the American Minister Robert R. Livingston, the negotiator of the Louisiana Purchase for President Jefferson. In 1804, Livingston was succeeded by his brother-in-law and Kosciuszko's good friend, John Armstrong. Kosciuszko became the godfather of Armstrong's son in 1806, and the Pole bequeath a sum of money for the child whom Armstrong christened Kosciuszko in honor of his friend.[24]

Of all the Americans, Kosciuszko held Thomas Jefferson most

dear. After his return to France in 1798 and for the remaining nineteen years of his life, Kosciuszko kept up a continuing correspondence with Jefferson. Kosciuszko wrote his letters in his more fluent French. Jefferson's election to the presidency in 1801 elated Kosciuszko, and the Pole released a flood of emotional tributes:

> I congratulate the United States of America on the choice of your person for their President; there will be no more doubt that Republicanism must be inseparable with honesty, probity, and strict justice, and that man should be honored more for his virtues and knowledge, than for his luxury. Your ever memorable message made greatest impression in Europe, even people of opposing opinion admired it, they maintained only that such beautiful promises are not fulfilled in reality.
>
> Knowing well your way of thinking, your Genius, your ability, your knowledge, your Character, and your good Heart, I silenced some and allayed others.[25]

During his long sojourn in France, Kosciuszko never ceased to exert himself in the cause of Poland's rebirth. He encouraged the formation of Polish Legions in France. Napoleon offered him the command of the Polish force, but Kosciuszko, mistrusting the devious Emperor, insisted that he state his promise to restore the Polish state openly. Napoleon demurred. After Waterloo, Kosciuszko looked to Tsar Alexander I, who seemed to follow a pro-Polish foreign policy that was influenced by his Foreign Minister, Prince Adam Czartoryski. Alexander pledged to restore the Polish state, whereupon Czartoryski invited Kosciuszko to come to Vienna in 1815 when the Congress of Vienna met to determine the future of Europe. At the Congress, the Tsar's ministers, aided by England and the two partitioning powers, Prussia and Austria, all opposed the restoration. As a consequence, Alexander abandoned his promise to the Poles, and Kosciuszko was betrayed again. To Jefferson, Kosciuszko explained the delusion he experienced in Vienna:

> Tsar Alexander promised to enlarge the Duchy of Warsaw to the Dzwina and Dnieper, our former limits, but his ministers re-

fused to carry out his generous and magnanimous plans, and unfortunately the Kingdom of Poland is smaller by a good third than the Duchy of Warsaw...Tsar Alexander pledged me a constitutional government, liberal and independent, and even to enfranchise our unfortunate serfs and give them their land. That alone would have immortalized him, but it went up in smoke.[26]

From Vienna Kosciuszko traveled to Soleure, Switzerland, where the Peter Joseph Zeltner family settled. In 1801, Kosciuszko had joined the family at the Chateau de Berrville, near Fontainebleau. Zeltner then served as the first Swiss Minister to France. In time, Kosciuszko became an accepted member of the family and a favorite of the children. In Soleure now, Kosciuszko lived a very quiet life, removed from the politics of the day. He maintained his correspondence with Jefferson. Knowing that Kosciuszko had entered the twilight years, Jefferson in 1817 urged him to come to America, offering many possibilities. He suggested the Quaker city of Philadelphia, if Kosciuszko liked city life; but "if the country I would say come to Monticello, and be one of our family." Kosciuszko, however, objected in the past to living at Monticello "as incroaching on your independence." So, Jefferson suggested that he should "come and build a house, or rent a house so near as to dine with us every day." And Jefferson closed with these memorable words:

> ...think seriously of this, my dear friend, close a life of liberty in a land of liberty, come and lay your bones with mine in the Cemetery of Monticello. This too will be the best way of placing your funds and yourself together; and will enable me to give you in person those assurances of affectionate friendship and respect which must now be committed to the hazard of this letter.

Undoubtedly Kosciuszko was deeply touched by Jefferson's warm sentiments of friendship and his fervent pleas for joining him at Monticello. Kosciuszko, however, remained the great patriot that he was. In his final letter to Jefferson on 15 September 1817, he wrote:

> I greatly and with all my gratefulness appreciate your gracious invitation, but my Country lies heavy upon my heart, and there

are also my friends, my acquaintances, and sometimes I like to give them my advice. I am the only true Pole in Europe, all others are by circumstances subject to Different Powers.[27]

Kosciuszko found relief from his painful memories of the loss of Poland while riding horseback across the pleasant countryside around Soleure. On one occasion, he overextended himself and caught fever. After a brief illness, he died peacefully, aged 71, in the presence of the Zeltner family on 15 October 1817. A funeral service took place in the Catholic Church of Saints Ursus and Victor in Soleure, and his body was interred temporarily in a vault of the local Jesuit Church.[28]

On 29 October 1817, Francis Xavier Zeltner, Kosciuszko's host, informed Thomas Jefferson of the death of the general: "This great man who has honored me with his friendship and confidence for over twenty years retired two years ago to the bosom of my family where he hoped to pass his life, unless circumstances more favorable than he ventured to hope would allow the rebirth of his unhappy Country." Although Jefferson had earlier been informed of Kosciuszko's death by John Barnes, who read the announcement in newspapers, the former President answered Zeltner with a great tribute to Kosciuszko:

> To no country could that event be more afflicting nor to any individual more than to myself. I had enjoyed his intimate friendship and confidence for the last 20 years, & during the portion of that time which he past in this country, I had daily opportunities of observing personally the purity of his virtue, the benevolence of his heart, and his sincere devotion to the cause of liberty, his anterior services during our revolutionary war had been well known & acknowledged by all.[29]

After a career of brilliant performance, Kosciuszko lived out his life in seclusion; and in the words of American writer Israel Losey White, "leaving him a man without a country, a soldier of liberty without a battle-field, a liberator without an opportunity to benefit his fellow-men." Yet, his noble ideals inspired a nation to gain the freedom he so valiantly had fought for. In death, he returned to his beloved Poland. Kosciuszko's remains were moved to Krakow in 1818 and laid to rest in the Cathedral of Wawel Castle, among the kings and national heroes.[30]

To Kosciusko

Good Kosciusko, thy great name alone
Is a full harvest whence to reap high feeling;
It comes upon us like the glorious pealing
Of the wide spheres—an everlasting tone.
And now it tells me, that in worlds unknown,
The names of heroes, burst from clouds concealing,
And changed to harmonies, for ever stealing
Through cloudless blue, and round each silver throne.
It tells me too, that on a happy day,
When some good spirit walks upon the earth,
Thy name with Alfred's, and the great of yore
Gently commingling, gives tremendous birth
To a loud hymn, that sounds far, far away
To where the great God lives for evermore.

—JOHN KEATS

EPILOGUE

THE KOSCIUSZKO-CARTER
CONFRONTATION

GENERAL KOSCIUSZKO'S
MANOEUVRES OF HORSE ARTILLERY

KOSCIUSZKO'S ENDURING FAME

THE AMERICAN WILL
OF THADDEUS KOSCIUSZKO

IS THIS KOSCIUSZKO'S PISTOL ?

GENERAL THADDEUS KOSCIUSZKO
Painting from the Josef Grassi School. Courtesy of the Embassy
of the Republic of Poland, Washington, D.C.

EPILOGUE

The Kosciuszko – Carter Confrontation

Incident at a Court Martial
White Plains, New York
7 September 1778

1. *Background.*

In *General Horatio Gates, A Biography (1976),* author Paul David Nelson includes the accounts of two duels over a matter of personal honor between General Horatio Gates and his former adjutant general, Colonel James Wilkinson. At the first duel at York, Pennsylvania, in February 1778, no one was hurt. Later, in September, Wilkinson again challenged Gates over derogatory remarks that the general allegedly made about him. Gates asked his friend Colonel Thaddeus Kosciuszko to be his second. Wilkinson's second was John Church, son-in-law of General Philip Schuyler. Church also used the name of John Carter. The dueling pair met at Harrison, New York, 4 September 1778. Wilkinson fired three times and missed. Gates did not fire. The seconds stepped in and declared that honor had been upheld, and all shook hands. Nelson writes:

> Gates signed a paper, which Kosciuszko gave to Church, declaring that Wilkinson had "behaved as a gentleman" at York. But, when Colonel Wilkinson refused to deliver a similar statement about Gates, Kosciuszko demanded that Church return the one Gates had signed.

The matter escalated into a serious disagreement between Kosciuszko and Church.

2. Incident at the Court Martial.

Nelson describes the scene at the court martial of Major General Arthur St. Clair:

> Both Kosciuszko and Church had been summoned to testify at St. Clair's trial, and by unfortunate chance they appeared in court on the same day. The two men, by now furious with each other, came prepared. No sooner had they entered the room where the court was sitting than they came at each other with pistols and swords. Guards were summoned quickly to clear the room, and Church, a civilian, ran to his horse and quickly rode away to avoid prosecution for disturbing a military tribunal. Kosciuszko, instead of pursuing his opponent, swaggered about the room bragging about his prowess and magnifying his alleged victory over Church. No one else seemed impressed with the performance of either the young Pole or the other men involved.[1]

Historian Francis C. Kajencki was surprised and disturbed over Nelson's description of Kosciuszko's behavior since Kosciuszko always behaved with decorum and modesty. On this occasion, however, was he so emotionally aroused as to swagger and brag? Kajencki decided to get to the bottom of the episode.

3. Contact with Author Nelson.

Kajencki wrote Dr. Nelson at Berea College, Berea, Kentucky, on 30 August 1995. He pointed out that Kosciuszko's alleged behavior appeared to be out of character with his consistent modesty. Nelson answered in a letter of 11 September 1995. He agreed with Kajencki, saying, "I acquiesce to your judgment in saying that such behavior was uncharacteristic of Kosciuszko." Nelson's focus on an exception to Kosciuszko's otherwise exemplary character seems unusual. After all, Nelson wrote about Gates and makes only several brief references to Kosciuszko's service under the general. However, at the court martial Nelson portrays Kosciuszko as a bully and braggart.

Nelson's description of the confrontation at the court martial is so detailed that the information could come only from an eyewitness. Kajencki decided to examine the six publications cited by Nelson in support of the paragraph describing the incident.

They are listed below and in Note 20 of page 197 of *Horatio Gates, A Biography.** The first three works briefly mention the duel between Gates and Wilkinson but not the scene at the trial. James Ripley Jacobs in *Tarnished Warrior,* however, wrote of the court martial episode, as follows:

> Both Kosciuszko and Church took up the wrangle where their principals had left off. It concerned the bedeviling certificate. Daily their anger grew. When summoned to give testimony for St. Clair, they had scarcely entered the court room before they made for each other with sword and pistol. Some one yelled for the guard. When it came tumbling in, Church made for his horse and rode away like the wind; he was determined not to be taken in hand as a civilian for disturbing an army tribunal. Kosciuszko did not pursue; he gloated over his fanciful victory, making much of the ignominious flight of his enemy.[2]

How did Jacobs know that Kosciuszko "gloated" and made much of Church's flight? Perhaps a newspaper correspondent witnessed the confrontation, and his story was printed in the *New York Packet* and *Continental Journal and Weekly Advertiser.* Jacobs cites these papers in his Note 31, and Nelson does likewise in Note 20 of his book.

Kajencki obtained microfilm copies of the three issues of the *Packet* and the one of the *Continental Journal.* The latter newspaper in Boston merely reprinted the stories previously published in the *Packet.* The 24 September 1778 issue of the *Packet* published Kosciuszko's open letter to Mr. John Carter, in which Kosciuszko included the episode at the court martial:

> But it seems you thought it was necessary to fight me some way or other; and wisely judged that types were safe weapons; in

* a. *Magazine of American History*, VII (July 1881), p. 65, and VIII (May 1882), p. 368.
  b. Edmund Pendleton to William Wooford, 4 October 1778, in David John Mays, ed., *The Letters and Papers of Edmund Pendleton*, 1734-1803, Vol. 1.
  c. James Thacher, *A Military Journal During the American Revolutionary War*, p. 145.
  d. James Ripley Jacobs, *Tarnished Warrior: Major-General James Wilkinson*, pp. 57-58.
  e. *New York Packet* (Fishkill), 17 and 24 September, and 8 October 1778.
  f. *Continental Journal and Weekly Advertiser* (Boston), 12 November 1778.

this you discover a degree of cowardice, not indeed so great as when you drew your pistol upon me at the Court Martial, when I was unarmed, and when the appearance of a guard (by order of the court) to apprehend you as an assassin, and the indignant shouts of the spectators, put you to an ignominious flight.[3]

From the above account, Kajencki noted two facts: one, Carter drew his pistol and threatened Kosciuszko; two, Kosciuszko did not draw his pistol, assuming he had one, nor did he draw his sword.

Carter answered Kosciuszko in a letter published in the *Packet*, 8 October 1778. With respect to the court martial, Carter wrote the following:

Such is his representation of what passed at the Court-Martial a few days after, when meeting me (not unarmed, as he declares, but with his sword on) he became abusive, and kept his hand in his pocket as I supposed holding a pistol; I immediately drew one from my holsters and told him that if he made any attack upon me I would blow his brains out; the Court-Martial was diffused and ordered out a guard, and as I did not belong to the army preferred riding out rather than be taken into custody by the guard;...this he calls an ignominious flight.[4]

To Kajencki's surprise, the *New York Packet* did not publish any other account. Therefore, the information about the confrontation can be drawn only from the published letters of Carter and Kosciuszko. Carter disputed Kosciuszko's claim that he was unarmed. Carter said his opponent wore his sword, but he did not assert that Kosciuszko drew his sword and waved it menacingly. It was appropriate for Kosciuszko to wear his formal military uniform, with sword sheathed in a scabbard, at a formal court martial. The sword was an officer's item of dress.

Carter stated that he *assumed* Kosciuszko had a pistol hidden in his pocket. Carter grew fearful to the point that he whipped out his pistol and openly threatened to blow Kosciuszko's brains out. Carter's outburst alarmed the court martial board and the spectators, and the guard was called out to seize him. To avoid arrest, Carter fled.

The two accounts clearly show that only one weapon was displayed, Carter's pistol. Nevertheless, both Jacobs and Nelson transformed the confrontation into melodrama. Jacobs writes: "…they made for each other with sword and pistol." And Nelson multiplies the number of weapons, writing: "…they came at each other with pistols and swords." Both authors maligned the truth. Furthermore, Jacobs really did not know whether Kosciuszko "gloated on his fanciful victory." He was not there, and the *Packet* did not publish an eyewitness account. Nelson is even more offensive with his description (pulled out of thin air) that the Pole "swaggered about the room bragging about his prowess and magnifying his alleged victory over Church."

In his letter to Kajencki, Nelson said that he cannot find his notes to corroborate the basis of his account of the confrontation. "I am convinced that I did not make it up," he protested, "for it is a sort of aside that is neither here nor there for the story of Gates"! But, in fact, Nelson did make it up. Both Jacobs and Nelson slid from the level of careful and objective history to one of fiction writing. They gratuitously damaged Kosciuszko's sterling character.[5]

MANŒUVRES

OF

HORSE ARTILLERY,

BY

GENERAL KOSCIUSKO.

WRITTEN AT PARIS IN THE YEAR 1800,

AT THE REQUEST OF GENERAL WM. R. DAVIE,

THEN ENVOY FROM THE UNITED STATES TO FRANCE.

———

TRANSLATED, WITH NOTES AND DESCRIPTIVE PLATES,

BY JONATHAN WILLIAMS,

COL. COMDT. OF THE CORPS OF ENGINEERS, AND PRESIDENT
OF THE U. S. MILITARY PHILOSOPHICAL SOCIETY.

———

PUBLISHED BY DIRECTION OF THE SOCIETY.

———

LONDON:

RE-PRINTED FOR T. EGERTON, MILITARY LIBRARY,

NEAR WHITEHALL.

———

1809.

Title page of Thaddeus Kosciuszko's treatise, Manoeuvres of Horse
Artillery, written in French in 1800 and translated into English
by Colonel Jonathan Williams, Superintendent of the United States
Military Academy. Published in New York in 1808 and in London in
1809 (before the War of 1812), the Manoeuvres served as the "bible"
for the United States Army in organizing and employing artillery units
in the second war against Great Britain.

EPILOGUE

General Kosciuszko's
Manoeuvres of Horse Artillery

UNLIKE MANY OFFICERS of the American Revolution, General Thaddeus Kosciuszko wrote sparingly. Perhaps his limited knowledge of English inhibited him. To those Americans who knew French, he wrote them in that language, like his correspondence with Thomas Jefferson. Kosciuszko did not write his memoirs; he was too modest to talk about himself. However, he did compose a valuable treatise, *Manoeuvres of Horse Artillery,* which he wrote in 1800 at the request of General William R. Davie, the Pole's comrade-in-arms in the Southern Army. At the time of his request, Davie served as American envoy to France. Kosciuszko did the treatise in French and gave the completed work to Davie, who carried it with him to the United States. In 1808, Davie contacted the president of the United States Military Philosophical Society of West Point, Colonel Jonathan Williams. In addition to being president of the Society, Williams served as the Commandant of the Corps of Engineers (Superintendent of the United States Military Academy). Davie asked the colonel to have the manual translated into English and published.

In his letter to the Society, General Davie stressed the importance of Kosciuszko's work. He said that it was "compiled by an officer who was completely master of the subject and whose whole life has been devoted to military science. The publication would be of great importance to our country. It is perhaps the only treatise on this subject in the world."

Williams translated Kosciuszko's book, adding notes and descriptive plates, and Campbell & Mitchell of New York published the 77-page manual with eighteen plates in 1808. The publisher assessed the importance of the treatise in the Introduction:

> The regulations were drawn up by a man who rendered essential personal service in the days of difficulty and danger and no one can be more capable of instructing us; the performance has therefore the double merit of friendship in the motive and talents in the execution.[1]

Colonel Williams offered a copy of the published *Manoeuvres of Horse Artillery* to President Thomas Jefferson, who acknowledged the receipt on 28 October 1808: "I thank you for the copy of General Kosciuszko's treatise on the flying artillery. It is a branch of military art which I wish extremely to see understood here, to the height of the European level."[2]

At the time of the War of 1812 with Great Britain, the War Department introduced *Manoeuvres of Horse Artillery* to the United States Army for the training of artillery units. The government paid the sum of $200 to the Military Philosophical Society for the copyright to Kosciuszko's book. The Secretary of War ordered on 1 August 1812:

> The exercises for cannon and field ordnance and Manoeuvres for horse artillery, as altered from the Manual of General Kosciuszko and adapted to the service of the United States, are hereby ordered for the government of the several Corps of Artillery in the said service.

The value of Kosciuszko's "flying artillery" was recorded by Lieutenant William Edward Birkhimer in *Historical Sketch of the Organization, Administration, Materiel and Tactics of the Artillery, United States Army,* published in 1884:

> ...a second war with Great Britain found the United States without any recognized system of instruction save Baron Steuben's infantry regulations and a system of horse-artillery manoeuvres written at Paris in 1800 by General Kosciusko....War was declared

without the Government having at its disposal any system of manoeuvres for the artillery except that of Kosciusko.

Thus, Kosciuszko continued to be of service to his adopted country long after the American Revolution. In 1932, the *Field Artillery Journal* published the excellent essay of Elizabeth Camille Brink, "Kosciuszko—Forefather of American Artillery." She describes *Manoeuvres of Horse Artillery* and credits the Pole with the early establishment of the organization and employment of field artillery.[3]

EPILOGUE

Kosciuszko's Enduring Fame

Hero of Two Continents

DURING HIS SEVEN YEARS in the Continental Army, Thaddeus Kosciuszko served with many fine American officers, upon whom he made lasting impressions. These Americans passed on the name of Kosciuszko to their children and grandchildren, as well as to friends and associates. General John Paterson, for example, delighted in relating the story of Kosciuszko and Agrippa Hull to his grandchildren. It was natural, therefore, for great grandson Thomas Egleston to include the amusing incident in his biography, *The Life of John Paterson*. Before Paterson, General Samuel Parsons commanded West Point, and Kosciuszko roomed with the general and Dr. Timothy Dwight, army chaplain and distinguished theologian and scholar. Dwight became president of Yale College from 1795 to his death in 1817. The friendship between Kosciuszko and General Anthony White has been noted. White's grandson, Anthony Walton White Evans, wrote a *Memoir* about Kosciuszko for the Society of the Cincinnati in 1883. Evans included many detailed and heartwarming facts, because "as a boy, I heard his praises sung and accounts of his deeds in war related by my grandmother, who considered him second only to Washington." Evans expanded on his source of information: "I used to sit as a boy, and listen with rapt attention, while my grandmother (who was of the fiery, but kind and gentle blood of the Huguenots of South Carolina) told her personal reminiscences of Kosciuszko, tales oft repeated, and never got tired of it by relater or listener." Among the many of Evans' anecdotes, the one about Kosciuszko's horse reveals the Pole's altruistic character. In Switzerland, living with the Zeltner family in Soleure, Kosciuszko frequently rode into the countryside. He gave money to the poor peasantry and offered a couple of bottles of old wine for the sick. His horse became so used to his master's ways that the animal stopped upon the sight of a poor man. Evans related: "On one occasion he sent young Zeltner to carry a message, and told him to ride his horse; he soon found he could not get the horse past a poor man until he had opened his purse, and before he got home he found himself cleaned out of all his cash." There were earlier enthusiastic admirers of Kosciuszko, like John Armstrong, Otho Williams, Horatio Gates, and Thomas Jefferson. Many Revolutionary War officers, most of whom knew Kosciuszko personally, became members of Congress, governors, justices, and leaders in their communities. They kept the name of Kosciuszko alive in America. And with the additional fame springing from his courageous battles in Poland against rapacious neighbors, Kosciuszko gained worldwide acclaim. It was not his military performances so much as his altruistic character, like that of Cincinnatus and Timoleon, that endeared him to the people. Indeed, Kosciuszko became a hero of two continents.[1]

Among Kosciuszko's many American friends, his relationship with Thomas Jefferson is especially noteworthy. Their friendship had developed into mutual trust and respect. Prior to departing America in 1798, Kosciuszko designated Jefferson the executor of his will, in which he specified the proceeds of his American estate of some $12,000 be used for the emancipation of slaves and their education. On the recommendation of Jefferson, Kosciuszko entrusted the money to Philadelphia banker John Barnes. Through careful investment, Barnes increased the principal over the years. The annual interest provided Kosciuszko with his livelihood.

After completing his second term as President in 1809, Jefferson found himself financially embarrassed. He looked desperately for means to relieve himself of debt. Barnes suggested that Jefferson borrow from Kosciuszko's investment. Some $4500 in eight percent certificates were maturing, and Barnes would reinvest them again. He now proposed that Jefferson borrow this money at eight percent. Jefferson did. Some years later Jefferson repaid the loan.

So confident was Jefferson that Kosciuszko would agree that he took the money without asking permission first. But, on 26 February 1810, Jefferson wrote Kosciuszko in Paris, explaining his dire circumstances and the need to take some of his friend's investment. Kosciuszko responded with wholehearted approval, asking only that the interest be paid regularly. Nathan Schachner in his biography of Jefferson asks, "One wonders what would have happened had Kosciuszko refused?" The mutual trust between Jefferson and Kosciuszko was greater than that implied in Schachner's question. No one lost money and both gained. Kosciuszko was happy to help his friend.[2]

Modesty was a pronounced characteristic of Kosciuszko. How others saw and described him is perhaps the best definition of his character. General Greene could never praise Kosciuszko enough. Greene wrote General William Irvine: "What besides greatly distinguished him was an unparalleled modesty and entire unconsciousness of having done anything extraordinary. Never making a claim or pretension for himself and never omitting to distinguish and commend the merits of others."[3]

In addition to Greene and others of Kosciuszko's comrades-in-arms, Europeans lauded his character. In Paris, Kosciuszko met the Countess Wirydjana Kwilecka, who had come to assist the Polish exiles in organizing the Polish Legions during 1801–1803. She had married Count Antoni Kwilecki in 1789, but the union fell apart over differences of estate and money. While associating with the exiles, she became acquainted with Brigadier General Stanislaw Fiszer whom she later married in 1806. In Paris, the countess was also delighted to meet the world-renowned Pole. She was graceful in body and spirit, highly intelligent, and a witty conversationalist. Attracted by her charm, Kosciuszko frequently invited the countess to ride the carriage along the tree-lined boulevards of Paris. On one occasion, Kosciuszko suggested that they visit the American Minister, Robert R. Livingston. Arriving at the Minister's house, they found a ball in progress. Countess Kwilecka would not enter. She protested she was not dressed properly for the occasion. Kosciuszko tried to explain that the people at the ball were not French but Americans who were less formal. She would not budge. She told him to call on the Minister himself while she waited for him in the carriage. Kosciuszko pretended to agree. He entered, but shortly he emerged with a group of young Americans who "threatened" to carry her in if she did not accede to their invitation voluntarily. The countess conceded defeat and afterwards admitted she had a very enjoyable visit. In her *Memoirs,* she describes Kosciuszko:

> He was of middle stature, lean, with a soldierly bearing; his movements were quick. He was not talkative and spoke quietly, but laconically, sometimes with discreet irony, often in a jocular mood. Exacting but tender and jovial, he would not humble a person although he commanded obedience. Kosciuszko was very cordial among friends but reserved among strangers. If he felt hurt by something, he left the company without offering an explanation. However, he was not touchy. He never took offense at the innocent jokes of others or their inattention. Notwithstanding his modesty and plain appearance, he maintained a sense of personal dignity, and one glance of his eyes or ironic silence was sufficient to subdue those who dared to be too familiar.[4]

The Frenchman, Duke de Rochefoucault-Liancourt, reinforced Kosciuszko's characteristic of modesty. "Simple and modest," he said, "he even sheds tears of gratitude, and seems astonished at the homage he receives." The Duke's impression of him was that of a noble person:

> In a word, elevation of sentiment, grandeur, meekness, force, goodness, all that commands respect and homage, appear to me concentrated in this celebrated and interesting victim of misfortune and despotism. I have met few men whose appearance so much excited in me that effect.[5]

In France, the Marquis de Lafayette remained a staunch friend of Kosciuszko. Both being idealists, they easily coalesced into a firm and abiding friendship. Dr. Jules Cloquet, Lafayette's longtime physician, explained the Marquis' choice of friends. "Real friends are made not by wit or understanding," Cloquet wrote, "but by the qualities of the heart." Lafayette spent his winters in Paris, where he frequently associated with Kosciuszko and other Poles. The two Revolutionary War generals especially liked to attend American functions. To a friend, Lafayette said, "The American dinner, on which you congratulate me, was in every respect very agreeable, particularly by your friend. Three of my messmates were Kosciusko, Barbe-Marbois, and myself." Lafayette attended the celebration of Kosciuszko's patron saint sponsored by the Polish exiles. He came, he said, "in order not to deprive the Poles of that only occasion to show the world how much they honor their common country through him." Upon Kosciuszko's death, Lafayette attended the Memorial Mass for him in St. Roche Church in Paris, 31 October 1817. He joined with many Poles who had fought in the Polish Insurrection under Kosciuszko, and many Frenchmen from the American Revolutionary War. Lafayette came to the service to pay his respects to a man that he admired as "a perfect type of courage, honor, and Polish patriotism."[6]

Throughout his life, Lafayette treasured the memory of many friends. At his chateau in Lagrange, he displayed engraved or sketched portraits, including Kosciuszko's, and he surrounded himself with mementos. He placed his writing desk in the center of his spacious bedroom, where he faced a bust of George Washington modeled in clay by Houdon. Immediately above the bust, he hung a portrait of Kosciuszko "presented by the Poles to General Lafayette on the birth-day of that illustrious defender of Polish patriotism." His bedroom looked like an art gallery. He was proud to display a "large frame containing a vignette representing the titular angel of Poland in prayer, with these words written underneath—'Homage of Gratitude,' followed by the signatures of 75 Poles who presented the vignette to Lafayette."[7]

Lafayette, indeed, maintained cordial relations with the

Polish exiles. He admired and respected these former officers in Kosciuszko's Army of Insurrection for their courage, and they responded to his warm feelings. At Lagrange, Lafayette displayed American and Polish flags. His wardrobe included a complete uniform of a grenadier of the Warsaw National Guard, presented by the Poles, and which Lafayette frequently wore. On one occasion he personally conducted a lottery to raise funds for a Polish cause in 1831. A celebrated French marine artist created a painting of an African landscape with a cloudy and stormy sky. He sent it to Lafayette with the request that the marquis raffle it off, "the amount of which was to be transmitted to the noble sons of Poland." Lafayette seized the opportunity of doing a good deed. Cloquet wrote: "Lafayette himself undertook to write the lottery tickets, which he soon disposed of among his friends, and the profits of which exceeded even his hopes. The money was sent to the Polish committee." Lafayette's generous character brought him great respect and love from the people. When he died in Paris on 20 May 1834, the whole nation mourned his passing, and the Poles lost a great friend. Among the eight pall bearers at the funeral, General Ostrowski represented Poland.[8]

In the United States perhaps the first visible tribute to Kosciuszko occurred at West Point. In 1802, during the Presidency of Thomas Jefferson, the federal government established the United States Military Academy. Although it was initially set up to train army engineers, the academy developed into a full-fledged military school. Living in the environment of Kosciuszko's fortifications, the cadets undoubtedly felt a kinship with that engineer, and they decided to honor his memory. Cadet S. J. Linden was the first to suggest a monument in 1825. To pay for the estimated cost of $5000, the Corps of Cadets voluntarily taxed itself. Each cadet contributed twenty-five cents per month from his pay. The cadets offered a prize of $50 or a gold medal of that value for the best design. By a happy coincidence, John H. B. Latrobe, former cadet of the Class of 1822, won the competition. He chose the prize of a gold medal that was struck at the United States Mint in Philadelphia.[9]

KOSCIUSZKO AT WEST POINT

Designed by Cadet John H. Latrobe, USMA Class of 1822, the monument was erected by the Corps of Cadets in 1828 to honor the Revolutionary War patriot. Serving as military engineer in the period 1778-1780, Kosciuszko made West Point over into an impregnable fortress on the Hudson River.

The statue atop the monument was added in 1913 by Polish American patriotic organizations. (U.S. Army photo)

Latrobe's design called for a slender column atop a square monument modeled after the Grecian school. The column is simple, reflecting the pure character of Kosciuszko; no embellishing was necessary. Furthermore, the column was patterned after those of the celebrated Doric Temple at Corinth. The stone was New York white marble. Latrobe provided drawings and instructions to Cadet J.S. Thompson, Chairman of the Committee on the Kosciuszko Monument. The proposed site of Kosciuszko's Garden was changed to a more conspicuous location, atop the parapet of Fort Clinton at the bend of the river. John Frazer made the pedestal and shaft, and Robert Eberhardt Schmidt von der Launitz executed the sculptured portions.[10]

The cadets dedicated the cornerstone on 4 July 1828. Cadet Charles Petigru of South Carolina delivered a stirring oration, in which he reminded the Corps of the attributes of Kosciuszko that prompted the erection of the monument. Petigru called him "a leader whose name, head and heart inspired confidence," and he praised the Pole's altruistic spirit: "He was pouring out his generous blood and wearing away the flower of his youth for the attainment of blessings of which neither himself nor any to whom he was related would ever partake." The orator succinctly described the honored general: "The history of the life of Kosciuszko is his proudest eulogium." Petigru was a member of the Class of 1829. Three famous Confederate generals of the American Civil War also were members of this Class: Robert E. Lee, Joseph E. Johnston, and Theophilus H. Holmes.

Following the laying of the cornerstone, the Cadet Committee wrote General Joseph G. Swift, Chief of Engineers, to resolve a matter of taste. On behalf of the Corps of Cadets, the committee of Charles Mason, Robert E. Lee, John Mackay, Charles Petigru, and William E. Bassinger asked the general whether the name Kosciuszko should be inscribed on the monument in bronze letters or be cut squarely into the marble. Builder Frazer advised inscribing the name on the marble for its elegant simplicity and permanence. General Swift answered: "According to my taste a legend upon a monumental stone should be plainly & deeply engraved into the stone & would be most durable cut prismatically & preferable to any wrought in bronze relief." The cadets adopted General Swift's recommendation. Erected later that year, the monument became a favorite spot for the gathering of cadets. Upper Classmen met there to sing songs and to discuss current events. During summer months generations of cadets in old Camp Clinton spent evenings sitting at the base of the monument. Visitors, too, admired the monument, when they stayed at the old West Point Hotel, located a short distance west and near the present location of Battle Monument. One must admire the patriotism of the cadets in the 1820 decade. They displayed their admiration and respect for Thaddeus Kosciuszko and his love and dedication to American independence. Although many monuments in the United States were subsequently erected in honor of Kosciuszko, the one at West Point undoubtedly stands preeminent.[11]

Kosciuszko also made his impression on Americans in unobtrusive ways. During the years he lived in America, he gained a reputation as an occasional portrait artist. He loved to sketch for relaxation. The one of Brigadier General Enoch Poor came about in an unusual way. Kosciuszko knew Poor from Fort Ticonderoga and Saratoga, where the general's brigade served. On one occasion Kosciuszko attended services at a Protestant church from a sense of respect and duty. Poor was there, too. As a Roman Catholic, the Pole did not feel inclined to follow the service. Instead, he took a hymn book and on the fly leaf sketched Poor, who sat in range. The writer of this story said that Kosciuszko preferred to sketch Poor "rather than listen to heretical doctrine." The sketch served a fortuitous purpose. In 1885, James E. Kelly, sculptor of the National Monument at Monmouth, New Jersey, sought the portraits of the generals who fought in the battle there during the American Revolution. No portrait of Enoch Poor was known to exist, except Kosciuszko's sketch on the hymn book. Miecislaus Haiman shows a likeness of Poor in *Kosciuszko in the American Revolution.*[12]

During Kosciuszko's visit to the United States in 1797–1798,

Thomas Jefferson

A Philosopher a Patriote and a Friend

Dessine par son Ami Tadée Kosciuszko

Et Gravé par Mr. Sokolnicki

Thaddeus Kosciuszko's painting of Vice President Thomas Jefferson in 1798. Kosciuszko's compatriot in Paris, Michal Sokolnicki, made an engraving from which the picture shown is a rare copy. Kosciuszko created the portrait in Philadelphia before his departure for France on a secret mission set up by Jefferson.(The Mabel Brady Garvan Collection, Yale University Art Gallery, New Haven, Connecticut)

and especially his residency in Philadelphia, the Pole frequently met with Thomas Jefferson. The Virginian was Vice-President, and Philadelphia served as the seat of the government at the time. Kosciuszko painted a water-color of Jefferson, aged fifty-five, as a token of their friendship. It was a caricature of Jefferson. When Kosciuszko departed on his secret mission to France, he took the painting with him. In Paris, Kosciuszko asked his compatriot, General Michal Sokolnicki, to make an engraving and prints. Alfred L. Bush believes that "the distortions of his image of Jefferson seem more a result of exaggerations in the transcription of it into the acquatint by Sokolnicki rather than the inferiority of the original image." Jefferson's friend William Thornton did not like the portrait. He believed that Kosciuszko did Jefferson an injustice. In July 1816, Thornton wrote Jefferson, "Nothing can be so bad, and when I saw it, I did not wonder that he lost Poland...."[13]

In addition to his most frequent caller Jefferson, Kosciuszko greeted other friends and admirers at the boarding house on Third Street. Some were young ladies who sought to have their portraits sketched by the world-renowned warrior. Upon Kosciuszko's secret departure from America, the Federalist press accused him of turning against America once he reached French soil. The editor of *Gazette of the United States* railed against Kosciuszko: "It is understood, however, that these amiable daughters of Columbia are witnesses of his clandestine exit from this country, and hearing of his ungrateful expressions and conduct in France, are determined with a spirit as patriotic as they are amiable, to consign to the flames *mementos* of a man who has practised upon them as well as their country the lowest deceptions." Perhaps the editor exaggerated the reaction of the young ladies.[14]

One of the young ladies, who did not "consign to the flames" her water-color drawing by Kosciuszko, was Lucretia Adelaide Pollock, daughter of Oliver Pollock, Esquire, of Carlisle, Pennsylvania. The father had distinguished himself in the American Revolution for zeal and services while a resident of New Orleans. The drawing of Lucretia is a profile sketch of a young face outlined in pencil and colored with a brush. She died in her twentieth year in Philadelphia, March 1804. The Pollock family treasured Kosciuszko's painting and included its photo in a family genealogy that was published in *Watson's Annals of Philadelphia*.[15]

As the nineteenth century advanced, the Americans who were most conscious of Kosciuszko passed on. Before the memory of Kosciuszko could fade, however, millions of new admirers appeared. These were Polish immigrants who left their oppressed land around the turn of the century and sought freedom and opportunity in a dynamically-growing country. They were well aware of Kosciuszko's role in Poland and admired him for his gallant fight to restore the freedom of their country. They were less knowledgeable of Kosciuszko's role in America. However, they were delighted to learn the extent of their hero's contribution to the independence of their adopted country.

The Poles' pride in Kosciuszko found new manifestations in America. They named their fraternal, social, and political societies after him (and his contemporary Casimir Pulaski). The more lasting expression of their pride resulted in the erection of numerous monuments throughout the United States, but principally in the East and Midwest, where Polish Americans settled in large numbers. Perhaps one of the first monuments erected through private donations of Polish Americans was dedicated in Perth, Amboy, New Jersey, in 1894. Others followed in quick succession: Cleveland, Ohio, and Chicago, Illinois, in 1904. The imposing and equestrian monument in Chicago was first placed in Humboldt Park, an area heavily populated by Poles. As a result of demographic changes, however, the city moved the monument to a more suitable location on Solidarity Drive near the Adler Planetarium. In 1905, the equestrian statue of Kosciuszko graced a public park in Milwaukee, Wisconsin. Led by the Polish National Alliance of the United States and other fraternal organizations, the Poles erected a beautiful monument in Washington, D. C. in 1910. With the approval of the federal government, it was placed in Lafayette Park, opposite the White House. A lifelike figure of Kosciuszko in Revolutionary War uniform stands atop the monument. Sculptor Antoni Popiel designed and executed the metal statuary. The monument is often the site for patriotic observances. The proud Poles of Yonkers, New York, displayed their reverence for Kosciuszko with a stone monument in 1912. At West Point, the Polish clergy and laity offered to add an Antoni Popiel statue to the column of the monument. The Secretary of War approved the plan on 19 July 1912, and the statuary was unveiled in a ceremony on 1 September 1913.* In 1926, the Polish community of Boston erected a monument in the heart of Yankee land—a fitting tribute, for Kosciuszko always prided himself on having many Yankee friends and called himself "more than half a Yankee."

In 1936, Polish Americans of Albany, Schenectady, Amsterdam, Troy, Cohoes, Watervliet, and surrounding communities erected a handsome monument of granite at Bemis Heights at the site of the decisive Battle of Saratoga. These New York compatriots of Kosciuszko were not affluent. Still their ardor motivated them to make small but numerous donations, despite the crushing weight of the Great Depression. In 1996, their descendants met at Saratoga National Historical Park to observe the sixtieth anniversary of the monument on September 28, and the next day they celebrated the event with a grand banquet in Schenectady. The numerous monuments in honor of General Thaddeus Kosciuszko undoubtedly will keep his accomplishments alive. Indeed, first and second-generation Polish Americans set a remarkable record.[16]

The name of Kosciuszko was not always known to Americans, even within a relatively short distance of a community named "Kosciusko." In Central Mississippi, William Dodd, the first representative from the area to the State Legislature, named the seat of Attala County in honor of Kosciuszko in 1833. Dodd's grandfather had served in the Revolutionary War and came home with praise for the Polish engineer. Years later an incoming cadet from Winona, Mississippi, became the roommate of the author.

---

* Today it seems the Kosciuszko statuary always stood atop the monument.

239

Russell Jackson Smith did not know who Kosciuszko was until he arrived at West Point. Jack said that as a high school senior in Winona he and a group of classmates used to drive the fifty miles to Kosciusko to attend dances. He explained that he thought Kosciusko was an old Indian name. In 1984, the town of Kosciusko, population 7000, opened the Kosciusko Information Center in honor of the Revolutionary War general. Located on the Natchez Trace Parkway, the Center soon became a favorite stopping place for tourists. By 1994, the yearly average of visitors reached nearly 43,000, and they came from all fifty states and eighty-six foreign countries.[17]

Other countries besides the United States and Poland honor the name of Kosciuszko. In 1838, Polish world-traveler, geologist, and researcher Pawel Edmund Strzelecki sailed across the Pacific Ocean, stopping to carry on research on Marquesas Islands, Hawaii, Tahiti, Tonga, New Zealand, and Australia. In 1840, he scaled the highest peak in the Australian Alps (he believed), located in New South Wales, and named it Mount Kosciusko (elevation 7310 feet). As a further tribute to Kosciuszko, the Australian government set aside a vast tract of land near the mount and named it Kosciusko National Park. Here at home, Polish geographer Stefan Jarosz conducted research on the Alaskan island of Kosciusko in the years 1935–1937. The island lies in the Alexander Archipelago and south of the capital Juneau. Jarosz produced a documentary film of the forests and geography of the island. (It is not known whether Jarosz or someone else named the island.)[18]

In the opinion of some writers, Kosciuszko should stand shoulder to shoulder with the famous generals in United States history. Ernest L. Cuneo, editor-at-large of *The Saturday Evening Post*, observed in a Bicentennial tribute: "It is one of the ironies of history that had General Thaddeus Kosciuszko been born with a name easily pronounced as Generals Robert E. Lee, Ulysses Simpson Grant or John J. Pershing, his name would resound throughout Western civilization as one of the foremost military geniuses of all time." Some of Kosciuszko's contemporary officers

MONUMENT IN HONOR OF
THADDEUS KOSCIUSZKO AT SARATOGA.

*The engineer chose the blocking position of Bemis Heights on
the Hudson River and fortified it into a bastion that insured
the decisive victory over the British Army under General John
Burgoyne in 1777. Erected in 1936 by Kosciuszko's compatriots from Albany, New York and the surrounding communities.
(Photo by the author, 16 September 1995).*

Bronze Plaque in the Sally port of Fort Ticonderoga in honor of the great men of its history. (Photo by the author, 17 September 1995).

1776   1929

THROUGH THIS ENTRANCE TO THE PLACE D'ARMES
OF THE FORT HAVE PASSED

George Washington	Ethan Allen
Benjamin Franklin	Seth Warner
Benedict Arnold	Major Robert Rogers
Horatio Gates	The Marquis de Montcalm
Anthony Wayne	The Duc de Lewis
Arthur St. Clair	Sir Jeffrey Amherst
Henry Knox	Sir Guy Carleton
Philip Schuyler	Major John Andre
Richard Montgomery	Sir John Burgoyne

Thaddeus Kosciusko

AND A HOST OF OTHER GREAT MEN OF OUR HISTORY
YOU WHO TREAD IN THEIR FOOTSTEPS REMEMBER
THEIR GLORY

DONOR
A. Stanley Miller

like Major William Jackson, aide-de-camp to General Washington, called him "Kosci."[19]

Despite his assumed handicap, Kosciuszko on occasion has joined an elite group of Americans. In 1929, A. Stanley Miller donated a bronze plaque to the restored Fort Ticonderoga. The plaque, mounted on a wall of the sally port, lists the names of nineteen famous individuals associated with the fort and includes French, British, American, and Thaddeus Kosciuszko, the engineer. Significantly, the name of Colonel Jeduthan Baldwin, chief engineer, is not listed, notwithstanding that the Fort Ticonderoga Association is partial to Baldwin. When the author first contacted Fort Ticonderoga in August 1995, he spoke by phone with Bruce Moseley, curator of the museum. The author explained that he planned to visit the fort in pursuit of his research on Thaddeus Kosciuszko. Moseley was quick to point out that Colonel Baldwin was the chief engineer. Despite the Association's loyalty to Baldwin, the chief engineer was not a professional, and he lacked tactical and strategic competence. Even the modest Kosciuszko told General Gates privately that Baldwin was fond of erecting blockhouses in the most improper places.[20]

The National Park Service has been fair and objective in portraying Kosciuszko's key roles, both at Saratoga National Historical Park, New York, and Ninety-Six National Historic Site, South Carolina. The Superintendent of the Saratoga Park displays in the Visitors Center a circular grouping of portraits of the key officers of the battles. Painted on aged wood, the display features striking likenesses of Generals Horatio Gates, Philip P. Schuyler, Benedict Arnold, John Burgoyne, Simon Fraser, Baron von Riedesel, Colonels Daniel Morgan and Thaddeus Kosciuszko. The engineer is shown prominently.

In American and English literature, too, Kosciuszko's name became lastingly recorded. Revolutionary War poet Joel Barlow associated Kosciuszko with Saratoga in lyrical expression:

> *But on the centre swells the heaviest charge*
> *The squares develop and the lines enlarge.*

> *Here Kosciuszko's mantling works conceal'd*
> *His batteries mute, but soon to scour the field.*[21]

In 1832, Samuel Lorenzo Knapp introduced Kosciuszko into the American novel. In *The Polish Chiefs, An Historical Romance*, Knapp centered his narrative around Kosciuszko and Casimir Pulaski. More recently, in 1933, novelist Kenneth Roberts included Kosciuszko in *Rabble in Arms, A Chronicle of Arundel and the Burgoyne Invasion*.

Kosciuszko appeared first in American literature as a result of his service in the American Revolution. Subsequently, Kosciuszko's brilliant generalship and valiant stand in Poland against the invading hordes of Russians and Prussians captured the attention of Europe and America. The English literati, in particular, began to extol his patriotism in poems and novels. Idealist and Romantic poet John Keats, for example, sang his praises in "To Kosciusko" and "Sleep and Poetry," and poets Thomas Campbell and Leigh Hunt likewise honored Kosciuszko. Similarly, Jane Porter's novel *Thaddeus of Warsaw* helped to establish the name of Kosciuszko. The novel attracted a very wide readership in England and the United States.

American poet Amy Lowell, commenting on John Keats' admiration for Kosciuszko, wrote in her 1925 biography *John Keats*:

> The Polish patriot, who had fought for the integrity of his own country against a rapacious Russia in vain...and [had] headed another national movement against Russia and Prussia combined, who had been defeated, wounded, and thrust into prison, and also, in the beginning of his career, gone to America and joined the revolutionary army there. Such a man could not fail of becoming an idolized hero in the eyes of the Liberals of the period.[22]

Francis E. Zapatka, Professor of Literature at American University, in "Kosciuszko and Keats" observes that the association Keats made between Kosciuszko and Alfred the Great was remarkably fitting. Zapatka points to the ardent patriotism of the two men who defended their countries against foreigners. In the American Revolution, Kosciuszko built fortifications, and in

THADDEUS KOSCIUSZKO BRIDGE. On Interstate Highway 87, it spans the Mohawk River nine miles north of Albany, New York. The Mohawk empties into the Hudson River, four miles to the east (right). General Philip Schuyler's Army retreated along the Hudson before General Burgoyne's British Army, taking up positions on Van Schaick's Island. Here Kosciuszko threw up fortifications to protect the Americans in August 1777. (Photo by the author, 21 September 1996).

England Alfred erected coastal defenses against enemy invasion. Furthermore, both men were compassionate to the poor and personally simple and kind. "So in these lines from 'Sleep and Poetry' and in the sonnet 'To Kosciusko,'" Zapatka concludes, "John Keats one of the greatest English poets writes of one of the greatest Poles in connection with one of the greatest English Kings."[23]

Numerous short biographical accounts of Kosciuszko are found in many publications, augmented by Monica Gardner's biography in 1920. Nevertheless, Miecislaus Haiman wrote the Pole's first scholarly and military biography in 1943.

Had Thaddeus Kosciuszko remained in the United States and made it his adopted home in 1798, his estate very likely would have survived to become a national shrine today. John Armstrong, residing on the Hudson River at Red Hook, New York, at the time, looked over likely land for his friend to purchase near the battle-field of Saratoga. He urged Kosciuszko to come and see for himself. But Kosciuszko could not act immediately for lack of money. When the federal government paid him some $19,000 in back pay, Kosciuszko could then afford to settle in the United States. Events in Europe, however, interfered with his plans. Vice President Thomas Jefferson asked him to carry out a secret diplomatic mission to France, and the patriotic Kosciuszko responded at once. He placed service to country above personal interest. The opportunity for a surviving estate here disappeared, but not completely.

Some 170 years later, an old and abandoned brick building at 301 Pine Street in Philadelphia was scheduled to be demolished. Philadelphia historian Edward Pinkowski discovered the building to be the same dwelling occupied by General Kosciuszko in 1797–1798. Pinkowski got the attention of Philadelphia industrialist Edward J. Piszek who purchased the property in 1970. Piszek offered to give it to the federal government if the National Park Service would renovate and maintain it as a national historic shrine. The National Park Service balked, and there followed a determined campaign of education, persuasion, and even Senate Committee hearings. The Polish American community won. In 1972, Congress passed a law accepting Piszek's gift and appropriating money for the restoration and maintenance of the building as the "Thaddeus Kosciuszko National Memorial."

During the planning for the work of restoration, the National Park Service determined that the adjoining twin house on Third Street was needed to provide necessary facilities for the Memorial. Without hesitation, donor Piszek bought the twin house and added it to his gift. The restoration was completed and dedicated on 4 February 1976, the 230th anniversary of Kosciuszko's birth. The event coincided with the Bicentennial of the American Revolution. The Thaddeus Kosciuszko National Memorial became another of the historical shrines of Independence National Historical Park.[24]

In published historical works by Americans, Thaddeus

Dual Portrait Painting of
GENERALS THADDEUS KOSCIUSZKO
and CASIMIR PULASKI

*Created by Polish-born artist Wanda de Turczynowicz
for the American Bicentennial Exhibit of the General
Casimir Pulaski Society of El Paso, Texas held in the Main
Public Library during October 1976.*

Kosciuszko has received unbiased treatment from most authors. To name two, Christopher Ward in *The War of the Revolution* and Lynn Montross, *The Story of the Continental Army*. These books were published about mid-twentieth century and perhaps represent the high-water mark of American historical objectivity. Toward the end of this century, some American historians found Kosciuszko's performance in the American Revolution to be less significant than that of prior colleagues. They brushed him off with a sentence or ignored him entirely. John S. Pancake, for instance, in describing how American patriots strove to impede Burgoyne's advance along Wood Creek during the Saratoga campaign, paints a picture of "a thousand axes" felling trees along the route of march and burying Kosciuszko in the process. In contrast stands the fair and even laudatory accomplishments of Kosciuszko by Dave Richard Palmer in his masterful book *The River and the Rock: The History of Fortress West Point, 1775– 1783,* published in 1969. Palmer's book is replete with facts and incisive evaluations of Kosciuszko's engineering work.

Some producers of television film demonstrated bias in portraying the American Revolution. Greystone Communications of Valley Village, California, produced a six-hour documentary film, *The American Revolution.* Written and produced by Don Cambou, the film was telecast on the Arts & Entertainment Network in July 1995. Not once was Thaddeus Kosciuszko, the architect of Fortress West Point, mentioned, even though the producer included a comprehensive coverage of the importance and construction of the fortress. The author wrote the historian/narrator of the segment on West Point, telling him of his deep disappointment that the historian had ignored Kosciuszko. The historian answered immediately that he, too, was disappointed, because he had mentioned the name of Kosciuszko more than once. He said that evidently the writer/producer had cut out the mention of Kosciuszko during the editing of the film footage in the cutting room.

Five months after the showing of Cambou's film, Real TV of Los Angeles, California, produced a six-hour documentary film likewise on the American Revolution. Entitled *The Revolutionary War,* the film was produced and directed by Carol L. Fleisher and telecast on The Learning Channel in November 1995. In contrast to Cambou's film, Fleisher included a segment that highlights Tadeusz Kosciuszko. The segment relates to General Nathanael Greene's race to the Dan River and the escape of the Americans from the British across the river on Kosciuszko's flotilla of boats. Charles Kuralt narrates the segment superbly.

It seems conclusive that the respect, gratitude, and love for Kosciuszko from Americans of an earlier day, coupled with the pride and reverence demonstrated by Polish Americans, should insure the enduring fame of the hero of two continents.

> *But do not trample upon the altars of the past,*
> *Even though you may more perfect ones erect;*
> *Upon them holy flames are still glowing*
> *And you owe them your reverence.*
>
> —ADAM ASNYK

EPILOGUE

The American Will
of Thaddeus Kosciuszko

BY JAMES S. PULA

*"THE AMERICAN WILL of Thaddeus Kosciuszko," published
in Polish American Studies, Vol. XXXIV, No. 1 (Spring 1977), is
republished herein with the permission and courtesy of James
S. Pula, author and editor.*

*One of the great legacies of Thaddeus Kosciuszko's service in
the American Revolution is his remarkable will of 5 May 1798
in which he left the proceeds for the emancipation and education of slaves. Unfortunately, the will never served its intended
purpose, due to delays in execution, conflicting wills made in
Europe, and the claims of kinfolk. The litigation continued into
the 1850 decade when the United States Supreme Court ruled
in favor of the relatives. As the author of the essay concludes,
"Clearly the ideal that motivated Kosciuszko's American will
survived the legal complications which struck it down."*

LIEUTENANT HENRY MUHLENBERG stood atop the parapet of
Fort Mifflin scrutinizing the diminutive sailing vessel that glided
upriver toward Philadelphia. It was the eighteenth of August,
1797. As the ship pulled abreast of the fort, Lieutenant Muhlenberg
shouted a command. Cannons flamed and roared, barking forth
a traditional salute of thirteen guns to honor a visiting foreign

dignitary. The little ship turned slowly, heading for its moorings along a dock packed tightly with politicians and well-wishers. Resounding cheers of "Long Live Kosciuszko!" echoed across the water.[1]

The hero of democratic revolutions on two continents, Thaddeus Kosciuszko had only recently been released from the prisons of Tsarist Russia where he had been confined for his efforts to free Poland from her neighbor's oppression. A source of suspicion among those who feared a new Polish uprising, Kosciuszko hoped to mislead his enemies into thinking that he planned to retire in the New World. Practical considerations also played a part in the decision to return to America. Aside from a wish to see again his colleagues in the Revolution, Kosciuszko hoped to improve his financial position by collecting debts owed him by the United States government. Once these obligations were settled, he planned to invest his funds to yield a steady, if modest, income to support his activities in Europe, chief among them the struggle for the independence of Poland.

Praised and applauded by the citizens of Philadelphia from the moment of arrival, Kosciuszko soon began to receive a flood of warm, congratulatory correspondence from friends and admirers. It was a tribute to the emerging mystique of the Revolution and to the esteem in which the young nation held him that he overcame for a moment the rising tide of factional dispute between Federalists and Republicans. He was not distracted, however, from the settlement of his financial affairs which centered upon money owed him for services in the Revolution. This debt was acknowledged by an Act of Congress which, in 1799, directed the Secretary of the Treasury to pay Kosciuszko $12,280.54, plus interest from January 1, 1793 to December 31, 1797.[2] During his absence in

---

[1] On Kosciuszko's life after the Revolution see Miecislaus Haiman, *Kosciuszko Leader and Exile* (New York: Polish Institute of Arts and Sciences in America, 1946), and other popular biographies.

[2] *Cases Argued and Decided in the Supreme Court of the United States* (Rochester, N.Y.: The Lawyer's Co-operative Publishing Company, 1926), Lawyer's edition, Book 14 Howard, 478. Hereafter cited as 14 Howard 478, etc.

Europe, one of Kosciuszko's most frequent correspondents had been Thomas Jefferson, and, not surprisingly, he turned to the Virginian for advice on investment opportunities. At the suggestion of his friend, Kosciuszko chose John Barnes, Jefferson's private banker, as his own advisor. Barnes invested $12,000 of the general's money in thirty shares of the Bank of Pennsylvania bearing an annual interest rate of eight percent.

Some years later, possibly in anticipation of the banking crisis of 1814, Jefferson sold the Pennsylvania bank stock and reinvested it in a government subscription loan at six percent. Historians have considered this a hedge against a faltering economy. There is, however, another explanation—the war with England, which put the government badly in need of funds. More probably, Jefferson sought to aid the United States Treasury than to protect Kosciuszko's investment. A letter from Jefferson to H.E.M. de Politica, the Russian Minister in Washington, dated May 27, 1819, offers some evidence on this point. In it, Jefferson cites his own "situation in the interior of the country" as the reason for suggesting that Barnes handle Kosciuszko's finances. He also states that it was he, Jefferson, who withdrew the money from the Bank of Pennsylvania and lent it to the Federal Treasury during the war.[3] Regardless, it is to the credit of Jefferson and Barnes that by the time of Kosciuszko's death in 1817, the original investment had grown to well over $17,000, exclusive of the interest which had been paid to him in Europe.[4]

Kosciuszko also realized the need to plan the disposition of his American property in the event of death. He wrote Jefferson about a proposed will in April 1798, and on May 5, 1798, he penned the final version of the document with John Barnes and John Dawson serving as witnesses. Jefferson was named executor. The text of the final declaration reads as follows:

> I, Thaddeus Kosciuszko, being just in my departure from America do hereby declare and direct that should I make no other

[3] 14 Howard 478.
[4] *Ibid.*

testamentary disposition of my property in the United States, I hereby authorize my friend Thomas Jefferson to employ the whole thereof in purchasing Negroes from among his own or any others and giving them Liberty in my name, in giving them an education in trades or otherwise and in having them instructed for their new condition in the duties of morality which may make them good neighbors good fathers or mothers, husbands, or wives and in their duties as citizens teaching them to be defenders of their Liberty and Country and of the good order of society and in whatsoever may make them happy and useful, and I make the said Thomas Jefferson my executor of this.[5]

Sentiments similar to these had prompted Jefferson earlier in the year to write General Horatio Gates: "...I see him [Kosciuszko] often, and with great pleasure mixed with commiseration. He is as pure a son of liberty as I have ever known, and of that liberty which is to go to all, and not to the few or the rich alone."[6]

Twenty years later, upon learning of the death of Kosciuszko, Jefferson faced the problem of submitting the will to probate. To a man of Jefferson's age this was no small problem, for, if conflicting claims surfaced, the litigation might go on for many years. Believing himself too old to complete the necessary work, Jefferson asked John Hartwell Cocke to act as executor instead. Cocke declined, citing , the great difficulties he would encounter in carrying out the provisions of the will. He noted that few schools then accepted blacks, and that the popular prejudices regarding the education of blacks might harm his (Cocke's) standing among his neighbors. Jefferson then submitted the will to the Circuit Court of Albemarle, Virginia, on May 12, 1821. The Court, in turn, delegated the handling of the estate to Benjamin L. Lear of

[5] The author wishes to thank Ms. Sarah Ringer of the University of Virginia Library and Mr. Shelby J. Marshall of the Circuit Court for Albemarle County, Virginia, for providing him with a copy of the original Kosciuszko will and allowing him to reproduce it here in its entirety.

[6] Jefferson to Gates, February 21, 1798, Jefferson Papers, Manuscript division, Library of Congress, quoted by Janina W. Hoskins, "'A Lesson Which All Our Countrymen Should Study: Jefferson Views Poland," *The Quarterly Journal of the Library of Congress,* 33, No. 1 (January 1933), 40-41, 46.

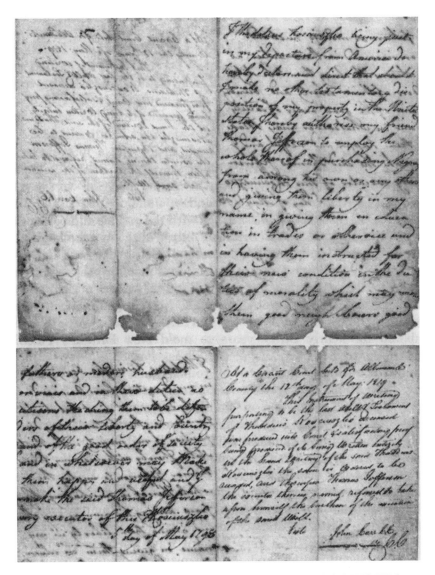

THE "AMERICAN WILL" OF THADDEUS KOSCIUSZKO
*From the manuscript copy deposited with the Circuit Court
of Albemarle County, Virginia.*

Washington, D.C. At the further request of Jefferson, William Wirt, the Attorney General of the United States, acted as counsel for the trust until his death in 1834.[7]

Following his examination of the will, Lear suggested that the funds be utilized to endow "The Kosciuszko School" then being planned by the African Education Society of New Jersey. In view of the difficulties he encountered with the prevailing prejudices in Virginia, Jefferson agreed to this alternative plan. The subsequent appearance of other claimants to the Kosciuszko estate, however, led to prolonged legal actions which prevented the implementation of Lear's proposal. The problem arose from the fact that Kosciuszko subsequently had authorized three additional wills. On June 28, 1806, he concluded a testament in Paris in which he charged his American estate with the payment of a legacy of $3,704 to Kosciuszko Armstrong, the son of a friend. A third will, dated at Soleure, Switzerland, on June 4, 1816, disposed of Kosciuszko's French properties. His final will, filed at Soleure on October 10, 1817, bequeathed specific legacies from funds invested in Switzerland and England, as well as providing for the bequest of his personal property in Switzerland to Mr. and Mrs. Zeltner, in whose home he resided. Thus, upon Kosciuszko's death, several conflicting claims were entered on behalf of different heirs seeking all or part of the Kosciuszko estate under the terms of the various wills.[8]

In thirty years of litigation the estate originally passed to Benjamin L. Lear doubled in size. The first executor of Kosciuszko's American legacy received to his care an estate valued at $25,931.435. Lear astutely reinvested Kosciuszko's funds in his own name so that by the time of his death in 1832 the total value of Kosciuszko's estate stood at $31,785.27. The position of executor passed then to Colonel Bomford who settled the outstanding accounts of Lear's

[7] Thomas Jefferson to H.E.M. de Politica, May 27, 1819; statement of William Wertenbaker, Deputy Clerk of the Circuit Court of Albemarle, May 1819, now on file in the Circuit Court of Aibemarle and the Library of the University of Virginia.
[8] 14 Howard 474, 481 486.

estate and held the funds of the Kosciuszko legacy for its eventual claimants. Bomford thus became the executor of Lear's estate, as well as the administrator *de bonis non* ("of goods not already administered") of Kosciuszko's estate.[9]

In 1852, the complicated international litigations reached the United States Supreme Court under the innocuous legal heading of *John F. Ennis vs. J.H.B. Smith, et. al.* Ennis represented the Polish relatives of Kosciuszko who claimed the American estate by virtue of the will of 1816, while Smith, *et. al.*, argued the case in favor of the primacy of the will of 1798 with regard to the American portion of Kosciuszko's legacy. Although many questions were laid before the Court, four were critical to the disposal of the American estate. They were: 1. Were the heirs to Bomford still liable for the funds of the Kosciuszko estate? 2. Did legal relatives of Kosciuszko really exist? 3. Was the will of 1798 still valid, or had it been superseded by any or all of the wills of 1806, 1816, and/or 1817? 4. Presupposing favorable answers to these questions, the heirs of Kosciuszko then sought clarification as to the legal residence of Kosciuszko at the time of his death. This was important because his legal domicile would determine under which nation's laws the Kosciuszko legacy would be settled.

With regard to the first question, Smith, *et. al.*, argued that according to the laws of the state of Maryland, which then also applied to the District of Columbia, any change in the form of a bequest by an executor meant that the estate was said to have been "administered." Thus, the defendants maintained, when the original form of the inheritance was changed by Lear's reinvestment, the legacy was no longer legally extant. Consequently, they held that Bomford's heirs were not liable for Kosciuszko's American funds. Further, they noted that there was a significant difference in the bonds which they held from the Bank of Columbia and those claimed by the applicants. The Court, in the written decision of Justice Wayne, disagreed with the

---

[9] *Ibid.*, 479.

executors, citing several legal reasons why Bomford, as the executor of Lear, could not lawfully claim the inheritance of Kosciuszko even though its form had been altered by Lear and came to Bomford as a portion of Lear's estate. Bomford's heirs were liable for the sum of Bomford's last accounting prior to his death in 1848, $43,504.40.[10] With this formality concluded, the substance of the claims became the focus of attention.

The defendants argued, in the second instance, that Kosciuszko had not been married, had no offspring and had no verified heirs to which the American estate could pass. The appellants, they argued, had no proof of their relationship to Kosciuszko. The claimants countered these assertions by producing decrees from the Assembly of Nobility of the Government of Grodno, dated May 7, 1843, and from the Court of Korbryn in the Province of Lithuania. Written in their original Russian, the two decrees were filed with the court in the District of Columbia. They both served to authenticate the relationship of Ennis' clients to Kosciuszko, and further stated their position as next of kin, and therefore legal claimants to Kosciuszko's estates. Both decrees were affixed with their respective official seals. As witnesses to attest to the authenticity and jurisdiction of the two entities, the claimants called Henryk Kalussowski and Jan Tyssowski, both Polish exiles who were familiar with Polish legal intricacies. Faced with this evidence, the Court ruled that the decrees proved that the claimants were collateral kinsmen of Kosciuszko and thus entitled to his estate.[11]

Undoubtedly the most important question that the Court had to decide was the legitimacy of the four separate Kosciuszko wills. The defendants in the case argued that the American estate of Thaddeus Kosciuszko was bequeathed under the will of 1798, and had not been subsequently revoked. If, however, it had been revoked, or if its trusts could not be carried out, they argued

---

[10] *Ibid.*, 476-80.
[11] *Ibid.*, 476, 486.

that the will of 1817 then bequeathed the estate to the Zeltners, thus intercepting and bypassing any claims put forth by the next of kin.

The claimants to the Kosciuszko estate noted that the 1816 will had previously been proved legitimate under French law, and that an authenticated copy of that will was in the possession of the court in the District of Columbia. The heirs, through Ennis, argued that the 1806 will did not follow the legal forms prescribed by French jurisprudence. Futhermore, they stated that the 1816 will, regardless of former wills, included a standard clause of revocation which read as follows: "Je revoque tous les testaments et codiciles que j'ai pu faire avant le present auquel seul je m'arrete comme contenant mes dernieres volantes."[12] This meant that all previous wills were null and void and the new will, that of 1816, was the only legal testament extant at that time. Since no disposition of the American property was made in the 1816 will, and because the 1817 will only bequeathed certain explicit portions of the Kosciuszko estate in general, the heirs of Kosciuszko concluded that the American portion of the Kosciuszko legacy was therefore *intestate*. That is, the American estate not having been bequeathed, it became the property of the next of kin.[13]

The Court agreed insofar as the revoking clause was concerned and declared that the will of 1816 did, in fact, supersede the 1798 will, thus making the 1798 provisions for Kosciuszko's American estate invalid. The defendants argued, however, that Clause II of the will of 1817 directed the Kosciuszko estate to the possession of the Zeltners. The clause read: "Je leque tous mes effets, ma voiture, et mon cheval y comprise a Madame eta Monsieur Zavier Zeltner, les homme ce dessus."[14] The defendants argued that the phrase "all of my effects" was not qualified by

---

[12] *Ibid.*, 481. Translation: "I revoke all the wills and codicils which I may have made previous to the present, to which alone I confine myself, as containing my last wishes."

[13] *Ibid.*, 476, 481.

[14] Translation: "I leave all of my effects, my carriage and my horse included, to Mr. and Mrs. Xavier Zeltner, the people I live with." *Ibid.*, 473.

the following phrase, "my carriage and my horse included," to mean only his personal effects. The defendants maintained that Kosciuszko only intended to make sure that the carriage and horse were not overlooked along with all of his other possessions.

The claimants insisted that in the French language the word *effets* referred only to property usually found about one's person, and that when linked with other qualifying phrases, as it was in this case, the rule of *ejusdem generis* ("of the same kind, class or nature") should apply. This would mean that the Zeltners were only entitled to Kosciuszko's personal possessions in the area of their immediate home, including his carriage and horse. The rest of the estate, including the American portion, would then go to the heirs represented by Ennis.[15]

The Court once again found in favor of the claimants noting that the use of the word *effets* could not be construed to include Kosciuszko's American property. "It would be a very strained construction," the Court concluded, "to make the words, all of my effects, comprehend his personal estate in the United States." Thus, the Court continued, the second article in the will of 1817 is not residuary and...has no relation to the funds in controversy."[16]

There remained the question of Kosciuszko's domicile for the purposes of division of property under the wills of 1816 and 1817. Smith, *et. al.,* maintained that Kosciuszko had no proved domicile other than Poland, where he was born, or Switzerland, where he died. The claimants argued that Kosciuszko was a resident of France at the time of his death. The French laws dealing with *intestate* legacies would give Ennis' clients possession of Kosciuszko's American funds; consequently, it was important that they prove this point. The Court noted that Kosciuszko, in his 1806 will, claimed that he was "at present residing in Paris." This, it held, was sufficient *prima facie* evidence of Kosciuszko's domicile in France. In addition to this, in his will of 1816

---

[15] *Ibid.,* 474, 477.
[16] *Ibid.,* 482.

Kosciuszko included the phrase: "I, the undersigned Thaddeus Kosciuszko, residing in Berville, in the township Genevraye, of the department of Seine and Marne [being now], or at present at Soleure, in Switzerland." The Court ruled this further evidence of residence in France. Although the defendants argued that Kosciuszko was, in fact, an exile from Poland who hoped to return, the Court rejected this appeal. The Justices found that Kosciuszko had not been forced to leave Poland by Tsar Paul; rather, the Pole had voluntarily chosen to leave for political reasons. Futhermore, the Court noted that a decree of the National Assembly of France had conferred citizenship upon Kosciuszko in August, 1792. Kosciuszko's legal domicile was, the Court concluded, France. Justice Wayne also accepted the printed version of the Code Civil of France as legitimate for the purposes of settling the estate. Under these precepts, the American legacy of Thaddeus Kosciuszko was ordered transferred to his heirs as established by the Court. The size of the award included two cash funds of $37,924.40 and $12,641.46 2/3 plus six percent interest since June 7, 1847. In addition, it also included $5,580 worth of stock in the Bank of Washington, plus dividends.[17]

Following the final disposition of Kosciuszko's American estate, some historians commented that Kosciuszko never really intended to use his funds to help alleviate some of the problems faced by slaves in the United States. These writers have relegated Kosciuszko's American will to a state of myth. The three succeeding wills, as shown by the Court, these historians contend, indicate that Kosciuszko himself certainly changed his mind about the destination of these funds. These conclusions are unwarranted. If Kosciuszko had changed his mind he certainly would have bequeathed his American estate to some other party or parties in one of his three other wills. He did not. Clearly, one could argue that Kosciuszko always intended his American estate for its original purpose. It appears that only the legal

---

[17] *Ibid.*, 483-84, 487.

intricacies of the revocation clause in the will of 1816 prevented the funds from being used for the purposes he set down in 1798. Each of Kosciuszko's wills dealt with a different portion of his estate and were intended to be equally valid. The standard revocation clause of the 1816 will was no doubt inserted as a matter of legal course, without a firm grasp of what implications it might have on former wills. Proof of Kosciuszko's continued concern for his American estate is seen in a letter which he wrote to Thomas Jefferson on September 15, 1817. With an impending sense of death, Kosciuszko wrote: "We all grow old, and for that reason, my dear and respectable friend, I ask you, as you have full power to do, to arrange it in such a manner that after the death of our worthy friend, Mr. Barnes, some one as honest as himself, may take his place, so that I may receive interest of my money, punctually; of which money, after my death, you know the fixed destination. As for the present, do what you think best."[18] This letter was written well after the will of 1816, and clearly indicates that Kosciuszko still considered his American will of 1798 to be in effect.

Similarly, some historians have scoffed at the importance of the will in view of its invalidation by the Supreme Court. This is also an erroneous conclusion for the will stands not only as testimony to the humanitarian principles of its author, but, of greater importance, it has served as an inspiration to Polish Americans and others for nearly two hundred years. One need only cite the following sentiments, taken from the memoirs of Wladimir Krzyzanowski, to prove the value of Kosciuszko's American will to succeeding generations.

> I am proud to say that the first man to recognize this [the need for education in the South], and to try to do something about it, was my countryman Tadeusz Kosciuszko. In 1800 when the Congress of the United States, recognizing his services to this country, voted him $15,000 and a land grant, Kosciuszko refused

---

[18] *Ibid*, 478-79.

to accept the money or the land. Instead, he attempted to donate it towards building schools for the education of the Negroes. But his good intentions bore no fruit. The Commonwealth of Virginia immediately passed laws forbidding the education of Negroes. Kosciuszko still refused to accept the gift. This gift was invested, and by the year 1853 it had grown to $65,000. Had Virginia established schools, and named them in Kosciuszko's memory, Virginia would have remembered him forever.... Perhaps Virginia would also have been able to avoid the later conflicts which raged within her borders.[19]

Clearly the ideal that motivated Kosciuszko's American will survived the legal complications which struck it down. Kosciuszko wrote the will in good faith and never intended that it be revoked. Rather, he expected even on the eve of his death that his original wishes be carried out. It is this spirit of humanity which has survived as a monument to its author and a goal for others to pursue.

---

[19] Wladimir Krzyzanowski, *Memoirs*, trans. Stanley J. Pula, ed. James S. Pula, pp. 19-20.

EPILOGUE

Is This Kosciuszko's Pistol?

BY WALLACE M. WEST

THE FOLLOWING ESSAY was published in the quarterly Polish Heritage, *Vol. XLVI No. 1 (Spring, 1995). It is republished herein through the courtesy and permission of the author and editor, Wallace M. West, and the American Council for Polish Culture.*

Beyond its fascinating contents, this short essay tells what happened to Agrippa Hull, Kosciuszko's faithful servant during the Revolutionary War.

A POLISH FLINTLOCK PISTOL in the arms collection of Frank J. Kelly, currently residing in Sun City Center, Florida. seemingly has all the earmarks of being the sidearm once belonging to American Revolutionary War Leader, Tadeusz Kosciuszko. The fascinating story behind this historical pistol was brought to my attention by a Clearwater, Florida resident, Leon Clark, whose American roots go back nine generations. Mr. Clark contacted me when he saw an article appearing in one of our local papers publicizing an art exhibit of the Kosciuszko Foundation Collection, sponsored by the American Institute of Polish Culture—Pinellas County at the Museum of Fine Arts in St. Petersburg, Florida.

Believing that I would be interested in hearing the wondrous story behind a rare flintlock pistol manufactured by a Polish gun maker during the second-half of the 18th Century, Mr. Clark put me in touch with the owner of the pistol, Mr. Frank Kelly.

Frank Kelly got the gun in 1956 in an exchange with a collector friend who had owned it for over twenty years, but had never tried to research the gun's history. The only information he could provide was that he had purchased the pistol in the early 1930s at an auction selling off some personal effects of a Dr. Lane.

This information did not seem very important at the time and the more Kelly thought about the gun the more determined he became to learn about its past history. Kelly intently read all articles published in gun magazines covering pistols used on both sides of the Revolutionary War but found no references to Polish arms. This lack of information on Polish weaponry puzzled him because he knew that the colonial forces had attracted some strong Polish allies in their struggle for independence from Great Britain.

The obvious first step in his fact-finding study was to get as much information as possible on the gun's maker whose name was inlaid in gold on top of the barrel "W. Miklaszewski w Warszawie" (W. Miklaszewski of Warsaw). The sidearm is superbly made as evidenced by the raised carving on the stock, pierced thimbles for the ramrod and silver front sight. The bore is rifled with nine lands and nine grooves and another fine groove down the center of each land.

In checking out all the lists of gun makers he could locate, Kelly found no mention of Miklaszewski. He wrote to museums, well-known gun collectors and dealers and showed the Polish pistol to knowledgeable old timers at gun shows. Discouragingly, none of these sources heard of Miklaszewski and none had even seen a Polish flintlock pistol before.

A letter was then sent to the Polish Consulate in New York

Pistol manufacturer's name on barrel of pistol.

requesting their assistance and they, in turn, referred Kelly to the Polish Army Museum in Warsaw.

A letter to them brought back a disappointing answer from Colonel Kazimierz Konieczny who wrote, "In reply to your letter of 24th September 1956, I inform you that Muzeum Wojska Polskiego (Polish Army Museum) does not find the name W. Miklaszewski among the names of known Polish gun makers and has no data concerning him." The Colonel went on to say that the museum was also interested in the history of Polish firearms and would welcome a more detailed description of the pistol. When positive identification of the gun's manufacturer and following the trail of ownership looked hopeless, Frank Kelly hung the gun on his wall and moved on to other pursuits.

Shortly afterwards, two precious bits of information came to light. A local Massachusetts newspaper, *The Berkshire Eagle,* published a historical article that referred to "…the ancient negro, Agrippa Hull of Stockbridge (Mass.) who was Kosciuszko's body servant during the Revolutionary War." This article provided Kelly with a valuable clue because Stockbridge is only seven miles from Great Barrington where the gun was bought at auction from Dr. Lane's estate. A visit to the Stockbridge Library proved to be very rewarding. They have an extensive file on Agrippa Hull.

Within that file, Kelly found one item that fascinated him—a letter written by Dr. Lane in 1932 to the editor of *The Berkshire Eagle*. In the letter, Dr. Lane wrote:

> I read with interest in last night's *Eagle* the announcement that the Stockbridge Library possesses a daguerotype and a portrait of Agrippa Hull, and was reminded of an anecdote told to me by the late Charles J. Taylor, historian of Great Barrington. Agrippa lived in a small house which stood on the south bank of the brook near the so called Goodrich place, where it stood when I came to Great Barrington in 1887.
>
> In Agrippa's visits to Great Barrington he was in the habit of calling on Mr. Taylor and relating to him his experiences. On one of these visits he told this story about himself while he was a servant of General Kosciuszko. One day when the General was away, Agrippa dressed himself in the General's uniform and paraded about the place. The General returned unexpectedly and when he saw Agrippa he saluted him and treated him as though he was really General Kosciuszko. When Agrippa finished his story, he said "Mr. Taylor, I was so ashamed I didn't know what to do." His chagrin was his only punishment. Mr. Taylor related this story to me as we were passing the cabin where Agrippa lived.
>
> Yours truly, Orville W. Lane

A little further research revealed that Charles Taylor was Dr. Lane's father-in-law. Now one could theorize a flow of the pistol's ownership: Kosciuszko to Hull, Hull to Taylor, Taylor to Lane, Lane's auction putting the pistol in the hands of a gun collector and eventually swapped to the current owner, Frank J. Kelly.

Now there was one more detail that needed clarification—the age of the gun and the identity of the maker. All previous attempts to find documentation that would identify Miklaszewski as a gun manufacturer were unsuccessful. Then, in the Summer of 1957, Kelly received a second letter from the Polish Army Museum which definitely identifies Miklaszewski as the maker of the flintlock pistol and secures the missing link between him and Kosciuszko.

The June 7, 1957 letter from Colonel Konieczny to Frank J. Kelly said: "Referring to your letter of 24th September 1956 and our letter no. 920 of 17th October 1956, I beg to inform you in the form of the following note about the Polish gun-maker, W. Miklaszewski, which contains the data we were able to collect in the meantime. W. Miklaszewski was one of the most eminent gun makers of the second half of the XVIII-th century. His workshop was counted among the biggest in Warsaw. It was situated in the building of "Korpus Kadetow"(Cadet

Frank Kelley explains how a flintlock pistol works to Polish Heritage editor, Wally West.

Corps) in the "Palac Kazimierowski" (King Casimir's Palace) in Krakowskie Przedmiescie (Krakow suburb), now the main building of the Warsaw University. This workshop worked for the Cadet Corps. In 1794 Miklaszewski (as well as other Warsaw gun makers) worked in the same workshop for the Kosciuszko Insurrection. He obtained orders and firing arms from the "Komisariat Kawalerii" (Commisariat of Cavalry). From his workshop, carbines, pistols, as well as rifles for the infantry came out prepared for the insurrectionists. We did not succeed in collecting more detailed data concerning his life and activity because of the destruction of Warsaw archives. The above information will appear soon in a book now about to be printed: "Uzbrojenie i Przemysl Zbrojeniowy w Powstaniu Kosciuszkowskim" (The Armament and the Armament Industry During the Kosciuszko Insurrection by Mr. Andrzej Zahorski). Our Museum of the Polish Army does not possess in its collections of arms of Warsaw gunmakers any example of Miklaszewski's work. We would be therefore very grateful for sending us some photographs of the gun made by him with the plate bearing his name. Very truly yours, Director of the Polish Museum, Col. Kazimierz Konieczny."

Despite the fact that a more detailed biography on Miklaszewski is unavailable because of war destruction of Warsaw's archives, one can reasonably conclude that in 1794 Miklaszewski was well established and may have known and worked for Kosciuszko decades earlier. Additionally, with regard to the evidence so diligently collected, it is logical to draw the following conclusions:

1. The flintlock pistol is contemporary with the American Revolution.

2. The side-arm was brought to America by a Polish ally in support of the Colonists' struggle for independence from England.

3. If the gun did belong to Kosciuszko, he apparently thought enough of Agrippa Hull to give it to him when he left America to return to Poland.

The third assumption is effectively strengthened by Kosciuszko's will. The original is in the Jefferson Papers of the Massachusetts Historical Society. It states:

> I Thaddeus Kosciuszko, being just on my departure from America do hereby declare and direct that, should I make no other testamentary disposition of my property in the United States, I hereby authorize my friend, Thomas Jefferson, to employ the whole thereof in purchasing negroes from his own or any others and giving them liberty in my name, in giving them an education in trade or otherwise and in having them instructed for their new condition in the duties of morality, which may make them good neighbors, good fathers and mothers, husbands and wives, in their duty as citizens, teaching them to be defenders of their liberty and country, of the good order of society, and in whatsoever may make them happy and useful and I make the said Thomas Jefferson executor of this.
>
> (signed) T. Kosciuszko
> 5th May 1798

The creditable investigation conducted by Frank Kelly in tracing the ownership of the Miklaszewski manufactured flintlock pistol does present us with strong prima facie evidence that the pistol was indeed once owned by Revolutionary War Hero, Tadeusz Kosciuszko. In view of this evidence, Frank Kelly's historical artifact is now safely stored in a Florida bank vault.

NOTES

Chapter 1. Prelude to Saratoga

1. James Wilkinson, *Memoirs of My Own Times*, 3 Vols. (Philadelphia: Printed by Abraham Small, 1816), I: 232; and Christopher Ward, *The War of the Revolution*, 2 Vols. (New York: The Macmillan Company, 1952), II:502. According to Major John Armstrong, Gates ordered Kosciuszko and Major Udney Hay, Quartermaster, to select a position on the west bank of the Hudson River, in General John Armstrong to Jared Sparks, Red Hook, New York, August 1837, *Sparks Manuscripts*, Serial 9, Vol. 1, par. 9, Harvard College Library, Cambridge, Massachusetts.
2. Henry B. Carrington, *Battles of the American Revolution, 1775-1781* (New York: A.S. Barnes & Company, 1877), p. 336; and Lynn Montross, *Rag, Tag and Bobtail: The Story of the Continental Army, 1775-1783* (New York: Harper & Brothers Publishers, 1952), p. 214.
3. Hoffman Nickerson, *The Turning Point of the Revolution or Burgoyne in America*, 2 Vols. (Port Washington, New York: Kennikat Press, Inc., 1967, first printed in 1928), II:289-90; Ward, *War of the Revolution*, II:502-03; and Rupert Furneaux, *The Battle of Saratoga* (New York: Stein and Day Publishers, 1971), p. 162.
4. Furneaux, *Saratoga*, pp. 13-32; and Carrington, *Battles of the Revolution*, pp. 303-07, 337.
5. Lieutenant-General John Burgoyne, *A State of the Expedition from Canada* (London, 1780; reprint ed., New York: Arno Press, Inc., 1969), Appendix, pp. iii-xii; Furneaux, *Saratoga*, p. 30; and Ward, *War of the Revolution*, I:398-400.
6. Gerald Howson, *Burgoyne of Saratoga, A Biography* (New York: Times Books, 1979), p. 145; Furneaux, *Saratoga*, pp. 31-32; and Burgoyne, *Expedition from Canada*, Appendix, pp. xii-xvii.
7. Howson, *Burgoyne of Saratoga*, p. 81; Ward, *War of the Revolution*, I:68; and Nickerson, *Turning Point of the Revolution*, I:129.
8. Miecislaus Haiman, *Kosciuszko in the American Revolution* (New York: Polish Institute of Arts and Sciences in America, 1943), p. 18; Ward, *War of the Revolution*, I:70; and Wilkinson, *Memoirs*, I:191.
9. Ward, *War of the Revolution*, I:101-02, 140.
10. Paul David Nelson, *General Horatio Gates, A Biography* (Baton Rouge: Louisiana State University Press, 1976), pp. 56, 58-59, 72, 75, 80; and Wilkinson, *Memoirs*, I:160-61. General Schuyler was aware of Kosciuszko's assignment to the Northern Department. In a letter to John Hancock,

President of Congress, 8 March 1777, Schuyler mentioned that "Col. Kusiuskow sets out this day in the place of Col. Pelisier," *Papers of the Continental Congress, 1774-1789*, National Archives, M247, R173, I 153, V3, p. 113.

11. Wilkinson, *Memoirs*, I:162-63.
12. Gates to Patterson, Albany, 8 May 1777, *Bancroft Collection*, V81, p. 133, Manuscript & Archives Section, New York Public Library. Also in *Gates Papers*, Reel 9, Box 19, New York Historical Society.
13. Thomas Williams Baldwin, ed., *The Revolutionary Journal of Col. Jeduthan Baldwin, 1775-1778*, (Bangor, 1906), p. 101.
14. Kosciuszko to Gates, 18 May 1777, *Gates Papers*, Reel 3 (Box 6), No. 190.
15. Wilkinson, *Memoirs*, I:164.
16. Kosciuszko to Gates, 18 May 1777, *Gates Papers*, Reel 3 (Box 6), No. 145; and Willard Sterne Randall, *Benedict Arnold: Patriot and Traitor* (New York: William Morrow and Company, Inc., 1990), p. 340.
17. Gates to John Paterson, 23 May 1777, *Papers of the Continental Congress*, National Archives, M247, R174, I 154, V1, p. 220.
18. *Baldwin's Journal* p. 103; and Wilkinson to Gates, 28 May 1777, *Gates Papers*, Reel 3 (Box 6), No. 181.
19. John Trumbull, *Autobiography, Reminiscences and Letters, 1756-1841* (New York: Wiley and Putnam, 1841), p. 31.
20. General John Armstrong to Jared Sparks, Red Hook, New York, August 1837, in *Sparks Manuscripts*, Serial 49, Vol. 1, par. 9.
21. Furneaux, *Saratoga*, p. 59; Montross, *Story of the Continental Army*, p. 196; *Sparks Manuscripts*, Serial 49, Vol. 1, par. 9; and Schuyler to Congress, Albany, 8 June 1777, *Papers of the Continental Congress*, M247, R173, I 153, V3, p. 144.
22. Wilkinson to Gates, 31 May 1777, *Gates Papers*, Reel 3 (Box 6), No. 188; and *Baldwin's Journal*, p. 104.
23. *Baldwin's Journal*, pp. 104-05.
24. Trumbull, *Autobiography*, p. 29.
25. Wilkinson, *Memoirs*, I:175.
26. Schuyler to Congress, 8 June 1777, and St. Clair to Schuyler, 18 June 1777, in "Proceedings of a General Court Martial...for the Trial of Major General Arthur St. Clair," *Collections of the New York Historical Society for the Year 1880*, pp. 19, 104-05.
27. "Proceedings of a General Court Martial," p. 109.
28. Kosciuszko's Deposition, "Proceedings of a General Court Martial," pp. 58-59.
29. Livingston's testimony, "Proceedings of a General Court Martial," p. 114.
30. Nickerson, *Turning Point of the War*, II:452.
31. Furneaux, *Saratoga*, p. 62. Furneaux does not mention Kosciuszko, who planned and built the fortifications.
32. "Journal of Du Roi the Elder," *German-American Annals*, New Series, Vol. 9 (1911); and Ward, *War of the Revolution*, I:406-07; II:523.
33. John C. Miller, *Triumph of Freedom 1775-1783* (Boston: Little, Brown and

Company, 1948), p. 177; and Carrington, *Battles of the Revolution*, p. 311.
34. Furneaux, *Saratoga*, pp. 40-41, 45-47.
35. Furneaux, *Saratoga*, p. 45.
36. Ward, *War of the Revolution*, p. 385; Wilkinson, *Memoirs*, I:181:82; and Furneaux, *Saratoga*, pp. 47, 49.
37. Howson, *Burgoyne at Saratoga*, pp. 166-67; Ward, *War of the Revolution*, I:410-11; Wilkinson, *Memoirs*, I:184-85; and Kosciuszko's testimony, "Proceedings of a General Court Martial," p. 60.
38. John S. Pancake, *1777: The Year of the Hangman* (University: University of Alabama Press, 1977), pp. 124-25; Furneaux, *Saratoga*, p. 58; and George Clinton to James Duane, 27 August 1777, in John Armstrong to Jared Sparks, Red Hook, New York, 4 December 1831, *Sparks Manuscripts*, Ser. 49, Vol. 1, par. 7.
39. Kosciuszko to Arthur St. Clair, Fort Edward, undated [July 1777], *Collections of the Manuscripts Division*, Library of Congress; and "Proceedings of a General Court Martial," pp. 58-61.
40. Burgoyne, *Expedition from Canada*, Appendix, pp. xxvii-xxix; " Proceedings of a General Court Martial," pp. 58-61; and Nickerson, *Turning Point of the War*, II:177.
41. Jane Clark, "Responsibility for the Failure of the Burgoyne Campaign," *American Historical Review*, Vol. 35 (1930), p. 554; Burgoyne, *Expedition from Canada*, p. 60; and Ward, *War of the Revolution*, I:421

Chapter 2. Saratoga: The Turning Point

1. Nickerson, *The Turning Point*, p. 173.
2. Wilkinson, *Memoirs*, I:200.
3. Letter Book of General Philip Schuyler, June 26-August 18, 1777, p. 53, American Antiquarian Society, Worcester, Massachusetts; and Montross, *Story of the Continental Army*, pp. 203-04, 213.
4. Don Higginbotham, *The War of the American Independence* (New York: The Macmillan Company, 1971), p. 190; Pancake, *1777, The Year of the Hangman*, p. 125; Burgoyne, *State of the Expedition from Canada*, pp. 126-27, Appendix, p. xxxv; Ward, *War of the Revolution*, I: 419-20; Nickerson, *The Turning Point*, pp. 176, 179; and Thomas Anburey, *With Burgoyne from Quebec: An Account of the Life at Quebec and of the Famous Battle of Saratoga*, Sydney Jackman, ed. (Toronto: Macmillan of Canada, 1963), p. 152.
5. John Armstrong Memorial for M.A. Jullien, 1818, in Henry A. Washington, ed., *The Writings of Thomas Jefferson*, VIII: 495.
6. Orderly Book of Henry B. Livingston, 19 July 1777, p. 52, and 29 July 1777, p.72, American Antiquarian Society, Worcester, Massachusetts.
7. Jared Sparks, ed., *The Writings of George Washington*, 12 Vols. (New York: Harper & Brothers, Publishers, 1847), IV: 503n; and Jared Sparks, *Correspondence of the American Revolution*, I: 427.

8. Carrington, *Battles of the American Revolution*, pp. 322-25.
9. Ward, *War of the Revolution*, I: 422-31; and Burgoyne, *Expedition from Canada*, Appendix, pp. xli-xliii.
10. John Hancock to George Washington, Philadelphia, 4 August 1777, and Washington to Horatio Gates, Headquarters, Philadelphia, 4 August 1777, *Gates Papers*, Reel 3, Nos. 44 and 45; and Furneaux, *Saratoga*, pp. 145-46.
11. Nickerson, *The Turning Point*, p. 289; Furneaux, *Saratoga*, p. 151; and Colonel Red Reeder, *Bold Leaders of the American Revolution*, (Boston: Little, Brown and Company, 1973), p. 51.
12. Washington to Gates, Head Qrs., Bucks County, 20 August 1777, *Gates Papers*, Reel 3, No. 49.
13. Pancake, *1777*, p.154.
14. Benson J. Lossing, *The Pictorial Field Book of the American Revolution*, 2 Vols. (New York, 1850-52), I: 49; Ward, *War of the Revolution*, II: 504-05; and Pancake, *1777*, p. 115.
15. Burgoyne, *Expedition from Canada*, pp. 58, 106; and Sir Edward S. Creasy, *The Fifteen Decisive Battles of the World from Marathon to Waterloo* (New York: A. L. Burt, Publisher, 1858), pp. 339-40.
16. Ward, *War of the Revolution*, II:505.
17. Carrington, *Battles of the American Revolution*, p. 341; Wilkinson, *Memoirs*, pp. 236-39: and Ward, *War of the Revolution*, II:506-12.
18. Burgoyne, *Expedition from Canada*, p, 162; Carrington, *Battles of the Revolution*, p. 340; Anburey, *With Burgoyne from Quebec*, p. 175; and Furneaux, *Saratoga*, p. 192
19. John Sweetman, *Saratoga 1777* (New York: Hippocrene Books, Inc., 1973), pp. 39-40, 46; and Anburey, *With Burgoyne from Quebec*, p. 176.
20. Sweetman, *Saratoga,1777*, pp. 47-51.
21. Sweetman, *Saratoga 1777*, pp. 52-53; and Pancake, *1777*, pp. 186-87.
22. Sweetman, *Saratoga 1777*, pp. 54-62.
23. Higginbotham, *War of American Independence*, p. 195; and Ward, *War of the Revolution*, II: 513-20.
24. Burgoyne, *Expedition from Canada*, p. 160.
25. Howson, *Burgoyne of Saratoga*, pp. 230-34.
26. Sweetman, *Saratoga 1777*, p. 65; Clark, "Responsibility for Failure of Burgoyne," *American Historical Review*, p. 555; and Burgoyne, *Expedition From Canada*, p. 118.
27. Furneaux, *Battle of Saratoga*, p. 163.
28. Armstrong's Letter, *Sparks Papers*, Ser. 49, VI, par. 9; and Haiman, *Kosciuszko in the American Revolution*, p. 29.
29. Montross, *Story of the Continental Army*, p. 227; Edward Channing, *A History of the United States* (New York: The Macmillan Company, 1921), III: 278; Furneaux, *Saratoga*, p. 293; and John Armstrong to Jared Sparks, Red Hook, New York, 8 July 1832, in *Sparks Manuscripts*, Ser. 49, VI, par. 7.
30. *The Memoirs of Rufus Putnam*, Rowena Buell, comp. (Boston: The Riverside Press, 1903), p. 73. Rufus Putnam was a cousin of General Israel

Putnam. Colonel Putnam and his regiment joined Kosciuszko at West Point in 1778.

31. Pancake, *1777,* p. 218; and Nickerson, *The Turning Point,* III: 404.
32. Sir George Otto Trevelyan, *The American Revolution,* 4 Vols. (New York: Longmans, Green, and Co., 1907), III: 162-63.
33. Sir John Fortescue, *A History of the British Army,* 13 Vols. (London: Macmillan and Co., 1899-1930; reprint ed., New York: AMS Press, 1976), III: 233.
34. James Lunt, *John Burgoyne of Saratoga* (New York: Harcourt Brace Jovanovich, 1975), p. 221.
35. Major General Von Riedesel, *Memoirs, Letters and Journals of Major General Riedesel,* William L. Stone, trans. (Albany: J. Mansell, 1868), p. 143.
36. Howson, *Burgoyne of Saratoga,* pp. 206-07.
37. Sweetman, *Saratoga 1777,* p. 26.
38. Ward, *War of the Revolution,* II: 507.
39. Burgoyne, *Expedition from Canada,* p. 106.
40. Wilkinson, *Memoirs,* I: 234.
41. Furneaux, *Battle of Saratoga,* pp. 157, 222-23.
42. Higginbotham, *War of American Independence,* p. 194.
43. Willard Sterne Randall, *Benedict Arnold: Patriot and Traitor* (New York: William Morrow and Company, Inc., 1990), p. 364.
44. Nickerson, *The Turning Point,* p. 303.
45. Howson, *Burgoyne of Saratoga,* p. 206.

Chapter 3. From Poland to America

1. Plutarch, "Timoleon," *The Lives of the Noble Grecians and Romans* (Chicago: Encyclopedia Britannica, Inc., 1952), pp. 195-213, of Book 14, *Plutarch, Great Books of the Western World,* Robert Maynard Hutchins, editor-in-chief.
2. Stephen P. Mizwa, "Tadeusz Kosciuszko," *Great Men and Women of Poland* (New York: The Kosciuszko Foundation, 1941), pp. 126-29. When the vengeful Germans ruthlessly and needlessly destroyed Old Town Warsaw in 1944, the Poles relied on Canaletto's paintings for the restoration of the historic site.
3. Jan Stanislaw Kopczewski, *Kosciuszko and Pulaski* (Warsaw: Interpress Publishers, 1976), pp. 54-60; and Antoni Gronowicz, *Gallant General: Tadeusz Kosciuszko,* translated by Samuel Sorgenstein (New York: Charles Scribner's Sons. 1947), p. 33.
4. Haiman, *Kosciuszko,* pp. 5-6. Stephen P. Mizwa gives another account of the route traveled by Kosciuszko to France. Mizwa writes that Kosciuszko rode a barge down the Vistula River to Gdansk on the Baltic Sea and from there sailed for France. In *Great Men and Women of Poland,* p. 130.
5. *Journals of the Continental Congress,* Worthington Chauncey Ford, ed.,

34 Vols. (Washington: Government Printing Office, 1906), V:719; and Haiman, *Kosciuszko*, p. 9.

6. John Hancock, President of Congress, to Monsieur Kermovan, Philadelphia, July 16, 1776, *Papers of the Continental Congress*, M247, R23, V1, p. 238; Haiman, *Kosciuszko*, p. 10; *Journals of Congress*, V: 443, 613-14; and Lyman H. Butterfield, "Franklin, Rush, and the Chevalier de Kermovan: An Episode of '76," in *Library Bulletin of the American Philosophical Society* (1946), pp. 33-44.

7. *Journals of Congress*, VI: 888; and Haiman, *Kosciuszko*, p. 9.

8. Washington to President of Congress, 9 December 1776,in John C. Fitzpatrick, *The Writings of George Washington from the Original Manuscripts, 1749-1799*, 39 Vols, (Washington, D.C.: Government Printing Office, 1931-1944), VI:340.

9. Peter Force, *American Archives*, Ser. 5, III: 1151; and Washington to John Hancock, 9 and 20 December 1776, Fitzpatrick, *Writings of Washington*, VI: 340, 405.

10. Henry Hobart Bellas, "The Defences of the Delaware River in the Revolution," *Proceedings and Collections of the Wyoming Historical and Genealogical Society*, Wilkes Barre, Pennsylvania, Vol. V (1900), pp. 50-51.

11. Nelson, *Horatio Gates*, p. 77; and *Journals of Congress*, VII: 202.

Chapter 4. Kosciuszko and the French Engineers

1. Elizabeth S. Kite, *Brigadier-General Louis Lebeque Duportail* (Baltimore: The Johns Hopkins Press, 1933), pp. 12, 24-25.

   Kite writes as an apologist for Duportail. A trustee of the Institut Francais de Washington, she was assisted by the Institut. Kite mistakenly places General Nathanael Greene, commander of the Southern Army, and his chief engineer, Colonel Thaddeus Kosciuszko, at the surrender of British General Lord Cornwallis at Yorktown, Virginia, 19 October 1781.

2. Dave Richard Palmer, *The River and the Rock: The History of Fortress West Point, 1775-1783* (New York: Greenwood Publishing Corporation, 1969), pp. 132-33.

3. Duportail to Congress, Philadelphia, 8 July 1777, *Papers of the Continental Congress*, M247, R51, I 141, V8, p. 9.

4. Washington to President of Congress, Whitemarsh, 10 November 1777, in Fitzpatrick, *Writings of Washington*, X: 35.

5. Kite, *Duportail*, pp. 31-33.

6. On one occasion at West Point, Kosciuszko preferred court martial charges against Lieutenant Timothy Whiting of the Quartermaster Department for a breach of discipline. Whiting was found guilty and sentenced to be dismissed from the army. Thinking the punishment too severe, Kosciuszko interceded with General Alexander McDougall, who restored Whiting to duty. Evening Order of 29 December 1778, Orderly Book No. 95, *McDougall Papers*, New-York Historical Society, New York.

7. "Report of the Board of War," 14 November 1777, *Papers of the Continental Congress,* M247, R145, I 136, V1, p. 479.
8. John Laurens to Henry Laurens, 9 February 1778, *The Army Correspondence of Colonel John Laurens in the Years 1777-8;* reprint ed. (New York: The New York Times & Arno Press, 1969), p. 121.
9. Kosciuszko studied in France for four years at Mezieres (the engineering school of Duportail) or *Ecole Militaire,* in Mizwa, *Great Men and Women of Poland,* p. 129.
10. Palmer, *River and the Rock,* p. 132; and Washington to General Putnam, Skippack Camp. 7 October 1777, and to Lieutenant Colonel Lewis de La Radiere, 8 October 1777, Fitzpatrick, *Writings of Washington,* IX: 325, 339.
11. Palmer, *River and the Rock,* p. 133; Report of the Board of War, 14 November 1777, *Papers of Congress,* M247, R145, I 136, V1, p. 479; and La Radiere to Congress, New Windsor, 13 December 1777, *Papers of Congress,* M247, R101, I 78, V9, p. 189.
12. Ward, *War of the Revolution,* II: 519-20, 539; and Palmer, *River and the Rock,* p. 134.
13. Kite, *Duportail,* pp. 84-88.
14. Kite, *Duportail,* p. 85.
15. Parsons to Washington, 7 March 1778, in Charles S. Hall, *Life and Letters of Samuel Holden Parsons* (New York: From the Archives of James Pugliese, 1968), p. 155; Washington to La Radiere, Valley Forge, January 25, 1778, Fitzpatrick, X:349; Kite, *Duportail,* pp. 88-90; Parsons to McDougall, 29 March 1778, *McDougall Papers;* and Frank Landon Humphreys, *Life and Times of David Humphreys: Soldier–Statesman–Poet,* 2 Vols. (New York: G.P. Putnam's Sons, 1917), I: 114.
16. *Public Papers of George Clinton,* Hugh Hastings and J.A. Golden, eds., 10 Vols. (Albany, New York: James B. Lyon, State Printer, 1899-1914), II: 712, 848.
17. Jared Sparks, ed., *Correspondence of the American Revolution,* 4 Vols. (Boston, 1853), II: 30; and *Papers of Clinton,* III: 85-86.
18. Washigton to McDougall, 16 and 21 March 1778, Fitzpatrick, XI:95, 119; Kite, *Duportail,* pp. 90-91; and Charles E. Miller, Jr., Donald V. Lockey, and Joseph Visconti, Jr., *Highland Fortress: The Fortification of West Point during the American Revolution, 1775-1783* (West Point, New York: Department of History, United States Military Acdemy, 1979), p. 87.
19. Washington to McDougall, 6 April 1778, *McDougall Papers,* MF Reel 3 (Vol. 3), New-York Historical Society; and Fitzpatrick, *Writings of Washington,* XI: 222. Fitzpatrick shows a slightly different version of the letter.
20. Parsons to McDougall, 28 March 1778, and "McDougall's Diary," 28 March 1778, *McDougall Papers,* MF Reel 2.
21. McDougall to Washington, Fishkill, 13 April 1778, *George Washington Papers,* Library of Congress.
22. Washington to McDougall, 22 April 1778, Sparks, ed., *The Writings of George Washington,* XI:298.
23. Kite, *Duportail,* p. 93.

24. Kite, *Duportail,* pp. 110-11. In November 1777, when Congress asked Washington for his views on the worth of the French engineers, Washington stated his belief that they would be valuable to the army. And he pointed to the engineering performance of Kosciuszko. Washington also took this occasion to bring the Pole to the attention of Congress, saying, "From the character I have had of him he is deserving of notice, too." Some historians interpret Washington's favorable comment to be a recommendation for Kosciuszko's promotion to brigadier general. If so, it was an oblique and subdued recommendation. However, Washington habitually corresponded with Congress with restraint and reserve, in Fitzpatrick, *Writings of Washington,* X: 35.

25. Greene to John Hancock, President of Congress, Middle Brook, 1 July 1777, *Papers of Congress,* M247, R175, I 155, V1, p. 35; Francis Vinton Greene, *General Greene,* (New York: D. Appleton and Company, 1893; reprint ed., New York: Research Reprints, Inc., 1970), pp. 71-75; and *Journals of Congress,* VIII: 531.

26. *Journals of Congress,* VIII: 537.

27. Greene to John Hancock, l0 July 1777, *Papers of Congress,* M247, R175, I 155, V1, p. 39; *Journals of Congress,* VIII: 630; and Mark Mayo Boatner III, *Encyclopedia of the American Revolution* (New York: David McKay Company, Inc., 1966), p. 1117.

28. Greene to Washington, Camp Charlotte, 7 December 1780, in George Washington. Greene, *The Life of Nathanael Greene,* (New York: Hurd and Houghton, 1871), III: 544.

29. Kosciuszko to Colonel Robert Troup, 17 January 1778, *Gates Papers,* Reel 4 (Box 9), No. 20.

30. Haiman, *Kosciuszko,* p. 51.

31. Duportail to Congress, Camp White Plains, 27 August 1778, *Papers of Congress,*M247, R51, I 141, V8, p. 54.

32. Washington to President of Congress, White Plains, 31 August 1778, Fitzpatrick, *Writings of Washington,* XII: 376.

33. Washington to Duportail, White Plains, 27 August 1778, and Washington to Colonel Malcolm, 7 September 1778, Fitzpatrick, *Writings of Washington,* XII: 363, 408.

34. Duportail to Washington, White Plains, 13 September 1778, in Kite, *Duportail,* pp. 96-101; Henry Guerlac, "Vauban: The Impact of Science on War," in *Makers of Modern Strategy: From Machiavelli to Hitler,* Edward Meade Earle, ed. (Princeton, New Jersey: Princeton University Press, 1952), pp. 40-41; and Miller et al, "Highland Fortress," p. 129.

The three West Point officer-instructors commented adversely about Kosciuszko's absence from West Point on September 9 and 10, 1778. In their otherwise excellent manuscript, they state: "The date of Duportail's arrival at West Point was known in advance."[!] "When he reached the post on September 9th Kosciuszko had already departed to White Plains in a thinly-veiled maneuver to escape the Frenchman's criticism." (p. 129). Undoubtedly, Kosciuszko did not wish to meet Duportail on any occasion. Duportail sniped at and derogated Kosciuszko's competence at every opportunity. As the three officers wrote, "No love was lost between any of the French engineers and the Pole" [except for Gouvion, Villefranche, and Dalzien (Dellisumne), who got along well with the Pole. In fact, Villefranche lived with Kosciuszko in his hut at West Point. Dalzien served Kosciuszko loyally as assistant throughout the war].

The three authors cast a slur on Kosciuszko's character. But he was too good a soldier to avoid responsibility, however distasteful. Nevertheless, did Kosciuszko know of Duportail's upcoming inspection and, therefore, fled West Point "in a thinly-veiled maneuver to escape the Frenchman"? What are the facts?

General Washington directed Duportail to make a series of inspections in the Highlands in his letter of 27 August 1778.[1] Washington did not notify Colonel William Malcolm, West Point commander, until September 7. Washington informed Malcolm to expect a visit from Duportail shortly and instructed him: "It is my wish that Colo. Koshiosko may communicate every thing to this Gentleman, who is the Head of the department, which he may find requisite for the purpose he is sent upon."[2] Malcolm probably received the letter the next day, September 8, and on the following day Duportail reached West Point. His inspection took place on 9 and 10 September 1778. Malcolm acknowledged Washington's instructions on September 10. He wrote the commander-in-chief: "General Duportail arrived yesterday...Kosciuszko is not returned from the plains, but the general has been shown all the works."[3]

Kosciuszko had left West Point for army headquarters at White Plains, New York, in response to a summons from the president of the court martial board for the trial of General Arthur St. Clair. He testified in St. Clair's behalf on September 7 and 8, but he was at White Plains a few days earlier. More than likely he departed West Point not later than September 3 because the next morning, September 4, he acted as General Horatio Gates's second at the general's duel with Colonel James Wilkinson at nearby Harrison, New York.[4]

Based on the evidence, clearly Kosciuszko did not know of Duportail's planned inspection, for Kosciuszko had left before Colonel Malcolm received Washington's alert. With respect to the duel, Gates likely asked Kosciuszko to be the second upon the engineer's arrival at army headquarters.

Did Duportail himself notify Kosciuszko unofficially as a matter of coordination between senior engineers? There is no evidence, and such

[1] Washington to Duportail, 27 August 1778, Fitzpatrick, *Writings of Washington*, XII: 363.
[2] Washington to Malcolm, 7 September 1778, Fitzpatrick, *Writings of Washington*, XII: 408.
[3] Malcolm to Washington, 10 September 1778, *Washington Papers*, Series 4, Reel 51, Library of Congress.
[4] Paul David Nelson, *General Horatio Gates, A Biography* (Baton Rouge: Louisiana State University Press, 1976), p. 196.

friendly behavior was not part of Duportail's modus operandi. He leaned on rank to get things done, as he had explained to the President of Congress.[5]

35. Washington to Duportail, West Point, 19 September 1778, Fitzpatrick, *Writings of Washington,* XII: 469; and Palmer, *River and the Rock,* p. 178.
36. Kosciuszko to Gates, West Point, 6 October 1778, *Gates Papers,* Reel 5 (Box 10), No. 108.
37. Washington to Marquis de Lafayette, New Windsor, 8 April 1781, Fitzpatrick, *Writings of Washington,* XXI: 433.
38. Duportail to Washington, Morris Town, 16 January 1780, *Papers of Congress,* M247, R170, I 152, V8, p. 337; and Kite, *Duportail,* p. 245-46.
39. Duportail to Washington, Camp before York, 24 October 1781, *Papers of Congress* M247, R188, I 169, V8, p. 256; and Washington to Duportail, Camp near York, 26 October 1781, Fitzpatrick, *Writings of Washington,* XXIII: 269.
40. Duportail to Washington, Camp near York, 27 October 1781, in "Correspondence of George Washington and Comte de Grasse," 71st Congress, 2d Session, Senate Document No. 211, pp. 146-47; and Kite, *Duportail,* pp. 215-17. Senate Document No. 211 contains Washington's certificate of merit and Duportail's letter to Washington of 27 October 1781.
41. Washington to President of Congress, Headquarters near York, 31 October 1781, *Papers of Congress,* M247, R171, I 152, V10, p. 365; and John Hanson to Duportail, Philadelphia, 17 November 1781, *Papers of Congress,* M247, R24, I 16, p. 123.
42. Kosciuszko to Gates, 8 April (1782), *Gates Papers,* Reel 8 (Box 16), No. 28.
43. Kite, *Duportail,* p. 59.

Chapter 5. West Point: Key to the Continent

1. *Journals of Congress,* IX: 864-68, 971-72; Washington to Putnam, Whitemarsh, 11 November and 2 December 1777, and Washington to George Clinton, 3 December 1777, Fitzpatrick, *Writings of Washington,* X: 40, 129-33, 135-36, 307-08, and Washington to Robert R. Livingston, Valley Forge, 12 March 1778, Fitzpatrick, XI: 70.
2. Horace M. Reeve, "West Point in the Revolution, 1778-1783," *The Centennial of the United States Military Academy at West Point, New York, 1802-1902* (Washington: Government Printing Office, 1904), I:156; and Charles S. Hall, *Life and Letters of Samuel Holden Parsons* (New York, 1968), p. 185.
3. *Public Papers of George Clinton,* II:729, 848.
4. *Public Papers of George Clinton,* II:708-09; Palmer, *River and the Rock,* pp. 150-53; and James Thacher, M. D., *Military Journal of the American Revolution* (Hartford, Connecticut: Hurlbut, Williams & Company, 1862), p. 216.

[5] Kite, *Duportail,* pp.31-33.

5. Palmer, *River and the Rock,* p. 154; and Hall, *Life of Parsons,* p. 157.

6. Washington to Parsons, 18 March 1778, Fitzpatrick, XI: 103-04; "McDougall's Diary," 8-11 April 1778, *Alexander McDougall Papers,* New-York Historical Society; and Palmer, *River and the Rock,* p.161.

7. *The Memoirs of Rufus Putnam,* pp. 75-76.

8. Washington to St. Clair, New Windsor, 20 July 1779, Fitzpatrick, XV: 442-43; Palmer, *River and the Rock,* p. 204; and Kosciuzko to McDougall, 6 April 1779, *McDougall Papers,* MF Reel 2. Kosciuszko's three original sketches of Redoubt No. 4 are the possession of The New-York Historical Society.

9. Reeve, *Centennial of USMA,* pp. 161-63.

10. Reeve, *Centennial of USMA,* p. 155.

11. George Clinton to Gates, 8 April 1778, *Papers of George Clinton,* III: 151; Troup to Gates, Fishkill, New York, 18 April 1778, *Gates Papers,* MF Reel 4 (Box 9), No. 85; Reeve, *Centennial of USMA,* p. 164; Palmer, *River and the Rock,* p. 164; and Miller, et al, "Highland Fortress," p. 205.

12. *Journals of Congress,* X: 354-55; Washington to Gates, Valley Forge, 24 April 1778, *Gates Papers,* MF Reel 3 (box 5), No. 58; McDougall to George Clinton, 11 May 1778, *Papers of George Clinton,* III: 294; "McDougall's Diary," 10-20 May 1778, *McDougall's Papers,* MF Reel 2; Washington to Gates, 29 June 1778, and Washington to John Glover, Haverstraw, 18 July 1778, Fitzpatrick, XII: 129, 188; John Glover to Gates, 2 July 1778, Manuscripts Division, New York Public Library; and Palmer, *River and the Rock,* p. 167.

13. "Returns of West Point, Commanded by Colonel William Malcolm," 25 July 1778, *Papers of Congress,* M247, R99, I 78, p. 373; and Palmer, *River and the Rock,* p. 168.

14. Washington to Colonel William Malcolm, White Plains, 21 and 27 July 1778, Fitzpatrick, XII: 196, 239; George Athan Billias, *General John Glover and His Marblehead Mariners* (New York: Henry Holt and Company, 1960), pp. 161-62; and Hall, *Life of Parsons,* p. 185.

15. Malcolm to Congress, West Point, 1 August 1778, *Papers of Congress,* M247, R99, I 78, p. 369; and Palmer, *River and the Rock,* pp. 171-72.

16. Ward, *War of the Revolution,* II: 587-93.

17. Washington to Comte D'Estaing, 11 September 1778, and Washington to President of Congress, White Plains, 12 September 1778, Fitzpatrick, XII: 426-27,434- 437; and Washington to Gates, 7 October 1778, Fitzpatrick, XIII: 43-44.

18. Kosciuszko to Gates, West Point, 3 March 1779, *Gates Papers,* MF Reel 5 (Box 11), No. 60; and Gates to Washington, 11 September 1778, *Washington Papers,* MF Reel 51, Library of Congress.

19. Washington to Gates, 11 September 1778, and Washington to Gates, 7 October 1778, Fitzpatrick, XII: 419-20, XIII: 44.

20. Kosciuszko to Gates, West Point, 12 September 1778, *Gates Papers,* MF Reel 5 (Box 10), No. 76; and Kosciuszko to Colonel John Taylor, 14 September 1778, in Metchie J.E. Budka, ed., *Autograph Letters of Thaddeus*

Kosciuszko in the American Revolution (Chicago: The Polish Museum of America, 1977), p. 28.

21. Haiman, Kosciuszko, pp. 97-98; and Palmer, River and the Rock, p. 181.

22. Washington to McDougall, 24 November and 16 December 1778, Washington to Malcolm, 7 December 1778, Fitzpatrick, XIII: 320- 21, 375, 399; and "Diary of a French Officer, 1781," The Magazine of American History, Vol. IV (1880), p. 306.

23. Thomas Egleston, The Life of John Paterson, pp. 308-10.

24. Haiman, Kosciuszko, p. 77; Palmer, River and the Rock , pp. 181- 82; and Washington to McDougall, 16 December 1778, Fitzpatrick, XIII: 400.

25. Washington to Malcolm, 8 November 1778, Fitzpatrick, XIII: 218; McDougall to Major Dobbs, 22 December 1778, Paterson to McDougall, 21 and 24 December 1778, Kosciuszko to McDougall, 2 January 1779, McDougall to Kosciuszko, 18 March 1779, McDougall Papers, MF Reel 2; and Palmer, River and the Rock, pp. 184-86.

26. Kosciuszko to McDougall, Fort Arnold, 28 December 1778, MF Reel 2, Kosciuszko to McDougall, 6 February and 24 April, 1779, Reel 3, McDougall Papers, and McDougall's "Evening Orders," 29 December 1778, Manuscript Department, New-York Historical Society. Kosciuszko's letter of 28 December 1778 is unusual not only for its frank content but also its level of English expression, better than his normal capability. Undoubtedly, the engineer had help, probably from General Paterson himself.

27. McDougall to Washington, Peekskill, 10 December 1778, McDougall Papers, Reel 2.

28. McDougall's instructions to Gouvion, 17 and 20 December 1778, McDougall Papers, Reel 2; Washington to McDougall, Middle Brook, 9 February 1779, Fitzpatrick, XIV: 84; McDougall to Washington, 15 April 1779, and Report of McDougall, Henry Knox, and Duportail to Washington, West Point, 20 August 1779, McDougall Papers, Reel 3.

29. Duportail to John Jay, President of Congress, 11 May 1779. Papers of Congress, M247, R181, I 164, p. 342; and Palmer, River and the Rock, p. 190. Duportail behaved in a manner that military men describe with a derogatory term, when an officer tries to cover his tracks and escape possible blame.

30. Washington to McDougall, Middle Brook, 28 May and 2 June 1779, Fitzpatrick, XV: 167, 214.

31. Joseph Johnson, Traditions and Reminiscences Chiefly of the American Revolution in the South (Charleston, Walker & James, 1851); reprint ed., Spartanburg, South Carolina: The Reprint Company, 1972), p. 415; and Major General James Pattison to Lord Viscount Townshend, Camp at Stoney Point, 9 June 1779, Papers of George Clinton, V: 23, 26.

32. General Orders, Army Headquarters, New Windsor, 30 June 1779, McDougall's Orderly Book, No. 74, McDougall Papers; and Fitzpatrick, XV: 341-42; Kosciuszko to Washington, 21 July 1779, George Washington Papers, Library of Congress; Washington to Kosciuszko, HeadQuarters, 9 September 1779, Fitzpatrick, XVI: 255.

33. Eugene P. Chase, ed. and trans., *Our Revolutionary Forefathers: The Letters of Francois, Marquis de Barbe-Marbois* (New York: Duffield, 1929), pp. 113-15.
34. Chase, *Letters of Barbe-Marbois*, pp. 116-18; and "Substance of Conference between the Chevalier de la Luzerne and General Washington," West Point, 16 September 1779, Fitzpatrick, XVI: 294.
35. Chase, *Letters of Barbe-Marbois*, p. 117.
36. Edward Field, ed., *Diary of Colonel Israel Angell, Commanding the Second Rhode Island Continental Regiment during the American Revolution, 1778-1781*, Entry of 28 November 1779 (Providence: Preston and Rounds Company, 1899), pp. 96-97.
37. Heath to Clinton, 25 January 1780, *Public Papers of Clinton*, V:464-65; Washington to President of Congress, 5 January 1780, Washington to Heath, 27 November 1779, Fitzpatrick, XVII: 191- 92, 357; Palmer, *River and the Rock*, p. 221.
38. *Heath's Memoirs of the American War*, with intro. and notes by Rufus Rockwell Wilson, reprint of original edition of 1798 (Freeport, New York: Books for Libraries Press, 1970), pp. 239-42; General Washington's Order, Moore's House, 21 November 1779, in *Orderly Book of McDougall's Brigade*, 20 November-5 December 1779, New-York Historical Society; Washington to Heath, Morristown, 14 January 1780, Fitzpatrick, XVII:395-98; and Palmer, *River and the Rock*, p. 227.
39. Kosciuszko to General Nathanael Greene, West Point, 28 January 1780, in "Correspondence relating to the American Revolution of Maj. Gen. N. Greene," Vol. 1, No. 56, American Philosophical Society, Philadelphia; Kosciuszko to Colonel Richard K. Meade, West Point, 23 March 1780, *George Washington Papers*, Series 4, Reel 65, Library of Congress, and Meade to Kosciuszko, 30 March 1780, Fitzpatrick, XVIII: 182.
40. Washington to General Robert Howe, Morristown, 21 March 1780, Fitzpatrick, XVIII: 131-32; Palmer, *River and the Rock*, pp. 228-29; and Reeve, *Centennial of USMA*, p. 164n.
41. Washington to President of Congress, 3 April 1780, Fitzpatrick, XVIII: 209; Kosciuszko to Philip Schuyler, West Point, 12 May 1780, *Papers of Congress*, M247, R97, I 178, V13, p. 557; Washington to Robert Howe, 25 May 1780, and Washington to President of Congress, 27 May 1780, Fitzpatrick, XVIII: 413, 428-29.
42. Ward, *War of the Revolution*, II: 703, 715-16; and *Journals of Congress*, XVII: 508.
43. Gates to Major John Armstrong, (spring 1780), in Henry A. Washington, ed., *The Writings of Thomas Jefferson*, VIII: 496; and *Journals of Congress*, XVII: 510.
44. Gates to Washington, Travelers Rest, 21 June 1780, in Budka, *Kosciuszko Letters*, p. 43; and McDougall to Howe, West Point, 3 July 1780, *McDougall Papers*, MF Reel 3
45. Kosciuszko to Washington, West Point, 30 July 1780, *George Washington Papers*, Reel 68, Library of Congress; and Washington to Kosciuszko,

Peekskill, 3 August 1780, Fitzpatrick, XIX: 316.

46. Kosciuszko to Washington, West Point, 4 August and 7 August 1780, *George Washington Papers*, Reels 68 and 69, Library of Congress; Washington to Kosciuszko, 8 August 1780, Fitzpatrick, XIX: 316n; Washington to Gates, Orange Town, 8 August 1780, and Washington to Arnold, Peekskill, 6 August 1780, Fitzpatrick, XIX: 331, 339.

47. Palmer, *River and the Rock*, pp. 206-07.

48. Francois-Jean, Marquis de Chastellux, *Travels in North America in the Years 1780, 1781, and 1782*, 2 Vols. (Paris, 1786); reprint ed., with intro. and notes by Howard C. Rice, Jr. (Chapel Hill: The University of North Carolina Press, 1963), pp 89-94.

Chapter 6. Kosciuszko Joins the Southern Army

1. Washington to Heath, HeadQuarters near Passaic Falls, 31 October 1780, Fitzpatrick, *Writings of Washington*, XX:268; and Palmer, *River and the Rock*, pp. 271- 78.

2. Heath to Washington, West Point, 6 November 1780, "The Heath Papers," III: 126-27, *Collections of the Massachusetts Historical Society*, Boston.

3. Washington to Gates, Headquarters, Orange Town, 12 August 1780, Fitzpatrick, XIX: 362.

4. Clajon to Gates, 20 August 1780, *The State Records of North Carolina*, XIV: 565. The New-York Historical Society has Kosciuszko's original architectural plan for a new and more imposing Traveler's Rest. Due to misfortune, however, Gates did not build it. In 1790, he sold the Virginia estate and moved to New York City, in Nelson, *General Gates*, pp. 287-88.

5. Jefferson to Gates, 23 September 1780, *The Writings of Thomas Jefferson*, Andrew A. Lipscomb, ed., 20 Vols. (Washington, 1903-05). *IV: 106.*

6. Ward, *War of the Revolution,* II: 722-30; Journals of Congress, XVIII: 906; and Washington to Gates, Headquarters near Passaic Falls, 8 October 1780, and Washington to Gates, Prackness, 22 October 1780, Fitzpatrick, XX: 136-37, 236-37.

7. Smallwood to Gates, Salisbury, North Carolina, 20 October 1780, *Records of North Carolina*, XIV: 704; Council of War, Hillsborough, North Carolina, 29 October 1780, *Records of North Carolina*, XIV: 438, 719; R.W. Gibbes, *Documentary History of the American Revolution, 1776-1782*, 3 Vols. (New York: D. Appleton & Co., 1857), III: 276-77; and Colonel Otho Holland Williams, "A Narrative of the Campaign of 1780," Appendix B of William Johnson, *Sketches of the Life and Correspondence of Nathanael Greene*, 2 Vols. (Charleston: A.E. Miller, 1822), I: 506.

8. Council of War, New Providence, North Carolina, 25 November 1780, *Papers of Congress*, M247, R174, I 154, V2, p. 337.

9. General Orders of General Gates, Charlotte, 3 December 1780, and of General Greene, 5 December 1780, *Papers of Congress*, M247, R190, I 171, p. 358-59.

10. Brown to Gates, Hillsborough, 16 November 1780, *Records of North Carolina,* XIV: 740; and Johnson, *Life of Greene,* Appendix B, I: 510.
11. Haiman, *Kosciuszko,* p. 104.

Chapter 7. The Race to the Dan

1. Greene to Kosciuszko, December 8, 1780, *Greene Papers,* GR 775, Huntington Library, San Marino, California; Greene to Samuel Huntington, President of Congress, Camp at the Cheraws, December 28, 1780, *Papers of the Continental Congress,* M247, R175, I 155, V1, p. 498, National Archives; Ward, *War of the Revolution,* II: 749-50; George W. Greene, *Life of Nathanael Greene,* III: 83-84; and Christopher L. Ward, *The Delaware Continentals, 1776-1783* (Wilmington, Delaware: The Historical Society of Delaware, 1941), p. 366.
2. Greene to Samuel Huntington, Camp at the Cheraws, December 28, 1780; Ward, *War of the Revolution,* II: 750-54; and George W. Greene, *Life of General Greene,* III: 131.
3. Greene to Kosciuszko, December 8, 1780, *Greene Papers,* GR 749, Huntington Library; Francis Vinton Greene, *General Greene,* p. 175; Ward, *War of the Revolution,* II: 751-52; Johnson, *Life of Greene,* I: 336; and General Greene to Samuel Huntington, Camp Charlotte, December 7, 1780, *Papers of Congress,* M247, R191, I 178, V1, pp. 18-19.
4. Greene to Kosciuszko, January 1, 1781, "Nathanael Greene Letter Book," Jan-Feb 1781, pp. 11-12, Manuscript Division, Library of Congress.
5. Ward, *War of the Revolution,* II: 755-62.
6. Lewis Morris to Kosciuszko, Mark's Ferry, February 1, 1781, *Greene Papers,* GR937, Huntington Library; and Johnson, *Life of Nathanael Greene,* I: 404. The name "Dellyenn" undoubtedly refers to Captain Dalzien.
7. Ward, *War of the Revolution,* II:765, 770.
8. Greene to Washington, Camp Guilford Court House, February 9, 1781, *Papers of Congress,* M247, R175, I 155, V1, p. 566; and Ward, *War of the Revolution,* II: 771.
9. "Council of War," Guilford Court House, February 9, 1781, *Papers of Congress,* M247, R175, I 155, V1, p. 569.
10. Greene to Washington, Camp Guilford Court House, February 9, 1781, p. 567; Ward, *War of the Revolution,* II: 772-73; and Charles Royster, *Light-Horse Harry Lee and the Legacy of the American Revolution* (New York: Alfred A. Knopf, 1981), pp. 11-12, 192.
11. Greene to Washington, Camp Irwin's Ferry on the Dan River, February 15, 1781, *Papers of Congress,* M247, R191, I 172, V1, p. 55; and Johnson, *Life of Nathanael Greene, I: 431.*
12. Johnson, *Life of Nathanael Greene, I:* 431-35; Ward, *War of the Revolution,* II: 774-76; and Washington to Greene, Head Quarters, New Windsor, March 21, 1781, Fitzpatrick, XXI: 345. The race to the Dan River and Kosciuszko's key role are portrayed dramatically in the television film

The Revolutionary War, Carol L. Fleisher, Executive Producer and Director, shown on The Learning Channel in November 1995.

13. Greene to Kosciuszko, February 16, 1781, *Greene Papers*, GR996, Huntington Library; Greene to General Richard Caswell, Camp at Halifax Court House, Virginia, February 16, 1781, and Greene to North Carolina Board of War, February 15, 1781, *Greene Papers*, Nos. 19:15 and 19:17, William L. Clements Library, University of Michigan, Ann Arbor, Michigan; and Greene to Washington, Camp Irwin's Ferry on the Dan River, February 15, 1781, *Papers of Congress*, M247, R191, I 172, V1, p. 59.

14. Kosciuszko to Greene, Halifax, North Carolina, February 19, 1781, *Greene Papers*, HM 8054, Huntington Library; and Haiman, *Kosciuszko*, pp. 109-10. The letter encloses a map sketch of the proposed defense of Halifax.

15. George W. Greene, *General Greene*, III: 176-190; and Ward, *War of the Revolution*, II: 784-85.

16. George W. Greene, *General Greene*, III: 193-202, 219.

17. Ward, *War of the Revolution, II: 802-08.*

18. Henry Lumpkin, *From Savannah to Yorktown: The American Revolution in the South* (Columbia: University of South Carolina Press, 1981), p. 184.

Chapter 8. Siege of Ninety-Six

1. Henry Lumpkin, *From Savannah to Yorktown*, p. 192; and Ward, *War of the Revolution*, II: 816.

2. Lt. Col. Joseph B. Mitchell, *Decisive Battles of the American Revolution* (New York: G.P. Putnam's Sons, 1962), p. 196; Ward, *War of the Revolution,* II: 816; and Lumpkin, *From Savannah to Yorktown,* p. 192.

3. Ward, *War of the Revolution,* II: 816-17.

4. "Kosciuszko's Notes," *Otho Holland Williams Papers*, Mss. 979, Maryland Historical Society, Baltimore; and Johnson, *Life of Nathanael Greene*, II: 143.

5. Henry Lee, *Memoirs of the War in the Southern Department of the United States* (New York: University Publishing Company, 1869; reprint ed., Arno Press, 1969), p. 359; and Johnson, *Life of Nathanael Greene*, II: 142.

6. Henry Guerlac, "Vauban: The Impact of *Science on War,"pp.* 26-48.

7. Lumpkin, *From Savannah to Yorktown*, pp. 198-99; and *Williams Papers*.

8. Kosciuszko, *Williams Papers*, Mss. 979; and Lumpkin, *From Savannah to Yorktown*, pp. 198-200.

9. Greene to President of Congress, June 9, 1781, *Papers of Congress*, M247, R175, I 155 V2, p. 113.

10. Lee, *Memoirs*, p. 359; Ward, *War of the Revolution,* II: 818-20; and Lumpkin, *From Savannah to Yorktown*, p. 200.

11. Charles Stedman, *The History of the Origin, Progress, and Termination of the American War*, 2 Vols. (London: J. Murray et al, 1794), II: 370; George W. Greene, *Life of Nathanael Greene*, III: 235-36; and Haiman, *Kosciuszko*, p. 116.

12. Lumpkin, *From Savannah to Yorktown*, pp. 200-01; Williams' report of casualties to Congress, 20 June 1781, p. 191, *Papers of Congress*, M247, R175, I 155, V2, p. 191; and Stedman, *History of the American War*, II:370.

13. Stedman, *History of the American War*, II: 369-70; and Lumpkin, *From Savannah to Yorktown*, p. 201.

14. Ward, *War of the Revolution*, II: 820-21; and Lumpkin, *From Savannah to Yorktown*, p. 202.

15. Ward, *War of the Revolution*, II: 821-22; and Lumpkin, *From Savannah to Yorktown*, p. 202.

16. General Greene to President of Congress, Camp at Little River near Ninety-Six, June 20, 1781, *Papers of Congress*, M247, R191, I 172, V1, p. 186; Stedman, *History of the American War*, II: 372-73; Ward, War of the Revolution, II: 822; Lossing, *Field Book of the Revolution*, II: 689-94; Kosciuszko's Notes, *Williams Papers*, Nos. 107, 978, 979; David Ramsay, *History of the Revolution in South Carolina*, 2 Vols. (Trenton, 1785), II: 242; and Colonel Williams' Notes, No. 978, Maryland Historical Society.

17. Lee, *Memoirs*, p. 371n.

18. Lumpkin, *From Savannah to Yorktown*, pp. 204-05.

19. Johnson, *Life of Greene*, II: 141-42; and Henry Lee, Jr., *The Campaign of 1781 in the Carolinas: With Remarks Historical and Critical on Johnson's Life of Greene* (Philadelphia, 1824); reprint ed., Chicago: Quadrangle Books, Inc., 1962), pp. 404-05. In his book Lee emphasizes the secondary title.

20. Lee, *Campaign of 1781*, p. 405; Joseph Johnson, *Traditions and Reminiscences Chiefly of the American Revolution in the South*, p. 405; and William Johnson, *Life of Greene*, II: 461.

21. George W. Greene, *Life of Nathanael Greene*, III: 305-17.

22. Alexander Garden, *Anecdotes of the Revolutionary War in America* (Charleston: A.E. Miller, 1822), pp. 65, 79; and Cecil B. Hartley, *Life of Major General Henry Lee, Commander of Lee's Legion in the Revolutionary War* (New York: Derby & Jackson, 1859), p. 207.

23. Noel B. Gerson, *Light-Horse Harry Lee: A Biography of Washington's Great Cavalryman, General Henry Lee* (Garden City, New York: Doubleday & Company, 1966), p. 136; and Boatner, *Encyclopedia of the American Revolution*, p. 590.

24. General Greene's Orderly Book, June 20, 1781, Huntington Library; and George W. Greene, *Life of Nathanael Greene*, III: 316.

25. Ward, *War of the Revolution*, II: 821-22; George W. Greene, *Life of Nathanael Greene*, III: 313-14; Lossing, *The Pictorial Field-Book*, p. 693; and Boatner, *Encyclopedia of the American Revolution*, p. 807.

Chapter 9. Eutaw Springs: Greene's Last Major Battle

1. Francis Vinton Greene, *General Greene*, p. 259.

2. Elswyth Thane, *The Fighting Quaker: Nathanael Greene* (Mattituck, New York: Aeonian Press, Inc., 1972), pp. 244-45; and Ward, *War of the*

Revolution, II: 825. The High Hills of the Santee are located several miles
north of the village of Stateburg, South Carolina. The southern area where
Greene encamped his army is today (1996) the site of fine residential
homes on spacious lots.

3. Kosciuszko to Gates, High Hills of Santee, July 29, 1781, *Gates Papers*,
Reel 8 (Box 16), No. 57.
4. Greene to Governor Thomas Burke, Headquarters on the High Hills of
the Santee August 12, 1781, *State Records of North Carolina*, XV: 606;
and Budka, *Kosciuszko Letters*, p. 64.
5. Johnson, *Life of Nathanael Greene*, II: 244; Ward, *War of the Revolution*,
II: 894-95; and Greene to General Marion, High Hills, September 17, 1781,
in Gibbes, *Documentary History*, pp. 166-67.
6. Greene to General Washington, Camden, August 26, 1781, *Greene Papers*,
42:36. William C. Clements Library, University of Michigan, Ann Arbor.
In 1912, the Eutaw Chapter of the Daughters of the American Revolution (DAR) marked the site of the Battle of Eutaw Springs, South Carolina.
A display board, with a sketch of the deployed forces, describes the battle.
The DAR stated: "In August 1781, George Washington sent a dispatch to
General Nathanael Greene, commander of the Southern army, which convinced him to strike a blow against the British forces in South Carolina
and prevent them from sending aid to Lord Cornwallis in Virginia. Without waiting for the end of the malaria season, Greene broke camp in the
High Hills of the Santee, moved up the flood-swollen rivers to Camden,
crossed and headed south." Notwithstanding, Greene's correspondence
with Washington indicates ignorance of Washington's plans for Virginia.
7. George W. Greene, *Life of Nathanael Greene*, III: 384-89.
8. George W. Greene, *Life of Nathanael Greene*, III: 390-404; and General
Greene to President of Congress, Head Quarters, Martins Ferry, near
Ferguson's Swamp, South Carolina, September 11, 1781, *Papers of Congress*, M247, R175, I 155, V2, pp. 317-28.
9. Greene to President of Congress, September 11, 1781.
10. Kosciuszko to Molineri, Nemours, France, March 17, 1809, Rare Books
and Manuscripts Division, New York Public Library; and Haiman,
Kosciuszko, p. 123.

Chapter 10. The War Subsides

1. Francis V. Greene, *General Greene*, p. 281.
2. Francis V. Greene, *General Greene*, pp. 278-83.
3. Haiman, *Kosciuszko*, pp. 123-24; Francis V. Greene, *General Greene*,
p. 284; Ward, *War of the Revolution*, II: 838-39; George W. Greene, *Life of
Nathanael Greene*, III: 421, 423; and "The Military Journal of Major
Ebenezer Denny," *The Memoirs of the Pennsylvania Historical Society*,
Vol. VII (1860), p. 250.
4. Ward, *War of the Revolution*, II: 839; and Kosciuszko to Williams

(Documents 145 and 258), and Susan Hayne to Williams, June 2, 1784 (Document 304), *Otho Williams Papers*.

5. Johnson, *Life of Nathanael Greene*, II: 331, 339-41, 344; Gibbes, *Documentary History of the American Revolution*, II: 216- 17; George W. Greene, *Life of Nathanael Greene*, III: 470; "Revolutionary Services of Captain John Markland," *The Pennsylvania Magazine of History and Biography*, Vol. IX (1885), p. 109; and Kosciuszko to Williams, no date (March 1782), Document 171, *Williams Papers*.

6. Markland, "Revolutionary Services," p. 110; Secretary Philip Prioleau, Minutes of South Carolina Council, October 14, 1782, and Army Council of War, Ashley Hill, South Carolina, October 16, 19, 1782, *Papers of Congress*, M247, R175, I 155, V2, pp. 569, 579; and Johnson, *Life of Nathanael Greene*, II: 344- 45.

7. Greene to Governor John Matthews, Headquarters, October 22, 1782, enclosing Pinckney's dissenting opinion, *Papers of Congress*, M247, R175, I 155, V2, pp. 563, 587; George W. Greene, *Life of Nathanael Greene*, III: 469; and *Journals of Congress*, XXIII: 825-27.

8. Budka, *Autograph Letters of Kosciuszko*, p. 84; and Harry Emerson Wildes, *Anthony Wayne: Trouble Shooter of the American Revolution* (New York: Harcourt, Brace and Company, 1941), pp. 202, 295-96.

9. Markland, "Revolutionary Services," pp. 110-11; and Johnson, *Life of Nathanael Greene*, II: 345. Colonel Mark Boatner mentions the last bloodshed of the Revolutionary War, but he limits his account to the death of Captain Wilmot. Boatner ignores Kosciuszko's role and incorrectly places the fighting on St. Johns Island, 4 November 1782, in *Encyclopedia of the American Revolution*, p. 559.

10. Garden, *Anecdotes*, pp. 91-93; and Edward McGrady, *The History of South Carolina in the Revolution*, 1780-83 (New York and London, 1902), pp. 662-67.

11. Colonel Lewis Morris to Miss Nancy Elliott, December 13, 1782, *South Carolina Historical and Genealogical Magazine*, XLI (1940), p. 12; Johnson, *Life of Nathanael Greene*, II: 366-67; Haiman, Kosciuszko, p. 138; John Markland, "Revolutionary Services," p. 111; George W. Greene, *Life of Nathanael Greene*, III: 488; and General Greene to Robert R. Livingston, December 19, 1782, *Papers of Congress*, M247, R175, I 155, V2, p. 599.

12. Kosciuszko to Greene, December 26, 1782, Miscellaneous Manuscripts, New York Public Library; and Johnson, *Life of Nathanael Greene*, II: 391.

13. Thane, *The Fighting Quaker*, p. 268; Kosciuszko to Williams, Charleston, February 11, 1783, *Williams Papers*, No. 192; and "The Military Journal of Major Denny," p. 255.

14. Kosciuszko to Alexander Garden, Philadelphia, December 17, 1797, *The South Carolina Historical and Genealogical Magazine*, II (1901), pp. 126-27; Kosciuszko to Dear Madam [Mrs. Nathanael Greene] [James Island], Thursday Evening, and Kosciuszko to Dear General [Nathanael Greene] [James Island], Thursday Evening, *Greene Papers* HM 22728 and HM 8055,

Huntington Library, San Marino, California.

At the South Carolina Historical Society in Charleston on 9 May 1996, the author attempted to identify further the couple, Mr. and Mrs. Scott, who nursed the fever-ridden Kosciuszko to health. It was hardly possible to proceed without discovering Scott's given name. Unfortunately, the only available reference is the Society's published index that simply lists "Mr. Scott (James Island)."

15. Greene to Otho Williams, Headquarters, Charleston, April 11, 1783, *Williams Papers*, No. 200; George W. Greene, *Life of Nathanael Greene*, III: 489; Kosciuszko to Greene, Philadelphia, June 18, 1783, and Greene to Kosciuszko, Headquarters Charleston, July 10, 1783, both letters in Budka, *Autograph Letters of Kosciuszko*, pp. 150, 154; Denny, "Military Journal," p. 256; and Thane, *The Fighting Quaker*, p. 269. Thane incorrectly places Kosciuszko's time of travel to Philadelphia as July 1783.

Chapter 11. Kosciuszko Prepares to Depart America

1. Kosciuszko to Greene, Philadelphia, June 18, 1783, and Greene to Kosciuszko, Charles town, July 10, 1783, in Budka, *Autograph Letters of Kosciuszko*, pp. 150, 154.

2. Greene to President of Congress, Charles town, July 10, 1783, *Papers of Congress*, M247, R149, I 137, V2, p. 747; *Journals of Congress*, XXIV: 489; Morris to Greene, Office of Finance, August 1, 1783, in Budka, *Autograph Letters of Kosciuszko*, p. 156; Duportail to President of Congress, Philadelphia, October 6, 1783, *Papers of Congress*, M247, R94, I 78, V8, p. 31; and *Journals of Congress*, XXV: 668-69, 695, and XXIV: 290, 447.

3. The Address and Petition of the Officers of the Army of the United States to Congress, Cantonments, Hudson's River, December 1782, *Journals of Congress*, XXIV: 291-93; Robert Morris to Greene, Philadelphia, December 19, 1783, in Budka, *Autograph Letters of Kosciuszko*, p. 158; and Higginbotham, *War of the American Revolution*, pp. 411-12.

4. Nelson, *General Gates*, pp. 279-80; Proclamation of the President of Congress, June 24, 1783, in Edmund C. Burnett, ed., *Letters of Members of the Continental Congress*, VII: 195-96; and Kosciuszko to Williams, July 2, 1783, and Major William Jackson to Williams, July 2, 1783, *Williams Papers*, No. 216.

5. Haiman, *Kosciuszko*, pp. 155-56; and Garden, *Anecdotes of the Revolutionary War*, pp. 437-38.

6. Lincoln to President of Congress, Princeton, August 8, 1783, *Papers of Congress*, M247, R163, I 149, V3, p. 123; *Journals of Congress*, XXIV: 498n; and Nelson, *General Gates*, pp. 276- 77, 281.

7. Kosciuszko to Washington, Philadelphia, September 26, 1783, and Washington to President of Congress, Rocky Hill, October 2, 1783, MF Reel 93, Series 4 (General Correspondence), Nos. 213 and 249, Library

of Congress; and Fitzpatrick, XXVII: 178-79.

8. *Journals of Congress*, XXV: 673.

9. Fitzpatrick, XXVII: 222.

10. Thacher, *Military Journal*, pp. 346-47.

11. *Journals of Congress*, XXVI: 43-44, 65-66; and *American State Papers*. "Documents, Legislative and Executive of the Congress of the United States, Class IX, Claims," p. 207.

12. George W. Greene, *Life of Nathanael Greene*, III: 522; Reverend William Gordon to Nathanael Greene, April 5, 1784, "Gordon Letters," *Massachusetts Historical Society Proceedings*, Vol. LXIII (1930), pp. 503-04; and George Champlin Mason, *Reminiscences of Newport* (Newport, Rhode Island, 1884), Massachusetts Historical Society, Boston, pp. 390-91.

13. *Journal of the General Meeting of the Cincinnati in 1784*, Major Winthrop Sargent, ed., "Contributions to American History," Historical Society of Pennsylvania, Philadelphia, Vol. VI (1858); George W. Greene, *Life of Nathanael Greene*, III: 526; Clark Kinnaird, *George Washington: The Pictorial Biography* (New York: Bonanza Books, 1967), p. 186; Edgar Erskine Hume, *Poland and the Society of the Cincinnati*, pp. 3-4, 18; and William Sturgis Thomas, *Members of the Society of the Cincinnati* (New York: Tobias A. Wright, 1929). p. 90.

14. Thomas, *Members of the Cincinnati*, pp. 7-13; Hume, *Poland and the Society of the Cincinnati*, pp. 7-8; and "Washington's Cincinnatus," *The Magazine of American History* (New York: A.S. Barnes & Company, 1880), IV: 158.

It is believed that Kosciuszko added his signature to the Engineers Roll at the General Meeting of the Society of the Cincinnati in Philadelphia, May 1784. Kosciuszko's signature follows that of Duportail on the Roll which was identified by G. Turner, Secretary ProTem, as a "Counterpart of the Institution signed by the Officers of the Engineers. Filed in Gen'l Meetg., May 1784."

The Society of the Cincinnati, Washington, D.C., kindly provided the author (January 30, 1997) an extract photo of the members of the Corps of Engineers. The statement above the signatures reads:

> We the subscribers officers of the American Army, all of us Belonging to the Corps of Engineers, do hereby voluntarily become parties to the aforegoing institution, and do bind ourselves to observe and, to be governed by the principles therein contained, for the performance whereof we so solemnly pledge to each other our sacred honour —
> Done in the cantonment on hudson's River the 24th of the month of May in the year 1783.

15. Kosciuszko to Robert Morris, New York, July 17(?), 1784, in *Bancroft Revolutionary Papers*, Vol. II, f. 479, New York Public Library.

16. Kosciuszko to Otho Williams, Philadelphia, July 9, 1784, and Major William Jackson to Otho Williams, July 20, 1784, *Williams Papers*, Nos.

262 and 265; Kosciuszko to Greene, New York, July 14, 1784, in Budka, *Autograph Letters of Kosciuszko*, p. 175.
17. Frank Landon Humphreys, *Life and Times of David Humphreys*, I:307, 313-14.
18. John Armstrong to Jared Sparks, Red Hook, New York, August 1837, *Sparks Manuscripts*, Ser. 49, Vol. 1, par. 9, Houghton Library, Harvard College, Cambridge, Massachusetts.

Chapter 12. Kosciuszko in Europe

1. *Journals of Congress*, XXXIV:133; Thomas Jefferson to Board of Treasury, Paris, May 16, 1788, in *The Writings of Thomas Jefferson*, Andrew A. Lipscomb, ed.-in-chief (Washington: The Thomas Jefferson Memorial Association, 1904), VII: 10; Count d'Oraczewski to Gouverneur Morris, Paris, August 15, 1792, in *American State Papers*, Class 1 (Foreign Relations) (Washington, 1833), I: 335; and Gouverneur Morris to Thomas Jefferson, Paris, August 17, 1792, in *The Papers of Thomas Jefferson*, John Catanzariti, ed. (Princeton, New Jersey: Princeton University Press, 1990), XXIV: 307.
2. Kosciuszko to Greene, Varsaw, January 20, 1786, in *Greene Papers* HM8056, Huntington Library; Francis V. Greene, *General Greene*, pp. 312-14; Kosciuszko to Haskell, Warsaw, May 15, 1789, in Budka, *Autograph Letters of Kosciuszko*, p. 185; and Humphreys to Kosciuszko, October 1, 1791, The Polish Academy of Sciences, Krakow, Poland, Mss. 1171, No. 88. Congress honored General Greene with a medal and a monument in Washington, D.C. (The author asks whether Kosciuszko's engraving of General Nathanael Greene has survived in any family of the recipients).
3. Kopczewski, *Kosciuszko and Pulaski*, p. 188; and President George Washington to David Humphreys, Philadelphia, July 20, 1791, Fitzpatrick, *Writings of Washington*, XXXI: 320.
4. Adam Zamoyski, *The Last King of Poland* (New York: Hippocrene Books, 1997), pp. 375-78, 381; and Miecislaus Haiman, *Kosciuszko: Leader and Exile* (New York: The Kosciuszko Foundation, 1977), pp. 9-12.
   British historian Norman Davies identifies the principal traitors among the Polish magnates who formed the Confederation of Targowica: Stanislaw-Szczesny Potocki, Franciszek-Ksawery Branicki, Seweryn Rzewuski, and the two Kossakowski brothers, Jozef and Szymon, in *God's Playground: A History of Poland*, 2 Vols. (New York: Columbia University Press, 1984), I: 535. Zamoyski adds another traitor to the list, Feliks Potocki, in *The Last King of Poland*, p. 356.
5. Haiman, *Kosciuszko: Leader*, pp. 15-20; and Kopczewski, *Kosciuszko*, p. 199.
6. Haiman, *Kosciuszko: Leader*, p. 26; and Zamoyski, *The Last King of Poland*, p. 45.
   The destruction of Poland was a great tragedy, plotted and executed

by Russia, Austria, and Prussia. Thomas Jefferson deplored the loss of political morailty in the eighteenth century, pointing to the Partitions of Poland. Her tragedy cannot be blamed alone on the three rapacious neighbor. The decline began internally and continued over a span of 200 years. Perhaps the eventual demise of Poland, a great power in Central Europe for several centuries, began with the death of King Zygmunt August, the last hereditary king, in 1572. The Polish magnates (*szlachta*) seized the occasion to make the kingship elective in order to gain more personal power. Unfortunately, European monarchs also took advantage of the periodic elections to promote their own candidates and meddle in Poland's internal affairs.There were some strong elected kings like the Hungarian Stefan Batory and Jan Sobieski, who saved Vienna and the Holy Roman Empire from the Turks in 1683. Upon Sobieski's death in 1698, two weak and ineffectual kings were elected, both from the principality of Saxony. As Kings of Poland, Augustus II followed by his son Augustus III reigned in name only over a span of nearly seventy years. The Saxons did not even bother to reside in the capital of Warsaw, preferring to remain in Dresden. As required by law, they presided over some national matters on Polish soil. On these few occasions they simply crossed the border into Poland, pitched their royal tents (in effect), conducted the business for a day or two, and then folded them and slunk back to Dresden. Under the Saxons the nation's moral fiber steadily eroded. Even the common folk spoke of the Germans with derision, The author's mother told her children: *"Za Krola Sasa, pij i popuszczaj pasa"* (Literal: "During the Saxon king, drink and let out your belt.")

Although King Stanislaw August was elected monarch with the strong backing of Empress Catherine of Russia in 1764, he neverthelss sought to rebuild the country and free it of Russian control. He was greatly impeded by Catherine who sought to keep Poland weak. The King was also hindered by traitorous Polish magnates. Still he might have succeeded if the country had continued to exist. As historian Adam Zamoyski writes: "Ultimately it was Poland's failure to survive that defeated him and condemned him to disgrace in posterity, and that failure cannot be ascribed to him." (*The Last King of Poland*, p. 462)

7. Thomas Campbell, *The Pleasures of Hope, with other Poems*, 4th edition (Glasgow: Printed by F. Mundell, Ayton Court, at the University Press, 1800), p. 30; Humphreys, *Life of David Humphreys*, II: 213; Noah Webster's editorial in *American Minerva*, reprinted in *Dunlap and Claypoole's American Daily Advertiser*, Philadelphia, February 26, 1795; Washington to Niemcewicz, Mount Vernon, June 18, 1798, Fitzpatrick, XXXVI: 297; Letter IV, "The Letters of Fabius," *The Political Writings of John Dickinson*, 2 Vols. (Wilmington, Delaware: Bonsol & Niles, 1801), II: 188-89; and Jefferson to John Adams, January 11, 1816, in Lipscomb, *Writings of Jefferson*, XIV: 394. Kosciuszko corresponded with Dickinson during his visit to America in 1797-98. Although he planned to visit Dickinson, he was unable to do so.

8. "Kosciuszko," *The Magazine of American History*, Vol. V(1880), p. 378; and Anne Cary Morris, ed., *The Diary and Letters of Gouverneur Morris* (New York: Charles Scribner's Sons, 1888), II: 238.
9. Haiman, *Kosciuszko: Leader*, pp. 31-34; and Edward P. Alexander, "Jefferson and Kosciuszko: Friends of Liberty and of Man," *Pennsylvania Magazine of History and Biography*, Vol. XCII (January 1968), pp. 88-89.
10. *The Philadelphia Gazette*, August 19, 1797; and Haiman, *Kosciuszko: Leader*, pp. 35-36.
11. Haiman, *Kosciuszko: Leader*, pp. 42-43.
12. Kosciuszko to Washington, Philadelphia, August 23, 1797, *Washington Papers*, MF Reel 111; Washington to Kosciuszko, and Washington to Secretary of State, Mount Vernon, both August 31, 1797, Fitzpatrick, XXXVI: 22, 23; and Haiman, *Kosciuszko: Leader*, pp. 49-50.
13. Kosciuszko to Gates, September 1, 1797, and Dr. Benjamin Rush to Gates, September 3, 1797, *Gates Papers*, MF Reel 9 (Box 18), Nos. 50 and 52.
14. Budka, *Under Their Vine and Fig Tree*, p. 19; Haiman, *Kosciuszko: Leader*, pp. 51-61; Hume, *Poland and the Society of the Cincinnati*, pp. 7-8; Nelson, *Horatio Gates*, p. 284; and Kosciuszko to Gates, 27 November 1797, *Gates Papers*, MF Reel 9 (Box 18), No. 55.
15. Jefferson to Gates, February 21, 1798, in Lipscomb, IX: 441; and Budka, *Under Their Vine and Fig Tree*, p. 33.
16. Armstrong to Gates, February 18, 1798, and Kosciuszko to Gates, February 22, 1798, *Gates Papers*, MF Reel 9 (Box 18), Nos. 61 and 62; Kosciuszko to Washington, Elizabeth Town, October 8, 1797, *Washington Papers*, MF Reel 111 (placed at end of the month of October); Washington to Kosciuszko, Mount Vernon, October 15, 1797, Fitzpatrick, XXXVI: 51; and *Laws of the United States of America from the 4th of March, 1789, to the 4th of March, 1815*, 5 Vols. (Washington City: R.C. Weightman, 1815), III: 25.
17. Asa Earl Martin, *History of the United States*, 1492-1865 (Boston: Ginn and Company, 1934), I: 310-15, 321-23; Haiman, *Kosciuszko: Leader*, pp. 73-74.
18. Kosciuszko to Jefferson, Philadelphia, undated [March 1798], *Collections of the Maine Historical Society*, Portland; Jefferson to General Thaddeus Kosciuszko, Philadelphia, June 1, 1798 in Lipscomb, *Writings of Jefferson*, X: 48n; and Alexander, "Jefferson and Kosciuszko," p. 92. Prior to his departure for France on his secret mission, 5 May 1798, Kosciuszko gave Jefferson a gift of remembrance—a rich fur overcoat. Jefferson wore it often. As President in 1805, he posed in the fur coat for portrait artist Rembrandt Peale. Later, the sculptor of Jefferson's figure in the Jefferson Memorial, Washington, D.C., portrays the President in Kosciuszko's fur coat.
19. Haiman, *Kosciuszko: Leader*, pp. 75-78; and James S. Pula, " The American Will of Thaddeus Kosciuszko," *Polish American Studies*, Vol. XXXIV, No. 1 (Spring 1977), pp. 17-18.
20. Budka, *Under Their Vine and Fig Tree*, pp. 65-66.
21. Niemcewicz to Jefferson, Federal City, May 27, 1798, and Jefferson to

Kosciuszko, June 18, 1798, *Jefferson Papers*, Library of Congress; Jefferson to Kosciuszko, June 1, 1798, Lipscomb, X: 47. The *Gazette of the United States*, November 6, 1798. hinted that Kosciuszko departed New Castle for Europe in the same vessel with Dr. John Logan and Volney.

22. The *Aurora and General Advertiser*, Philadelphia, September 10, 1798; *Gazette of the United States*, November 6, 1798; Nathaniel Cutting to Jefferson, Paris, August 27, 1798, *Jefferson Papers*, Library of Congress; Haiman, *Kosciuszko: Leader*, p. 86; Antoine Jullien, *Rys Zycia Wodza Polskiego Tadeusza Kosciuszki*, (translated from the French) (Sketch of the Life of Polish Leader Thaddeus Kosciuszko), (n.p., 1819), p. 30; and Kosciuszko to Jefferson, Paris, undated [December 1798], *Jefferson Collection*, Massachusetts Historical Society.

23. Martin, *History of the United States*, I: 322.

24. John Armstrong to Thomas Jefferson, Red Hook, New York, January 4, 1818, as quoted in Israel Losey White, "The Truth about a European Liberalist in America—General Kosciuszko," *The Connecticut Magazine*, XII (1908). p. 380.

    Earlier, in 1797, another American child was named after Kosciuszko. The general discovered the honor at Elizabeth town, New Jersey, as he returned to Philadelphia from his visit to Gates in New York. The Pole unexpectedly met the little son of Colonel Shepard Kollock, founder and proprietor of the *New Jersey Journal*. The editor of the *Magazine of American History*, relating the story, wrote: "The noble-hearted man was so pleased that he took the little fellow up in his arms and kissed him, placed around his neck or fastened to his coat a gold ornament (cross) which is still tenderly preserved in the family." The editor received the anecdote from a daughter of the Rev. Shepard Kosciuszko Kollock of Philadelphia, who was the little boy, in the *Magazine of American History*, Vol. VI (1881), p. 383.

25. Kosciuszko to Jefferson(in French), undated [June 1801], *Jefferson Collection*, Massachusetts Historical Society; and Haiman, *Kosciuszko: Leader*, p. 90. American historians have compiled and published the correspondence of Thomas Jefferson with prominent individuals. A compilation and editing of the Jefferson–Kosciuszko correspondence remains undone.

26. Kosciuszko to Jefferson (in French), Soleure, April 1816, *Jefferson Collection*, Massachusetts Historical Society; Haiman, *Kosciuszko: Leader*, pp. 104-06; and Henry A. Washington, ed., *The Writings of Thomas Jefferson*, VIII:497.

27. Jefferson to Kosciuszko, Monticello, June 15, 1817, *Herbert R. Strauss Collection*, Newberry Library, Chicago; Kosciuszko to Jefferson, Soleure, September 15, 1817, Jefferson Collection, Massachusetts Historical Society; and Haiman, *Kosciuszko: Leader*, p. 104.

28. Haiman, *Kosciuszko: Leader*, p. 115.

29. Zeltner to Thomas Jefferson, Soleure, Switzerland, October 29, 1817, *Thomas Jefferson Papers*, Missouri Historical Society, St. Louis, Missouri;

Jefferson to Zeltner, Monticello, July 23, 1818, *Jefferson Collection*, HM5884, Huntington Library; and Haiman, *Kosciuszko: Leader*, pp. 115-16.

30. White, "The Truth about a European Liberalist," p. 380.

Epilogue:

The Kosciuszko–Carter Confrontation

1. Nelson, *Horatio Gates*, p. 196.
2. Kajencki to Nelson, 30 August 1995; Nelson to Kajencki, 11 September 1995; and James Ripley Jacobs, *Tarnished Warrior: Major-General James Wilkinson* (New York: The Macmillan Company, 1938). p. 58.
3. *New York Packet*, 24 September 1778.
4. *New York Packet*, 8 October 1778.
5. Nelson to Kajencki, 11 September 1995. Historian Miecislaus Haiman devoted a full chapter to "The Carter Affair" in his pioneering work *Thaddeus Kosciuszko in the American Revolution* (1943).

Kosciuszko's *Manoeuvres of Horse Artillery*

1. Martin I. J. Griffin, "General Thaddeus Kosciuszko," *The American Catholic Historical Researches*, 2nd Series, Vol. VI (April 1910), p. 204.
2. President Thomas Jefferson to Colonel Jonathan Williams, Washington, October 28, 1808, Lipscomb, ed., *The Writings of Thomas Jefferson*, XII: 185; and Haiman, *Kosciuszko: Leader*, p. 92.
3. Griffin, "General Kosciuszko," p. 205; William E. Birkhimer, *Historical Sketch of the Organization, Administration, Materiel and Tactics of the Artillery, United States Army*, 1884; reprint ed., New York: Greenwood Press, Publishers, 1968), pp. 300-302; and Elizabeth Camille Brink, "Kosciuszko—Forefather of American Artillery," *Field Artillery Journal*, XXII (May-June, 1932), pp. 303-13.

   Birkhimer, West Point graduate and member of the Third Regiment, U.S. Artillery, was a prolific writer as wll as a military officer. In the Spanish–American War, the U.S. Army awarded him the Medal of Honor for gallantry at San Miguel de Mayoume, Luzon, 13 May 1899, "in charging and routing with 12 men 200 of the enemy." He was retired from the U.S. Army in 1906 after more than forty years of service with the rank of brigadier general, in Francis B. Heitman, *Historical Register and Dictionary of the United States Army* (Washington: Government Printing Office, 1903), I: 220.

Kosciuszko's Enduring Fame:

1. A.W.W. Evans, *Memoir of Thaddeus Kosciuszko: Poland's Hero and Patriot* (New York: Published by the Society of the Cincinnati, 1883), pp. 3, 24, 33.
2. Dumas Malone, *Jefferson and His Time: The Sage of Monticello* (Boston: Little, Brown and Company, 1981), pp. 39-41; and Nathan Schachner, *Thomas Jefferson, A Biography* (New York: Appleton-Century-Crofts, Inc., 1951), II: 900.
3. John Armstrong to Jared Sparks, Red Hook, New York, September 2, 1837, *Sparks Manuscripts*, Ser. 49, Vol. 1, par. 9, Houghton Library, Harvard College.
4. Wirydjana Fiszerowa, "Memoirs of a Polish Lady of Kosciuszko" (in French). *Historical Review*, Adam M. Skalkowski, ed., Warsaw, 2nd Series, Vol. XII (1934), pp. 261, 265.
5. *Duke de Rochefoucault-Liancourt's Travels in America from 1795 to 1797*, extract in *The Magazine of American History*, Vol. V (1880), p. 378.
6. Jules Cloquet, *Recollections of the Private Life of General Lafayette* (London: Baldwin and Cradock, 1835), pp. 40, 252; Lafayette to Jefferson, November 6, 1806, and Lafayette to unknown addressee, February 12, 1830, in *Memoirs, Correspondance et Manuscrits du General Lafayette*, 12 Vols. (Bruxelles: Societe Belge de Librairie, 1839), IX: 441, XI: 212; and General Franciszek Paszkowski, *Dzieje Tadeusza Kosciuszki, Pierwszego Naczelnika Polakow* (Annals of Kosciuszko, First Leader of the Poles (Krakow, Poland: Jagiellonian University Press, 1872), p. 202. The Marquis de Lafayette visited the United States in the period 1824-25. He was received by the President, Congress, and the people with great joy and respect. On 21 March 1825 he was in Savannah, Georgia, where he laid the cornerstones for the monuments to Generals Casimir Pulaski (Monterey Square) and Nathanael Greene (Johnson Square), in J. Bennett Nolan, *Lafayette in America Day by Day* (Baltimore: The Johns Hopkins Press, 1934), p. 278.
7. Cloquet, *Lafayette*, pp. 177, 248-49.
8. Cloquet, pp. 173, 183, 257-58, 282, 290.
9. Marie T. Capps, Maps and Manuscripts Librarian, USMA Library, to Independence National Historical Park, Philadelphia, June 24, 1986, in Special Collections, USMA Library, West Point, New York; and Cory Gillilland, "A Medal from the Alma Mater," *TAMS Journal*, October 1989, pp. 163-64. (The Token and Medal Society, Inc., Crawford, Indiana.)
10. Capps to Independence National Historical Park, June 24, 1986.
11. Printed Program, "Unveiling of the Kosciuszko Statue, United States Military Academy, West Point, New York, September 1st, 1913"(USMA Library); Letter from Committee of the Corps of Cadets on the Monument to Kosciuszko to General J.G. Swift, West Point, July 22, 1828, Special Collections, USMA Library; and Colonel George S. Pappas, "More to the Point: 1993—Dual Birthday for a Monument Honoring Kosciuszko,"

Assembly (July 1993), p. 54.

12. Griffin, "General Thaddeus Kosciuszko," p. 212; and Haiman, *Kosciuszko in the American Revolution*, p. 31.
13. William Howard Adams, ed., *Jefferson and the Arts: an Extended View*, (Washington: National Gallery of Art, 1976), pp. 47-48.
14. Budka, *Under Their Vine and Fig Tree*, pp. 54-55; and *Gazette of the United States* (Philadelphia), November 9, 1798.
15. *The Magazine of American History*, Vol. IX (1883), p. 73. John F. Watson's *Annals of Philadelphia* is found in the Historical Society of Pennsylvania. For a likeness of Lucretia Pollock, see Haiman, *Kosciuszko: Leader and Exile*, p. 65.
16. Griffin, "General Thaddeus Kosciuszko," p. 209; "Tadeusz Kosciuszko," an address (published) by Stephen Mizwa, President of The Kosciuszko Foundation, at a Members Day Program, New York, October 21, 1967; and Capps to Independence National Historical Park, January 24, 1986.
17. "Decade of Service from the Kosciusko Information Center, 1984-1994," *Kosciuszko Heritage Foundation*, Kosciusko, Mississippi.
18. *Encyklopedia Powszechna PWN* [General Encyclopedia] (Warszawa: Panstwowe Wydawnictwo Naukowe [National Educational Publishers], 1976), p. 304; *Wielka Encyklopedia Powszechna PWN* [Great General Encyclopedia] (Warszawa: Panstwowe Wydawnictwo Naukowe, 1965), VI: 106; and *Przeglad Geograficzny* [Polish Geographical Review] (Warszawa: Panstwowe Wydawnictwo Naukowe, 1958), XXX: 527-29. The *Polish American Journal* of Buffalo, New York, reported in its edition of September 1997 that the state government of New South Wales, Australia, restored the original spelling of Mount Kosciusko by adding a "z" to the name. "The new spelling of the name of Australia's highest mountain," the *Journal* reported, "corrects the longstanding error."
19. Major Ernest L. Cuneo, "General Thaddeus Kosciuszko: Master Military Mind of the American Revolution," *The Saturday Evening Post*, October 1975, p. 63; and Major William Jackson to General Otho Williams, July 2, 1783, *Williams Papers*, No. 216.
20. During the author's visit to Fort Ticonderoga in September 1995, he asked Museum Curator Bruce Moseley to see the Kosciuszko painting, the one that historian Miecislaus Haiman said in 1943 was displayed at the museum. Donated by Edward C. Wheeler in 1934, the painting had been put away pending restoration. Moseley brought out the painting from storage. Clearly it needed restoration; the canvas had become dark from pollutants in the air and the frame, unglued at the corners. The author offered to help solicit money for the restoration, if the curator would give him an estimate of the cost. Shortly after the author's visit, Moseley left Fort Ticonderoga for another position. The author repeated his offer to Moseley's replacement, Christopher Fox, who seemed to be cooperative. He said he would consult with a restoration artist for an estimate when the professional was expected to visit the fort in January 1996. Unfortunately, Fox never gave the author an estimate.

The author's second effort for information proved fruitless again. He wrote Anthony Pell of Weston, Massachusetts, and President of the Fort Ticonderoga Association, for data about the dedication of the bronze plaque in the sally port of the fort in 1929 and about the donor, A. Stanley Miller. Pell passed my letter to Nicholas Westbrook, executive director, who answered with a letter but offered no information. Westbrook said that he did not know who Miller was and had no record of the event. However, he held out a slim hope that something might turn up. "In my experience here," Westbrook wrote, "the answers often materialize just weeks after we ruefully write explaining that we have been able to find nothing."

21. Joel Barlow, *Columbiad* (London, 1809), p. 202.
22. Amy Lowell, *John Keats*, 2 Vols. (Boston: Houghton Mifflin Company, 1925), I: 232.
23. Francis E. Zapatka, "Kosciuszko and Keats," *Polish Studies Newsletter*, November 1992, p. 7.
24. Robert H. Wilson, *Thaddeus Kosciuszko and His Home in Philadelphia* (Philadelphia: Copernicus Society of America, 1976), p. 33.
25. The author claims that the mid-twentieth century set the high-water mark of American historical objectivity. As late as 1997, bias against Kosciuszko surfaced in the work of Richard M. Ketchum who injures Kosciuszko's reputation in *Saratoga: Turning Point of America's Revolutionary War* (p. 123). Ketchum concedes that the resident engineer at Fort Ticonderoga, Colonel Jeduthan Baldwin, "received some skilled help from Colonel Thaddeus Kosciuszko...but the help was a mixed blessing." On the contrary, the fact that Mount Independence became fortified at all resulted from Kosciuszko's engineering expertise. In the summer of 1776, General Philip Schuyler ordered that Mount Independence be fortified and made the center of the American defense. The following June 1777 he inspected the Mount with his brigadier generals and, to his consternation, found that almost nothing had been done under Baldwin for the past year. He at once ordered the new commander at Fort Ticonderoga, General Arthur St. Clair, to rush the defensive effort. St. Clair turned to the capable Kosciuszko, who carried out the task rapidly, having drawn up the plans for General Horatio Gates a month earlier.

Ketchum, furthermore, reveals his prejudice and ignorance of Kosciuszko's character when he states: "Kosciuszko's interest was less in Baldwin and his projects than in promoting his own agenda with General Gates, to whom he wrote fawning letters seeking a staff position while belittling Baldwin's efforts." One may ask, "What position was Kosciuszko seeking?" He already was Gates's engineer. Gates had selected him earlier in Philadelphia and brought him to Fort Ticonderoga. Gates's adjutant general, Major James Wilkinson, habitually referred to Kosciuszko as "Our Chief Engineer."

When Ketchum accuses Kosciuszko of belittling Baldwin's competence, Ketchum implies that Kosciuszko probably criticized Baldwin openly among his fellow officers at Fort Ticonderoga. Ketchum quotes from

Kosciuszko's letter to Gates, 18 May 1777: "I say nothing of what unnecessary works have been carried on, you'll be a judge yourself, my General. We are very fond here of making blockhouses & they are all erected in the most improper places. Nevertheless we'll conquer, headed by your Excellency." For the record, Kosciuszko's letter of 18 May 1777 was the only time he commented on Baldwin's lack of competence, and the frank statement, in private, was a proper response to General Gates's directive to his engineer—to assess the status of the work of fortifying Fort Ticonderoga. The commander has every right to know the conditions of his command.

Jeduthan Baldwin was not a schooled engineer, and his capability was limited to relatively small construction projects. He was not a military planner, with a grasp of overall military strategy in which he could carry out fortifications properly for the defeat of the enemy.

Despite the praise of some friends, Ketchum's *Saratoga* is not "absolutely reliable." Ketchum states with respect to Burgoyne's impending invasion of New York: "Arthur St. Clair had to assume—despite reassurances by Congress and General Gates to the contrary—that the British would be heading his way." But contrary to Ketchum's assertion, General Gates was well aware of the British threat. In his letter of 23 May 1777, Gates cautions General Paterson at Fort Ticonderoga to continue to strengthen the fort. "Perhaps the Enemy may give us Two Months before they come to look at Ticonderoga." And he urges Paterson "to order Lieut. Colonel Kosciuszko's plan to be immediately put into Execution, doing the most defensible parts first." Was Ketchum aware of Gates's letter? Perhaps Ketchum's research is flawed.

Adam Asnyk was a leading poet of the latter half of the nineteenth century (1832-1897), in Czeslaw Milosz, *The History of Polish Literature*, 2nd ed. (Berkeley: University of California Press, 1983), pp. 317-18.

Appendix

Acknowledgements

THE AUTHOR is grateful to the following individuals and libraries in Poland:

- Prof. Dr. Jerzy Wislocki
  Kornik Library, Polish Academy of Sciences

- Dr. Jadwiga Wroblewska
  Gdansk Library, Polish Academy of Sciences

- Dr. Karolina Grodziska
  Krakow Library, Polish Academy of Sciences

- National Library in Warsaw
  For permission to publish Thaddeus Kosciuszko's
  map of the Saratoga battlefield.

- Jan Tadeusz Staszewski
  Zambrow

The author is likewise grateful to the following individuals, libraries, and archival agencies in the United States:

- Jeffrey M. Flannery
  Manuscript Reference Librarian
  Library of Congress, Washington, D. C.

- Dave Richard Palmer
  Lieutenant General, U.S. Army Retired
  Walden University
  Minneapolis, Minnesota

- Seith F. Hudgins, Jr.
  Colonel, U. S. Army Retired
  President, Association of Graduates
  West Point, New York

- Alan C. Aimone
  Assistant Librarian for Special Collections
  United States Military Academy
  West Point, New York

- Paul Ackerman
  West Point Museum
  West Point, New York

- Betsy Gotbaum, Executive Director
  Wendy Haynes
  Richard Fraser
  Megan Hahn
  John Kuss
  New-York Historical Society
  New York, New York

- Susan J. Motyka
  Joyce Ann Tracy
  American Antiquarian Society
  Worcester, Massachusetts

- Jessica M. Pigza
  Maryland Historical Society
  Baltimore, Maryland

- Ron Vestal
  State Department of Cultural Resources
  Raleigh, North Carolina

- Dennis Northcutt
  Missouri Historical Society
  St. Louis, Missouri

- Laura Beardsley
  Ann Flemming
  Historical Society of Pennsylvania
  Philadelphia, Pennsylvania

- Rita Dockery
  The American Philosophical Society
  Philadelphia, Pennsylvania

- Louis L. Tucker, Director
  Virginia H. Smith
  Massachusetts Historical Society
  Boston, Massachusetts

- Alexander Moore, Director
  Peter A. Rarig
  South Carolina Historical Society
  Charleston, South Carolina

- Nicholas Noyes
  Maine Historical Society
  Portland, Maine

- Ellen McAllister Clark
  The Society of the Cincinnati
  Washington, D. C.

- Suzanne Warner
  Yale University Art Gallery
  New Haven, Connecticut

- Willa Sanders
  Kosciuszko Heritage Foundation
  Kosciusko, Mississippi

- Farrell Saunders, Superintendent
Eric Williams
Ninety-Six National Historic Site
Ninety-Six, South Carolina

- Judy Sargent
Chamber of Commerce
Ninety-Six, South Carolina

- Jeffrey J. LaBarge
Saratoga National Historical Park
Stillwater, New York

- Andrea C. Ashby
Karen D. Stevens
Independence National Historical Park
Philadelphia, Pennsylvania

- Francis E. Zapatka
Professor of Literature, American University
Washington, D. C.

- Jan Lorys, Curator
Polish Museum of America
Chicago, Illinois

- Jaroslaw Kurek
Press Attache
Embassy of the Republic of Poland
Washington, D. C.

- John Rhodehamel
Dan Lewis
The Huntington Library
San Marino, California

- Inter-Library Loan Office
University of Northern Illinois
De Kalb, Illinois

- Carolyn Kahl
  Inter-Library Loan Librarian
  University of Texas at El Paso

- Claudia A. Rivers, Special Collections
  Thomas Burdette, Military History
  Library, University of Texas at El Paso

- Rachel K. Onuf
  Rob Cox
  William L. Clemens Library
  University of Michigan
  Ann Arbor, Michigan

- Elaine Stefanko
  Osterhout Free Library
  Wilkes-Barre, Pennsylvania

- Marijean Murray
  Learning Resources Center
  U. S. Army Sergeants Major Academy
  Fort Bliss, Texas

- Jason Nichols
  Brent Prater
  Document Express, The General Libraries
  University of Texas at Austin

- Whitney Baker
  Harry Ransom Humanities Research Center
  University of Texas at Austin

- Ann Marshall May
  John McFarland
  El Paso Public Library, Texas

- Susan Greaves
  Lucy B. Burgess
  The Olin and Kroch Libraries
  Cornell University, Ithaca, New York

- Melanie Wisner
  Susan Halpert
  The Houghton Library
  Harvard University
  Cambridge, Massachusetts

- Julie Englander
  The Newberry Library
  Chicago, Illinois

- John D. Stinson
  Rare Books and Manuscripts Division
  New York Public Library
  New York, New York

- Pauline Pierce
  Curator, Historical Room
  The Stockbridge Library Association
  Stockbridge, Massachusetts

- Joseph E. Gore, President
  Ela Ingarden
  The Kosciuszko Foundation
  New York, New York
  For permission to place a likeness of "Tadeusz
  Kosciuszko at West Point" on the book cover.
  (Painting by artist B. J. Czedekowski at The
  Kosciuszko Foundation)

- Faith Freeman Barbato
  Harper Collins Publishers
  New York, New York

Bibliography

I. PRIMARY SOURCES

1. Government Documents

American State Papers, "Documents, Legislative and Executive of the Congress of the United States:"
Class I (Foreign Relations)
Class IX (Claims for Military Service)

Correspondence of George Washington and Comte de Grasse: Duportail to Washington, Camp near York, October 27, 1781, 71st Congress, 2nd session, Senate Document No. 211.

George Washington Papers, 1741-1799, MF, 124 Reels, 1964.

Journals of the Continental Congress, 1774-1789, Worthington C. Ford et al, eds., 34 Vols. Washington: Government Printing Office, 1904-1937.

Laws of the United States of America, from the 4th of March, 1789, to the 4th of March, 1815, 5 Vols. Washington City: R. C. Weightman, 1815

Public Papers of George Clinton, Hugh Hastings and J. A. Golden, eds, 10 Vols. Albany, New York: James B. Lyon, State Printer, 1899-1914.

The Centennial of the United States Military Academy at West Point, New York, 1802-1902, Reeves, Horace M., "West Point in the Revolution, 1778-1783." Washington: Government Printing Office, 1904.

The Papers of the Continental Congress, 1774-1789, M247, Reels 1-204, National Archives.

The Writings of George Washington, from the Original Manuscript Sources, John C. Fitzpatrick, ed., 39 Vols. Washington: Government Printing Office, 1931-1944.

The State Records of North Carolina, Walter Clark, ed., 26 Vols. Raleigh: P. M. Hale, 1886-1907.

2. Thomas Jefferson Series

The Papers of Thomas Jefferson, John Catanzariti, ed., Vol. 24. Princeton, New Jersey: Princeton University Press, 1990.
The Writings of Thomas Jefferson, Andrew A. Lipscomb and A. E. Berg, eds., 20 Vols. New York, 1903-04.
The Writings of Thomas Jefferson, Henry A. Washington, ed., 9 Vols. Philadelphia: J. B. Lippincott, 1869-71.

3. Collections

American Antiquarian Society, Worcester, Massachusetts.
 Letter Book of General Philip Schuyler
 Orderly Book of Henry B. Livingston
American Philosophical Society, Philadelphia.
 Correspondence relating to the American Revolution of Maj. Gen. N. Greene, Vol. 1, No. 55.
Historical Society of Pennsylvania, Philadelphia.
 Major Winthrop Sargent, ed., *Journal of the General Meeting of the Cincinnati in 1784.*
Houghton Library, Harvard College, Cambridge, Massachusetts.
 Jared Sparks Manuscripts
Huntington Library, San Marino California.
 Nathanael Greene Papers
 General Greene's Orderly Book
 Jefferson Collection
Kosciuszko Heritage Foundation, Kosciusko, Mississippi.
 "Decade of Service from the Kosciusko Information Center, 1894-1994"
Library of Congress (Manuscript Division)
 Nathanael Greene Letter Book
 Thaddeus Kosciuszko to General Arthur St. Clair (in French), undated, [Fort Edward, New York, July 1777].
Library of the United States Military Academy, Special Collections.
 Committee of the Corps of Cadets on the Monument to Kosciuszko to General J. G. Swift, West Point, July 22, 1828.
 Cory Gillilland, "A Medal from the Alma Mater," *TAMS Jour-*

nal, October 1989. (The Token and Medal Society, Inc., Crawford Indiana.)

Marie T. Capps, USMA Library, to Superintendent, Independence National Historical Park, July 24, 1986.

Printed Program, "Unveiling of the Kosciuszko Statue, September 1st, l913."

Maine Historical Society, Portland.

Thaddeus Kosciuszko to Thomas Jefferson, Philadelphia, undated [March 1798]. John S. H. Fogg Collection

Maryland Historical Society, Baltimore.

Otho Holland Williams Papers

Massachusetts Historical Society, Boston

William Gordon Letters

William Heath Papers

Thomas Jefferson Collection

Newberry Library, Chicago

Thomas Jefferson to Thaddeus Kosciuszko, Monticello, June 16, 1817, Herbert R. Strauss Collection.

New-York Historical Society, New York

Alexander McDougall Papers

Alexander McDougall Orderly Book

Horatio Gates Papers

Kosciuszko's Drawing of Redoubt No. 4 at West Point

"Proceedings of a General Court Martial...for the Trial of Major General Arthur St. Clair," in *Collections of the New-York Historical Society for the Year of 1880,* Vol. III.

New York Public Library, Bancroft Collection

Horatio Gates to John Paterson, May 8, 1777

Kosciuszko to General Greene, Charles Town, December 26, 1782

Kosciuszko to Molineri, France, March 17, 1809

The Polish Academy of Sciences, Krakow, Poland

David Humphreys to Thaddeus Kosciuszko, Lisbon, October 1, 1791

The Society of the Cincinnati, Washington, D.C.

Edgar Erskine Hume, *Poland and The Society of the Cincinnati*

Yale University Art Gallery, New Haven, Connecticut

Thaddeus Kosciuszko's Painting (Engraving) of Thomas Jefferson

William L. Clemens Library, University of Michigan at Ann Arbor

Nathanael Greene Papers

4. Books

Anburey, Thomas. *With Burgoyne from Quebec: An Account of the Life at Quebec and of the Famous Battle of Saratoga.* Sydney Jackman, ed. Toronto: Macmillan of Canada, 1963.

Baldwin, Thomas Williams, ed. *The Revolutionary Journal of Colonel Jeduthan Baldwin, 1775-1778.* Bangor, Maine: De Burians, 1906.

Budka, Metchie, J. E. ed. *Under Their Vine and Fig Tree,* being the published account of Julian Ursyn Niemcewicz's *Travels through America in 1797-1798,* with some further account of life in New Jersey. Elizabeth, New Jersey: The Grassman Publishing Company, Inc., 1965.

_____ . *Autograph Letters of Thaddeus Kosciuszko in the American Revolution.* Chicago: The Polish Museum of America, 1977.

Buell, Rowena, comp. *The Memoirs of Rufus Putnam and Certain Official Papers and Correspondence.* Boston: The Riverside Press, 1903.

Burgoyne, Lieutenant-General John. *A State of the Expedition from Canada.* London, 1780; reprint ed., New York: The New York Times, 1969.

Burnett, Edmund C. *Letters of Members of the Continental Congress.* Vol. VII. Washington, D. C.: Carnegie Institution, 1934; reprint ed., Gloucester, Massachusetts: Peter Smith, 1969.

Campbell, Thomas. *The Pleasures of Hope, with other Poems,* 4th edition. Glasgow: Printed by F. Mundell, Ayton Court, at the University Press, 1800.

Chase, Eugene P., ed. and trans. *Our Revolutionary Forefathers: The Letters of Francois, Marquis de Barbe-Marbois.* New York: Duffield, 1929.

Chastellux, Francois Jean, Marquis de. *Travels in North America in the Years 1780, 1781, and 1782,* 2 Vols. Paris, 1786; reprint ed. with intro. and notes by Howard C. Rice, Jr. Chapel Hill: The University of North Carolina Press, 1963.

Cloquet, Jules, M. D. *Recollections of the Private Life of General Lafayette.* London: Baldwin and Cradock, 1835.

(Denny, Ebenezer). "The Military Journal of Major Ebenezer Denny," *The Memoirs of the Historical Society of Pennsylvania,* Vol. VII (1860).

Dickinson, John. *The Political Writings of John Dickinson,* 2 Vols. Wilmington, Delaware: Bonsal and Niles, 1801.

Eelking, Max von. *Memoirs, Letters and Journals, of Major General Riedesel During His Residence in America,* 2 Vols., translated by William M. Stone. Albany: J. Munsell, 1868; reprint ed., New York: New York Times & Arno Press, 1969.

Field, Edward, ed. *Diary of Colonel Israel Angell, Commanding the Second Rhode Island Regiment during the American Revolu tion, 1778-1781.* Providence: Preston and Rounds Company, 1899.

Force, Peter, ed. *American Archives,* Fifth Series. Washington, D. C., 1837-1853.

Garden, Alexander. *Anecdotes of the Revolutionary War in America.* Charleston, South Carolina: A. E. Miller, 1822.

Grzelonski, Bogdan. *Jefferson-Kosciuszko Correspondence,* edited and with Intro. and Notes by Bogdan Grzelonski. Warsaw: Interpress Publishers, 1978.

Heath, William. *Memoirs of Major-General Heath.* Boston: I. Thomas and E. T. Andrews, 1798; reprint ed., Freeport, New York: Books for Libraries Press, 1970.

Heitman, Francis B. *Historical Register and Dictionary of the United States Army.* Washington: Government Printing Office, 1903.

Lafayette, Marquis de. *Memoirs, Correspondance et Manuscrits du General Lafayette,* published by his family, 12 Vols. Bruxelles: Societe Belge de Librarie, 1839.

Laurens, John. *The Army Correspondence of Colonel John Laurens in the Years 1777-78;* reprint ed., New York: New York Times & Arno Press, 1969.

Lee, Henry, Jr. *The Campaign of 1781 in the Carolinas: With Remarks Historical and Critical on Johnson's Life of Greene.* Philadelphia, 1824; reprint ed., Chicago: Quadrangle Books, Inc., 1962.

_____ . *Memoirs of the War in the Southern Department of the United States.* New York: University Publishing Company, 1869; reprinted as *The American Revolution in the South.* New York; Arno Press, 1969.

Mason, George Champlin. *Reminiscences of Newport.* Newport, Rhode Island, 1884. (Massachusetts Historical Society).

Morris, Anne Carey, ed. *The Diary and Letters of Gouverneur Morris,* 2 Vols. New York: Charles Scribner's Sons, 1888.

Sparks, Jared, ed. *Correspondence of the American Revolution,* 4 Vols. Boston: Little, Brown and Company, 1853.

_____ . *The Writings of George Washington,* 12 Vols. New York: Harper & Brothers, Publishers, 1847.

Tarleton, Lieutenant-Colonel. *A History of the Campaign of 1780 and 1781, in the Southern Provinces of North America.* London, 1787; reprint ed., New York: New York Times & Arno Press, 1968.

Thacher, James. *Military Journal of the American Revolution.* Hartford: Connecticut: Hurlbut, Williams & Company, 1862; reprint ed., New York: New York Times & Arno Press, 1969.

Thomas, William Sturgis. *Members of the Society of the Cincinnati: Original, Hereditary and Honorary.* New York: Tobias A. Wright, Inc., 1929.

Trumbull, John. *Autobiography, Reminiscences and Letters, 1756-1841.* New York: Wiley and Putnam, 1841.

Wilkinson, General James. *Memoirs of My Own Times,* 3 Vols. Philadelphia: Abraham Small, 1816; reprint ed., New York: AMS Press, Inc., 1973.

5. Periodicals and Magazines (Primary and Secondary Sources)

American Bar Association Journal
Louis Ottenberg, "A Testamentary Tragedy: Jefferson and the Wills of General Kosciuszko," Vol. 44 (January 1958).

American Historical Review
Jane Clark, "Responsibility for the Failure of the Burgoyne Campaign," Vol. 35 (1930).

Assembly (Association of Graduates, U. S. Military Academy)
Colonel George S. Pappas, "More to the Point: 1993—A Dual Birthday for a Monument Honoring Kosciuszko," July 1993.
Richard John Meyer, Jr., "Thaddeus Kosciuszko: Father of the U. S. Military Engineers," July/August 1997.

Field Artillery Journal
Elizabeth Camille Brink, "Kosciuszko—Forefather of American Artillery," Vol. XXII (May-June 1932)

German American Annals
"Journal of Du Roi the Elder," New Series, Vol 9 (1911)

Historical Review
Wirydjanna Fiszerowa, *Pamietnik Damy Polskiej o Kosciuszce* (Memoirs of a Polish Lady of Kosciuszko) (in French), Adam Skalkowski, ed., 2nd Series, Vol. XII (1934), Warsaw.

Library Bulletin of the American Philosophical Society
Lyman H. Butterfield, "Franklin, Rush, and the Chevalier de Kermovan, An Episode of '76," (1946).

Pennsylvania Magazine of History and Biography
John Markland, "The Revolutionary Services of Captain John Markland," Vol. IX (1885).
Edward P. Alexander, "Jefferson and Kosciuszko: Friends of Liberty and of Man," Vol. XCII (January 1968).
Polish American Studies
James S. Pula, "The American Will of Thaddeus Kosciuszko," Vol. XXXIV, No. 1 (Spring 1977).
Polish Heritage
Wallace M. West, "Is This Kosciuszko's Pistol?" Vol. XLVI, No. 1 (Spring 1995).
Proceedings and Collections of the Wyoming Historical and Genealogical Society
Henry Hobart Bellas, "The Defences of the Delaware River in the Revolution," Vol. V (1900).
South Carolina Historical and Genealogical Society
Kosciuszko to Alexander Garden, Philadelphia, December 17, 1797, Vol. II (1901).
Colonel Lewis Morris to Miss Nancy Elliott, December 13, 1782, Vol. XLI (1940).
The American Catholic Historical Researches
Martin I. J. Griffin, "General Thaddeus Kosciuszko," 2nd Series, Vol. VI (April 1910).
The Connecticut Magazine
Israel Losey White, "The Truth about a European Liberalist in America—General Kosciuszko," Vol. XII (1908).
The Magazine of American History
"Diary of a French Officer," Vol. IV (1880)
"Washington's Cincinnatus," Vol. IV (1880)
Extract of "Kosciuszko" from Duke de Rochefoucault-Liancourt's *Travels in America from 1795 to 1797,* Vol. V (1880)
"Kosciuszko," Vol. VI (1881)
"Kosciuszko as an Artist," Vol. IX (1883)

6. Newspapers

Continental Journal and Weekly Advertiser, Boston
Dunlap and Claypoole's American Daily Advertiser, Philadelphia
Gazette of the United States, Philadelphia
New York Packet, Fishkill
Polish American Journal, Buffalo
The Philadelphia Gazette

II. SECONDARY SOURCES

1. Books

Adams, William Howard, ed. *Jefferson and the Arts: An Extended View.* Washington: National Gallery of Art, 1976.

Arnold, Isaac N. *The Life of Benedict Arnold.* Chicago: Jansen, McClurg & Company, 1880.

Billias, George Athan. *General John Glover and His Marblehead Mariners.* Henry Holt and Company, 1960.

Birkhimer, William E. *Historical Sketch of the Organization, Administration, Materiel and Tactics of the Artillery of the United States Army,* 1884; reprint ed., New York: Greenwood Press, Publishers, 1968.

Boatner, Mark Mayo III, *Encyclopedia of the American Revolution.* New York: David McKay Company, Inc., 1966.

Carrington, Henry B. *Battles of the American Revolution, 1775-1781.* New York: A. S. Barnes & Company, 1877; reprint ed., New York: New York Times & Arno Press, 1968.

Channing, Edward. *A History of the United States, (Vol. III, The American Revolution).* New York: The Macmillan Company, 1921.

Creasy, Sir Edward S. *The Fifteen Decisive Battles of the World.* New York: A. L. Burt, Publisher, 1858.

Davies, Norman. *God's Playground: A History of Poland,* 2 Vols. New York: Columbia University Press, 1984.

Egleston, Thomas. *The Life of John Paterson: Major-General in the Revolutionary Army.* New York: G. P. Putnam's Sons, 1898.

Fortescue, Sir John. *History of the British Army,* 13 Vols. London: Macmillan and Co., 1899-1930.

Furneaux, Rupert. *The Battle of Saratoga.* Briarcliff Manor, New York: Stein and Day Publishers, 1971; reprint ed., Scarborough House, 1983.

Gerson, Noel B. *Light-Horse Harry: A Biography of Washington's Great Cavalryman, General Henry Lee.* Garden City, New York: Doubleday & Company, Inc., 1966.

Gibbes, R. W., M.D. *Documentary History of the American Revolution, 1776-1782,* 3 Vols. New York: D. Appleton & Company, 1857.

Greene, Francis Vinton. *General Greene.* New York: D. Appleton and Company, 1893; reprint ed., New York: Research Reprints, Inc., 1970.

Greene, George Washington. *The Life of Nathanael Greene,* 3 Vols. New York: Hurd and Houghton, 1871.

Gronowicz, Antoni. *Gallant General: Tadeusz Kosciuszko,* translated by Samuel Sorgenstein. New York: C. Scribner's Sons, 1947.

Grzelonski, Bogdan. *Poles in the United States of America, 1776-1865.* Warsaw: Interpress Publishers, 1976.

Guerlac, Henry. "The Impact of Science on War," in *Makers of Modern Strategy: Military Thought from Machiavelli to Hitler,* Edward Meade Earle, ed. Princeton, New Jersey: Princeton University Press, 1952.

Haiman, Miecislaus. *Kosciuszko in the American Revolution.* New York: Polish Institute of Arts and Sciences in America, 1943.

_____ . *Kosciuszko: Leader and Exile.* New York: Polish Institute of Arts and Sciences in America, 1946.

Hall, Charles S. *Life and Letters of Samuel Holden Parsons.* New York: From the Archives of James Pugliese, 1968.

Hamilton, Edward P. *Fort Ticonderoga: Key to a Continent.* Boston: Little, Brown and Company, 1964.

Hartley, Cecil B. *Life of Major General Henry Lee, Commander of Lee's Legion in the Revolutionary War.* New York: Derby & Jackson, 1859.

Higginbotham, Don. *The War of American Independence.* New York: The Macmillan Company, 1971.

Howson, Gerald. *Burgoyne of Saratoga, A Biography.* New York: Times Books, 1979.

Humphreys, Frank Landon. *Life and Times of David Humphreys: Soldier–Statesman–Poet, "Belov'd of Washington,"* 2 Vols. New York: G. P. Putnam's Sons, 1917.

Jacobs, James Ripley. *Tarnished Warrior: Major-General James Wilkinson.* New York: The Macmillan Company, 1938.

Johnson, Curt. *Battles of the American Revolution.* New York: Bonanza Books, 1984.

Johnson, Joseph. *Traditions and Reminiscences Chiefly of the American Revolution in the South.* Charleston, South Carolina: Walker & James, 1851; reprint ed., Spartanburg, South Carolina: The Reprint Company, 1972.

Johnson, William. *Sketches of the Life and Correspondence of Nathanael Greene, Major General of the Armies of the United States,* 2 Vols. Charleston, South Carolina: A. E. Miller, 1822; reprint ed., New York: De Capo Press, 1973.

Jullien, Antoine. *Rys Zycia Wodza Polskiego Tadeusza Kosciuszki* (Sketch of the Life of Polish Leader Thaddeus Kosciuszko) (translated from the French), n.p., 1819. (At the Library of the

Polish Academy of Sciences, Gdansk, Poland).

Ketchum, Richard M. *Saratoga: Turning Point of America's Revolutionary War.* New York: Henry Holt and Company, 1997.

Kinnaird, Clark. *George Washington: The Pictorial Biography.* New York: Bonanza Books, 1967.

Kite, Elizabeth S. *Brigadier-General Louis Lebeque Duportail: Commandant of Engineers in the Continental Army, 1777-1783.* Baltimore: The John Hopkins Press, 1933.

Kopczewski, Jan Stanislaw. *Kosciuszko and Pulaski.* Warsaw: Interpress, 1976.

Lodge, Henry Cabot. *The Story of the Revolution,* 2 Vols. New York: Charles Scribner's Sons, 1898.

Lossing, Benson J. *The Pictorial Field Book of the American Revolution,* 2 Vols. New York: Harper, 1851-52.

Lowell, Amy. *John Keats,* 2 Vols. Boston: Houghton Mifflin Company, 1925.

Lumpkin, Henry. *From Savannah to Yorktown: The American Revolution in the South.* Columbia: University of South Carolina Press, 1981.

Lunt, James. *John Burgoyne of Saratoga.* New York: Harcourt Brace Jovanovich, 1975.

Malone, Dumas. *Jefferson and His Time: The Sage of Monticello.* Boston: Little, Brown and Company, 1981.

Martin, Asa Earl. *History of the United States, 1492-1865,* Volume 1. Boston: Ginn and Company, 1934.

Mays, David John, ed. *The Letters and Papers of Edmund Pendleton, 1734-1803,* Volume 1. Charlottesville: The University Press of Virginia, 1967.

McGrady, Edward. *The History of South Carolina in the Revolution, 1780-83.* New York and London, 1902.

Miller, Charles E., Lockey, Donald V., and Visconti, Joseph Jr. "Highland Fortress: The Fortifications of West Point during the American Revolution, 1775-1783." West Point, New York: Department of History, U. S. Military Academy, 1979.

Miller, John. *Triumph and Freedom, 1775-1783.* Boston: Little, Brown and Company, 1948.

Milosz, Czeslaw. *The History of Polish Literature,* 2nd ed. Berkeley: University of California Press, 1983.

Mitchell, Lt. Col. Joseph B. *Decisive Battles of the American Revolution.* New York: G. P. Putnam's Sons, 1962.

Mizwa, Stephen P. "Tadeusz Kosciuszko," in *Great Men and Women of Poland.* New York: The Kosciuszko Foundation, 1941.

Montross, Lynn. *Rag, Tag and Bobtail: The Story of the Continental Army, 1775-1783.* New York: Harper & Brothers, Publishers, 1952.

Morrill, Dan L. *Southern Campaigns of the American Revolution.* Baltimore: The Nautical & Aviation Publishing Company of America, 1993.

Nelson, Paul David. *General Horatio Gates: A Biography.* Baton Rouge: Louisiana State University Press, 1976.

Nickerson, Hoffman. *The Turning Point of the Revolution, or Burgoyne in America*, 2 Vols. New York: Houghton Mifflin Company, 1928; reprint ed., Port Jefferson, New York: Kennikat Press, Inc. 1967.

Nolan, J. Bennett. *Lafayette in America Day by Day.* Baltimore: The Johns Hopkins Press, 1934.

Palmer, Dave Richard. *The River and the Rock: The History of Fortress West Point, 1775-1783.* New York: Greenwood Publishing Corporation, 1969.

Pancake, John S. *1777: The Year of the Hangman.* University, Alabama: The University of Alabama Press, 1977.

Paszkowski, General Franciszek. *Dzieje Tadeusza Kosciuszki, Pierwszego Naczelnika Polakow* (Annals of Thaddeus Kosciuszko: First Leader of Poles). Krakow: Jagiellonian University Press, 1872.

Plutarch. *The Lives of the Noble Grecians and Romans.* Chicago: Encyclopedia Britannica, Inc., 1952, Book 14 of *Great Books of the Western World.* Chicago: University of Chicago, 1952.

Ramsay, David. *History of the Revolution in South-Carolina,* 2 Vols. Trenton, New Jersey: I. Collins, 1785.

Randall, Willard Sterne. *Benedict Arnold: Patriot and Traitor.* New York: William Morrow and Company, Inc., 1990.

Reeder, Colonel Red. *Bold Leaders of the American Revolution.* Boston: Little, Brown and Company, 1973.

Roberts, Kenneth. *Rabble in Arms: A Chronicle of Arundel and the Burgoyne Invasion.* New York: Doubleday, Doran & Company, Inc., 1940.

Royster, Charles. *Light-Horse Harry Lee and the Legacy of the American Revolution.* New York: Alfred A. Knopf, 1981.

Rusinowa, Izabella. *Saratoga-Yorktown. Z Dziejow Wojny Amerykansko-Angielskiej* (Saratoga-Yorktown, History of the American-English War). Warszawa: Ministerstwo Obrony Narodowej, 1984 (Ministry of National Defense).

Schachner, Nathan. *Thomas Jefferson, A Biography,* 2 Vols. New York: Appleton-Century-Crofts, Inc., 1951.

Skowronek, Jerzy. *Ksiaze [Prince] Jozef Poniatowski.* Wroclaw: Zaklad Narodowy imienia Ossolinskich Wydawnictwo, 1984 [Ossolineum National Publishing House].

Stedman, Charles. *The History of the Origin, Progress and Termination of the American War,* 2 Vols. London: J. Murray et al, 1794; reprint ed., New York: New York Times & Arno Press, 1969.

Sweetman, John. *Saratoga 1777.* New York: Hippocrene Books, Inc., 1973.

Swiggett, Howard. *The Forgotten Leaders of the Revolution.* Garden City, New York: Doubleday & Company, Inc., 1955.

Thane, Elswyth. *The Fighting Quaker: Nathanael Greene.* Mattituck, New York: Aeonian Press, Inc., 1972.

Trevelyan, Sir George Otto. *The American Revolution,* 4 Vols. London: Longmans, Green, and Co., 1907.

Ward, Christopher. *The Delaware Continentals, 1776-1783.* Wilmington, Delaware: The Historical Society of Delaware, 1941.

_____ . *The War of the Revolution,* 2 Vols. New York: The Macmillan Company, 1952.

Wildes, Harry Emerson. *Anthony Wayne: Trouble Shooter of the American Revolution.* New York: Harcourt, Brace & Company, 1941.

Wilson, Robert H. *Thaddeus Kosciuszko and His Home in Philadelphia.* Philadelphia: Copernicus Society of America, 1976.

Zamoyski, Adam. *The Last King of Poland.* New York: Hippocrene Books, l997.

2. Historical Films

The American Revolution, Don Cambou, writer/producer. Greystone Communications, Valley Village, California, 1995.

The Revolutionary War, Carol L. Fleisher, director/producer. Real-TV, Los Angeles, California, 1995.

Index

Cross Creek (Fayetteville), North Carolina, 131
Cross of Virtuti Militari (Poland), 195
Crown Hill, West Point, 88
Crown Point, New York, 8, 14, 21
Cruger, Lt. Col. John Harris, 143, 147, 149-154, 159-161
Cuneo, Maj. Ernest L., 240
Cutting, Nathaniel, 209
Czartoryski, Prince Adam, 54, 56, 211

Dalzien, Capt. Joseph, 118, 132, 147, 158
Dan River, Virginia, 131-132, 134, 136, 138, 140, 248
Danbury, Connecticut, 98
Danton, 196
Daughters of the American Revolution, 163
Davidson, Brig. Gen. William, 125
Davie, Gen. William R., 157, 223
Davies, Norman, 290n4
Dawson, John L., 204, 206, 251
Deane, Silas, 56, 61, 70,
Dearborn, Maj. Henry, 34
Declaration of Independence, 16, 44, 124, 182, 196
Deep River, North Carolina, 133
De Kalb, Maj. Gen. Baron, 80, 124
Delaplace, Capt. William, 6
Delaware, 164, 170-171, 177
Delaware River, 57, 59, 199
D'Estaing, Admiral Comte Charles, 97-98
Dickinson, John, 197
Dietrich, Nicolas Baron de Ottendorf, 56
Dionysius (Greek tyrant), 53
District of Columbia, 255, 257
Dnieper River, Poland, 211
Dockery, Rita, 301
Dodd, William, 239
Dorchester, South Carolina, 170
Doric Temple at Corinth, Greece, 234
Dresden, Saxony, 56, 291n6
Duane, James, 22, 184-185
Duchy of Warsaw, 211-212
Duke of Brunswick, 21
Dunn, Maj. Isaac B., 17,
Du Coudray, Maj. Gen. Phillipe Charles,

70-71, 190
Dupont, Victor, 209
Duportail, Brig. Gen. Louis, 61, 63-64, 69, 72-80, 87, 89-90, 97. 102, 105-107, 110, 114, 117, 120, 128, 154, 180-181, 183, 188
Du Roi, Lt. August Wilhelm (The Elder), 19
Dutch, 8
Dwight, Dr. Timothy, 91, 227
Dwina River, Poland, 211

Easton, Brig. Gen. Pinkertham, 139
Ecole de Genie, France, 55, 75
Edisto River, South Carolina, 170
Edwards, Maj. ____, 183
Egleston, Thomas, 101, 227
Elizabeth(town), New Jersey, 182, 202
Ellis, Margaret, 201
Ellis, Mary, 201
England, 4, 42, 197-198, 204, 211, 244-245, 251, 254
Englander, Julie, 304
English Tories, 198
English Whigs, 198
Ennis, John F., 255-258
Esopus (Kingston), New York, 42-43
Estko, Anna Kosciuszko, 193
Europe, 63, 74, 145, 154, 186, 188, 196, 209, 211, 244, 246, 251
Europeans, 229
Eutaw Springs, South Carolina, 164, 169
Evans, Anthony Walton White, 227-228

Federal City (Washington), 208
Federalists, 199, 205, 208-210, 237, 250
Fellows, Brig. Gen. John, 41
Fermoy, Brig. Gen. Roche de, 9, 16, 28-29
Finland, 198
Fishkill, New York, 68, 88, 94, 104, 109
Fish Kill (Saratoga), 41
Fiszer, Brig. Gen. Stanislaw, 229
Flannery, Jeffrey M., 299
Fleisher, Carol L., 248
Flemming, Ann, 301
Fontainebleau, France, 212
Fort Arnold (West Point), 90-91, 94,

About the Author

FRANCIS CASIMIR KAJENCKI was graduated from the U.S. Military Academy and commissioned second lieutenant in January 1943. He served in the Pacific Theater in World War II, followed by staff and command assignments over a span of thirty years. He retired as Colonel and Assistant Chief of Information, Department of the Army, in 1973.

Kajencki earned three Masters degrees: from the University of Southern California in Mechanical Engineering, 1949; University of Wisconsin–Madison in Journalism, 1967; George Mason University in History, 1976. Upon retiring from the army, he took up historical research and writing that led to five published books on American history.

The author was born in Erie, Pennsylvania, November 15, 1918. A widower with four adult children, he resides in El Paso, Texas.

Typography, book design and jacket design by Vicki Trego Hill of El Paso, Texas. This book was produced electronically using a Power Macintosh computer. The pages were formatted using Aldus PageMaker. Photographs were retouched using Adobe Photoshop, and maps were produced using Adobe Illustrator. Text was set in 11pt Caslon Book; chapter headings were set in Caslon Medium Italic.

Printing/Binding by Thomson-Shore of Dexter, Michigan. The text was printed on 60-pound Glatfelter Supple Opaque Recycled Natural, an acid-free paper with an effective life of at least three hundred years. The color plates were printed on 70-pound RichGloss Enamel and tipped-in.